Doing Business in China
Third edition

Aimed specifically at Western and non-Chinese businesses and managers, this book offers a theoretical framework for understanding Chinese business culture and a practical guide to business practices, market conditions, negotiations, organisations, networks and the business environment in China and the factors that can lead to business success.

The authors guide the reader through the processes of market entry, marketing and managing operations in this unique social and cultural context by including:

- case studies and examples of business ventures as diverse as car washes, sausages and outdoor clothing
- discussion of the issues surrounding products, pricing, distribution and advertising
- advice on choosing business partners, negotiating and entering Chinese overseas markets
- guides to further resources in local cultures to help businesses tailor their strategies to local conditions.

Building on the strengths of the first two editions with new case studies, updated discussion of the evolving marketplace and its interactions with government and a new chapter on business law, the third edition of *Doing Business in China* will continue to be the number one resource for students of international business and management studies and for practitioners with an eye on China.

Tim Ambler is Senior Fellow at the London Business School.

Morgen Witzel is Honourary Senior Fellow at the School of Business and Economics, University of Exeter, and editor-in-chief of *Corporate Finance Review*.

Chao Xi is Assistant Professor at the Faculty of Law, the Chinese University of Hong Kong.

Doing Business in China
Third edition

Tim Ambler, Morgen Witzel
and Chao Xi

Routledge
Taylor & Francis Group

LONDON AND NEW YORK

First published 2000
by RoutledgeCurzon
Second Edition published 2004 by Routledge
Reprinted 2005 (four times)
Third Edition published 2009
2 Park Square, Milton Park, Abingdon, Oxon OX14 4RN

Simultaneously published in the USA and Canada
by Routledge
270 Madison Ave, New York, NY 10016

*Routledge is an imprint of the Taylor & Francis Group,
an informa business*

© 2000, 2004 Tim Ambler, Morgen Witzel;
2009 Tim Ambler, Morgen Witzel and Chao Xi

Typeset in Baskerville by Keyword Group Ltd
Printed and bound in Great Britain by TJ International
Ltd, Padstow, Cornwall

British Library Cataloguing in Publication Data
A catalogue record for this book is available
from the British Library

Library of Congress Cataloging in Publication Data

ISBN 13: 978-0-415-43631-1 (hbk)
ISBN 13: 978-0-415-43632-8 (pbk)
ISBN 13: 978-0-203-94649-7 (ebk)

ISBN 10: 0-415-43631-1 (hbk)
ISBN 10: 0-415-43632-X (pbk)
ISBN 10: 0-203-94649-9 (ebk)

Contents

Foreword

The dizzying pace of change in China makes it hard to keep up. Step off the plane in any of the major cities, be whisked into the city centre fast and efficiently (in Shanghai's case, faster than anywhere else in the world), and the chances are that a new building will have gone up since you were last there. New business districts are being built. Transport systems are being transformed. Cityscapes are changing daily.

So it is with the people in China. It is not just the fashion that has changed. With three decades of growth and modernisation has come a transformation of lifestyles and attitudes. Increasing numbers of people, who once would have set their sights on owning a bicycle, drive around in their own cars. A property-owning class has been created – a section of society which is growing all the time. Such aspirations would have been completely unthinkable 30 years ago.

Yet, on another level, anyone who visits China regularly will see that Chinese people take the changes in their stride. It is completely natural that, where 30 years ago the shops would have been drab and staffed by surly assistants who could not care less whether you bought the shops' products or not, today shoppers (at least in the cities) can flit between upmarket boutiques, high-tech malls and expensive restaurants. And, what is more, they can afford to buy what is in them. What were aspirations have become expectations.

Can this continue? Will China come grinding to a halt, or, as some suggest, will the shaky financial system implode? I certainly don't think so. But there are major challenges – particularly around the degradation of the environment and the growing social disparities – to suggest that a certain amount of caution is in order. At the very least, China will need what might be termed a new business model as it moves into the next phase of its economic development, one that embraces clearer notions of sustainability and more efficient use of resources.

The environment in which Western businesses operate has also changed markedly, if not completely beyond recognition. In the earliest days of 'opening up', what Western investors needed to do first and foremost was to identify, negotiate with (often at great lengths) and then cooperate with a suitable joint-venture partner. Such operations were invariably to establish low-cost, export-focused manufacturing. Indeed, it was a requirement that the majority, if not all, of manufactured output would be exported.

The reason for these requirements was to assist China to develop its export markets and generate foreign exchange earnings, as well as to attract foreign investment and technology.

China's planners could hardly have anticipated how successful this policy would be. Inward investment poured in, reaching at its peak around US$1 billion each week. Foreign exchange reserves mounted and mounted, to exceed US$1 trillion. The coastal provinces, where most of the investment was located, flourished. It was vindication, *par excellence*, of government strategy.

Yet, it was not all plain sailing. Western investors needed patience in abundance to deal with central, provincial and local bureaucracy. They certainly needed to think long-term before seeing a return on their investments. In the worst cases, investments were lost altogether. Some struggled with the culture and the language. China was not for the faint-hearted.

Today, there are different issues at play. No longer are Western investors required to enter into joint ventures, with some key exceptions. They can invest in wholly-owned and managed businesses. The requirements to export are tailing off. There is a greater access to more and more sectors, as a result of the momentous decision by China to join the World Trade Organisation in 2001. Investors can achieve a return on their investment in much shorter timeframes. Long-term relationships in business have been forged. Above all, China is now a known quantity: there is accumulated knowledge about business practice from which newcomers to the market can benefit.

There is also a wealth of expertise available, and I hope I will be forgiven for pointing out that the first port of call for any business approaching the China market is the China–Britain Business Council.

Yet, we can always learn more. There remain obstacles and challenges, not least in the difficult area of protection of intellectual property. Carefully conceived regulations at the central level are not always followed to the letter at the local level. There continue to be fraud scams, in which unsuspecting Western companies, believing that they have won huge orders from companies in China, are drawn into making advance 'gifts' of thousands of pounds in pursuit of fictitious orders.

The starting point must always be: do your research. Time spent researching and finding out about the business environment, the culture and the nature of China today will always be time well spent. I am delighted to endorse this new edition of *Doing Business in China*, which, as was the case with the previous editions, will prove extremely useful for those embarking on China business. Much has changed about the market, as I have suggested, but the fundamentals remain the same. My advice to the next generation of managers in China is to read, learn and assiduously digest the information so helpfully laid out in this volume.

Stephen Phillips
Chief Executive Officer, China–Britain Business Council

Acknowledgements

Books are always collaborative ventures, and this one more than most. Our many friends and colleagues, most of whom know far more about China than we ever will, have been incredibly generous with their time and knowledge. We must offer our deepest thanks to Sir Alan Donald KCMG, Ian Rae, C.F. Li, Ken Campbell, Zinan Liu and Tian Jun, who supported our course at London Business School and loyally came year after year to speak to our students and share their vast knowledge and experience. Giles Chance, Malcolm Warner, Michael Yahuda, Simon Powell, Rod Wye and many others also came to join the fun. Between them, they have many hundreds of years of experience of China and things Chinese, and we are honoured that they should have shared so much with us.

Special thanks should be tendered to John Beyer, formerly of the China–Britain Trade Group (now China–Britain Business Council), who visited the class and has been of great help in many other ways. His deputy, Mandi Sturrock, was also invaluable, particularly when giving feedback on the first year of the course. In general, we should like to thank all the CBTG/CBBC staff for their assistance over the years.

At the London Business School, our warmest thanks go to Wang Xiucun, who visited us on sabbatical from Beijing for a year, co-taught the course with us, and corrected with great kindness and politeness our more crass errors on things Chinese. Other assistance and material came from George Tian, Jonathan Thompson, Zhang Jing and Vivan Li Fang. Ken Simmonds and the late Philip Law also contibuted advice and ideas.

Following the first two editions, we received much valuable criticism and comments from many people. Space precludes us mentioning them all here, but we must particularly single out Benjamin Creuzfeldt, Frank-Juergen Richter and Ian Rae. Special thanks also to Ma Jia for her comments about the usefulness of the book while this edition was being prepared. Material for cases came from many sources. Our thanks go to Giles Chance, Greg Harris, Geoff Mills, Li Xuemin, Shan Jinglong, Gabrielle Sentilhes, T.Y. Wong, Jonathan Patrick, Larry Renaldi, Chen Derong, Jin Shen Yu, Michael Zhu and the staff of the Sun and Moon Spreading Company for their generously given help. George Adams, Barry Smith and Connie Ma are thanked for directing us to case material for the second edition. Thanks also to our lawyer friends in China for their advice on the third edition.

At Routledge, our thanks go to Vicki Smith, who commissioned the first edition, Craig Fowlie, who saw that project through and commissioned the second edition, and finally to Stephanie Rogers, who has helped the project along and commissioned the third edition. Family matters called her away just as we were getting ready to go to press, but we also thank Sonja van Leeuwen and Leanne Hinves for taking up the torch for the final leg.

Last but not least, we would like to thank our students at London Business School, the hundred or so men and women from all over the globe who took the 'Doing Business in China' course and contributed so much to it, year after year. Without them, this book would not have been possible.

Tim Ambler
Morgen Witzel
Chao Xi

March 2008

Introduction

What does anybody here know of China? Even those Europeans who have been in that Empire are almost as ignorant of it as the rest of us. Everything is covered by a veil, through which a glimpse of what is within may occasionally be caught, a glimpse just sufficient to set the imagination to work and more likely to mislead than inform.

(Lord Macaulay, *c*. 1790)

This is a big canvas, much of it still dark. Personal impressions are sometimes vivid, always incontestable; but they illuminate only part of the scene, and from one angle only. They are also outsiders' impressions. We each construct our vision of China from the limited materials available to us, from our direct experience and reading, our memories of certain conversations and scenes; and we cling tenaciously to it. But it remains China through a foreigner's distorting glass. The real China, whatever that may be, eludes us.

(Sir Percy Cradock, 1994)

Visitors to Disneyland in Hong Kong during the run-up to Chinese New Year in 2008 were likely to encounter an unexpected figure. Greeting visitors along the route down the middle of the park were not only those old favourites, Mickey Mouse and Donald Duck and their friends, but also the moustached and robed figure of Cai Shen Ye, the Daoist god of wealth. This caused something of a flurry of interest in the local and international press. Some thought the idea charming, but some Americans were uncomfortable with this adaptation of their own culture. Cynics said that Cai Shen Ye had been brought in simply to make Disneyland more acceptable to a Chinese audience, since attendances at Disneyland Hong Kong since its opening had not exactly been robust. Other cynics – the really hardened ones – thought that Disneyland and the god of wealth were perfectly suited to each other, and Walt Disney and his colleagues had missed a trick by not including him right from the beginning alongside Mickey and Donald.

The story provoked some mild outrage and a great deal of amusement, but the symbolism is clear. The West has finally learned, or is learning, two things. First, China is here to stay. Five years ago, predictions of a Chinese economic collapse were rife. Few still hold to this view today. The question now is how to ride the elephant, not how to make it go away. Incidentally, this does not mean that there will *not* at some point be an economic collapse or at least a downturn in China; it means simply that the evidence for one happening is at present weak. (We are not in the predicting game, however, and readers are encouraged to keep an open mind.)

The second point is that China, although modernising rapidly, is not going to become just like the West. Young Chinese may listen to Western pop music and dress in Western fashion, but these are fads, fancies, surface manifestations. Beneath, Chinese culture is as robust as ever, and arguably growing stronger as the Chinese people themselves grow more confident in their dealings with the West and lose the sense of inferiority that had been engendered by many years of foreign domination, first by the Manchus of the Qing dynasty, then by European colonial powers. If the West wants to do business with China, then it must recognise this strength and confidence and be prepared to adapt. From that perspective, including a Chinese god among the Disney pantheon is probably no more than a sensible adaptation to local needs.

But what are those needs? What do Chinese consumers want today? How do Chinese businesses operate? How do their managers think and behave? We are told often that China is a nation of a billion customers, but it is also a vast country with a shaky infrastructure. Where do we look for those customers and how do we find them? These are the hard questions, and the answers to them are often vague and lacking in detail. Above, we quoted the former British ambassador to China, Sir Percy Cradock, who in turn was paraphrasing St Paul, on the difficulties of identifying firm and solid facts about China. Westerners see China through a distorted lens, and not as it truly is. It comes as small comfort to know that many Chinese are looking back through that distorted lens in the opposite direction, and see us just as imperfectly.

Modern China: change and continuity

Ten years is a long time in modern China. Since the first edition of this book, many things have changed. The economy has continued its upward rise. Personal prosperity is now much more evident, especially in the big cities and the eastern coastal zone. Beijing, where once it was a struggle to get a decent meal in the evening, now boasts streets full of smart restaurants and its youth wear leather jackets and trendy haircuts. The mayor of Shanghai, visiting Beijing in the autumn of 2002 for the Sixteenth Congress of the Communist Party, was reportedly shocked by the high standard of living he found there, and asked his Beijing counterpart for advice on how Shanghai could catch up (but as this was reported in the local Beijing media, perhaps the story should be taken with a very large pinch of salt – the rivalry between Beijing and Shanghai in such matters is legendary). At all events, Shanghai itself has moved on apace. The building boom halted briefly in the early part of this decade after the Asian financial crisis, but then resumed. Guangdong and Tianjin are booming too.

In 2001, after years of wrangling, China joined the World Trade Organisation. The event was largely overshadowed by events post-9/11, with world attention focused on Afghanistan and the Middle East; but its significance as a symbol of China's reintegration into the world-system can hardly be doubted. In 2002, according to the *Financial Times*, China took in more than $52 billion in foreign investment, overtaking the USA as the country with the largest foreign capital inflows in the world. China's trade surplus that year reached $100 billion, while the US trade deficit with China reached $83 billion. Since then the trend has continued upwards. In 2007, bilateral trade between China and the UK alone reached $40 billion, or around £20 billion sterling. There were nearly 6,000 British investment projects in China, which in the year to November 2007 had pumped a further $7.5 billion into the Chinese economy. Among these investors was the London Stock Exchange, which opened a representative office in Shanghai alongside the already established NYSE and NASDAQ. There seems no end to China's growth, or its appetite for investment.

Signs of change are everywhere. Five years ago, much of the Pudong district of Shanghai was waste ground, waiting for development. Today those plots of ground are covered by skyscrapers. There has been a revolution in housing: following the liberalisation of the property market and a programme of assistance for the less well-paid, it is estimated that 80 per cent of the urban population now own their own homes, a figure almost beyond imagining five years ago. The statistic may not be accurate, but whether the true figure is 60 per cent or 90 per cent, this is still a massive advance. Bicycles have all but disappeared from the streets of Shanghai and Beijing, replaced by cars; while European cities like London strive to encourage their citizens to abandon their cars and take to bicycles, in Shanghai and Beijing, at least, the trend is in the opposite direction. Delightful, clunky old CCTV 9, the English-language state television station with its precarious-looking sets and presenters with terrible haircuts, has transformed into CCTV International, as slick and polished as CNN or BBC World, with young presenters who are equally slick and polished. An example is weather presenter Halla Mohiedeen: naturally, as a Muslim woman presenting the weather on Chinese state television, she speaks with a soft Scottish accent.

And yet, and yet. For those who travel and work in modern China, it is easy to spot the many and massive changes that are reshaping the country, its economy, its society and even its political system. But, by looking just a little more closely, it is just as easy to compile a list of things that have *not* changed, or are changing very little and very slowly. Huge regional economic disparities remain; per capita incomes in the west of the country are half or a third those of the east coast. The growth of industrialisation in the country has been explosive, and the proportion of Chinese GDP coming from agriculture has declined from more than 35 per cent to about 14 per cent, but this merely emphasises the plight of the hundreds of millions of rural inhabitants whose wages and standards of living still lag behind those of their urban counterparts.

The Communist Party, the death of which was widely foretold in the 1990s, is thriving. With 73 million members – up by 13 million in five years – it is the world's largest political organisation. The newly prosperous middle classes and the wealthy elite, far from shunning the Party, have embraced it. And the Party has evolved too. At the Sixteenth Congress in November 2002, the Party openly called on capitalists to join its ranks, and adopted President Jiang Zemin's philosophy of the 'three represents': the Party (and by implication the government) should work to represent the interests of the growing Chinese economy, the development of Chinese culture and the needs of the Chinese people. By co-opting capitalism, the Party was attempting to safeguard its own future, and also to ensure that the emerging Chinese capitalism retained a social dimension. Five years on, it looks to have succeeded handsomely as far as the first goal is concerned. The jury is still out on the second.

In the first edition of this book, we suggested that many of the lessons learned by Western businesses while doing business in China could be turned around and applied at home in the West, with good results. We also suggested that rather than adopting Western business methods wholesale, Chinese managers were picking and choosing those techniques which they found to work and discarding those they did not, combining their learning of Western methods with their own inherited Chinese systems of management. A hybrid model of management was beginning to emerge, part-Chinese and part-Western in terms of its components, but very strongly Chinese in terms of its philosophy and outlook. By the time of the second edition in 2004, some were going further and arguing that the emerging Chinese model of management would soon begin to influence Western management thought and practice, in much the same way that Japanese management did in the 1980s. Again, the jury is still out: certainly there are some valuable things that Western managers can learn from their Chinese counterparts, but there is no sign yet of a distinctive Chinese management philosophy that will be embraced by the West in the same way that, say, lean production and TQM were imported wholesale from Japanese industry in the late 1980s and early 1990s. But what we can say with confidence is that Chinese managers are developing their own ways of doing things, and sometimes those ways are very different from what we see in the West.

The third edition of this book continues by examining ongoing trends: the growth and increasing sophistication of Chinese consumer markets, and the growth of management training in China being two examples. But we also observe those things that have changed little, if at all. Despite China's rapid economic growth over ten years, many things remain fundamentally the same. That should be good news. If many things have remained the same in the past, then there is hope that at least some of those things will remain the same in the future, and this gives businesspeople some solid ground on which to build.

One thing that has not changed is the importance of cultural understanding. Part of what makes China unfamiliar is its culture and its history, which have given the Chinese people mental processes, outlooks and attitudes that can be very different from those imbued by Westerners. These differences often create misunderstandings and serve as powerful barriers, hindering or preventing Western and Chinese businesspeople from working together. But, to the Westerner prepared to devote the time to understanding China, many of these differences can be overcome. The reward, for those who succeed, is good relationships with Chinese partners, access to new markets and/or sources of supply, and an entrée into Chinese business networks. All of these can be powerful sources of competitive advantage.

While this book discusses marketing and advertising, organisation behaviour and the mechanics of joint ventures in China, they are placed in the context of Chinese history, philosophy and culture. These form the essential backdrop against which business in modern China makes sense. A better understanding of China not only helps to explain *how* things happen in that vast, complex and diverse country, but it can also suggest *why* they happen, and why they might (or might not) happen again.

And we look at the similarities between China and the West, not just the differences. The differences are important, but they are not all-pervasive. It is not necessary to reinvent the wheel to do business in China; instead, a process of adaptation is required. Many Western techniques and practices can be replicated in China. There is much to be said – as Wall's ice-cream (the Unilever subsidiary) did in Beijing in the early 1990s – for starting with the usual market entry formula and changing it only when you have to. Second, and a little more esoterically, by looking at these common features from a Chinese perspective, we learn more about the things we already do. In other words, by learning how to do business in China, we can also improve what we do in the West.

This book, therefore, has several purposes. For those businesspeople who deal directly with China, as traders, investors, expatriate managers or partners, it provides an introduction. For their colleagues, it provides some explanation of why things may take so long, why people come before business, why legalistic or contractual thinking has so little place, and explains the kind of help the expatriates and visitors will need. For teachers and trainers, the book can serve as a textbook. We have included some short cases and examples. In the past, China has contributed many of the world's most useful inventions, from paper to spaghetti to explosives, and it will provide many more in the future. In one sense or another, we are all students of China. To the extent that this book contributes to mutual understanding, it will have served its purpose.

Why China?

In 1995, China's post-economic reform boom was at its height. This was the time of the 'Wild East', with double-digit growth (and inflation) in China and Southeast Asia. Shanghai's Pudong district boasted some of the most expensive real estate on the face of the planet. Western companies were scrambling to get in, often exhibiting a mentality reminiscent of the nineteenth-century gold rushes. The reason for interest in China was obvious: it was the place to go to make money.

The Asia Crisis of 1997–8 was a wake-up call for many investors from both West and East who had predicted that the boom would go on forever. Most of the Southeast Asian 'Tiger' economies collapsed, and some such as Indonesia have not yet really revived. Some analysts predicted that China would go the same way. Other, shrewder heads believed it would not, and then prayed devoutly that they were right. It seems clear in the aftermath that China's leadership, by sticking to their guns and refusing to devalue the country's currency, helped boost confidence in the region and not only preserved China from the worst shocks but helped other Southeast Asian countries to recover on its coat tails. At the time, it was fascinating to watch as even the most ardent free-market enthusiasts in the West changed tack and came up with good reasons why China should not devalue (reasons, it seems, that Chinese premier Zhu Rongji and his advisers knew all along).

Since then, China has boomed again. Growth increased from 8–9 per cent in 2002 to 11 per cent in 2007. That does not mean there are no economic problems in the country. Many of the old state-owned enterprises (SOEs) have been disbanded or privatised, but many still resist. That problem, however, is much less critical than it was. More urgent are the social and economic divisions that persist in China, between city and country, underdeveloped west and developed – in some cases overdeveloped – east. Infrastructure remains a nagging headache, and despite the huge Three Gorges hydroelectric project, China still has trouble meeting its electricity needs. Property prices have skyrocketed, food prices have followed them. The environment remains a real concern, with pollution affecting the larger cities in particular. Yet, despite these problems, the economy continues to grow, and China remains both an opportunity and a challenge for Western firms. The passing of the overheated 'gold rush' days of the early 1990s is a good thing. There may be fewer quick profits to be made, but the prospects for firms that are able and willing to invest for the long term, build relationships and embed themselves in China, have probably never been better.

Will China become the world's dominant trading nation and economic powerhouse? At some point in the future, it seems very likely. Though problems do remain, the government has succeeded in its primary goal of maintaining political stability; the events of 1989 are slipping into memory now, and the generation that protested then is often intent on making money now. Political unrest does exist but it is exaggerated by most Western commentators. Two more obvious problems remain: corruption, and inequitable wealth distribution.

Corruption affects many aspects of business in China, as it has since ancient times. We will return to that throughout the book, but particularly at the end of Chapter 5 ('An ethical interlude'). Foreigners have to be especially careful as some businesspeople have the underlying idea that, as foreigners ripped off China in the past, they are now fair game. The gap between rich and poor – individuals, cities and regions – in China is large and growing. But China is hardly unique in this respect: one only has to look at the US, Brazil and India for examples of economic development being accompanied by extremes of wealth distribution: the bigger the country, the wider the disparity. Compare Hong Kong with Switzerland and one finds a similar disparity but not due to size. To what extent the relatively fatalistic social fabric will stand the strain remains to be seen.

Two centuries ago, getting to China meant travelling in a cramped, uncomfortable ship and eating bad food for several months. Today, getting to China means travelling in a cramped, uncomfortable aircraft seat and eating bad food, but only for nine or ten hours. The question should not be, 'why China?' but rather, 'is there any excuse for *not* going to China?'

The overseas Chinese

There are 60 million ethnic Chinese outside mainland China, concentrated mainly in the countries of Southeast Asia including Malaysia, Indonesia, Thailand, Singapore, Taiwan, the Philippines, Vietnam, Cambodia, Laos and Burma. Other smaller communities exist around the world. Taken together, these *huaqiao* (overseas Chinese) communities are a powerful economic force; were they a nation in their own right, their gross national product would be two-thirds that of Japan. In many of the countries that host them, they dominate the local economy, even though in every case except Taiwan, widely considered (by the Chinese) to be part of China anyway, and Singapore, they are a minority ethnic group. There are close ties between *huaqiao* communities in these different countries and, importantly, there are also close ties between them and the homeland, mainland China. The overseas Chinese have already played an important role in the economic growth of China since the reform process began, and despite the blip of the Asia Crisis of 1997–8, they will continue to do so. Their contribution has included not only investment capital but management expertise, gathered in the often rough-and-tumble free markets of Southeast Asia during the decades when the Chinese were immured in the Maoist command economy system. Any look at business in China today must consider these vibrant, volatile, powerful communities and their sometimes uneasy relationship with the motherland.

The focus of this book is on the People's Republic of China, and throughout the book when we refer to 'China' we generally mean the PRC. But we do refer to 'Greater China', sometimes for comparison and sometimes for contrast. This book is *not* a detailed guide to doing business in Malaysia, Indonesia, Singapore *et al.* (although Chapter 10 gives an overview of these countries), but it does describe the affinities that the *huaqiao* communities have with China. Generally these take place on two levels:

1   **Cultural**: the residents of the Chinese mainland and the overseas Chinese communities continue to share a strong cultural bond, and despite different regulations, market conditions and so on, their ways of doing business remain fundamentally similar.

2   **Business**: particularly since economic reform began, but before that as well, overseas Chinese and their mainland cousins have done business together and made money together. Since reform, the overseas Chinese have been far and away the largest investors in China, far outstripping the USA, Europe or even Japan.

Why another book on China?

As anyone studying or researching business in China will have realised, there are hundreds of books, and probably thousands of magazine and journal articles, in print. Does the world really need another book on China?

Indeed, there are a number of highly useful books, all of which illuminate some aspect of the problems of doing business in China. (In Chapter 1, we discuss some of the various types of recently published literature on China and make suggestions for further reading.) There are, for example, a number of 'road map' books, which help the first-time entrant to China figure out where to go and who to see when planning a first venture there. Likewise, there are books on etiquette and negotiation styles which explain some of the cultural hurdles to be crossed. Along with these are a few – far too few – memoirs by businesspeople, relating what happened to them in their early years in China. We need more of these tell-it-as-it-was accounts, especially as those above are a little dated. The large and often excellent body of academic work covers economics, organisational behaviour, corporate governance (joint ventures) and foreign trade. Very few, if any, deal with marketing, i.e. the basic business of making money.

There is also much that is of limited use. While few in the West really know China, that does not seem to restrict the number of opinions. Particularly in books on Chinese politics and in books by journalists, not to mention journalism in general, one can hear as one reads the sound of axes being ground. The Chinese mostly dislike these books, not because the facts are inaccurate but because they have been selected in ways they do not recognise. Fifty years ago, a group of British businessmen were proposing the first ever trade mission to 'Red China'. The most senior was summoned by their Foreign Minister, Sir Anthony Eden, and advised not to take part. Sir Alfred Owen responded: 'If you will take care of the politics, we will take care of the trade'.[1] We do not suggest that politics and trade are wholly divisible, but the focus of this book is on the latter.

This book has two broad aims. First, we want to take a broad view of doing business and managing organisations in China, bringing together the various accounts and surveys mentioned above. This approach is broad-based and holistic. Doing business in China, as indeed anywhere else, requires us to combine personal experience *and* macro-level knowledge. Personal experience, on subjects such as markets, negotiation styles, etiquette and so on, is necessary in the first instance, in order to deal with the people and things encountered in daily life in China. Personal knowledge helps us know *what* to do. Macro-level knowledge, on the other hand, provides depth to personal experience and explains *why* things happen and why particular responses may be more appropriate. As we shall see in the next few chapters in particular, macro-level knowledge is extremely important when doing business in China. Following on from this, our second aim is to suggest particular areas where readers should focus attention. This is important: China is far too vast and complex a subject for there to be 'one big book about China' which tells you all you need to know. Chapter 1 discusses sources of knowledge about China, but if you are going to China to do business, even on a small scale, some sort of personal learning about the country and its inhabitants is essential.

What the businessperson needs to know

Some of the questions that first-time business visitors to China generally ask, include:

- Where do I find information about China?
- How do I determine if there is a market for my firm's products/ services in China?
- Where should I make my first point of entry?
- Do I need a Chinese business partner or should I go it alone?
- If I decide I want a partner, how do I go about getting one?
- How do I deal with the language barrier?
- How do I market my products/services in China?
- How do I recruit staff in China?
- How will I personally adjust to living in China?

And here are some additional questions which should be asked:

- What will my Chinese business partners expect of me?
- What ethical issues might I encounter when doing business in China?
- Are there advantages to becoming involved in the overseas Chinese network, rather than going straight into China?
- When establishing a joint venture with a Chinese partner, what conditions should I insist on? Is it imperative that I retain control?
- How will I deal with various levels of government in China?
- How will I establish good relations with suppliers? with customers?
- Having recruited trained and skilled staff, how will I keep them?

- How should Western subsidiaries in China be structured? Can I expect my Chinese managers and staff to work to Western methods and principles?
- Why is my company going into China in the first place, and what does it hope to gain/expect to achieve?

We cannot hope to anticipate every question and are well aware of the dangers of claiming any expertise for ourselves in matters Chinese. The more one learns about China, the less one actually seems to know. We do, however, claim the expertise of others. During the years that we ran our course on business in China at the London Business School, and throughout the development of the third edition of this book, many Chinese and Western students, academics and businesspeople have contributed greatly. We are in their debt.

May we also claim your expertise? If you have a cautionary tale, or consider what we say to be misleading in any respect, please e-mail us at: tambler@london.edu or morgen@carucate.co.uk, or chaoxi@cuhk.edu.hk. We would be glad to hear from you.

David Hall and Roger Ames (1998: 30–1), in a fine introduction to Chinese philosophy, note that the Chinese character *zhi*, which means 'knowledge' or 'wisdom', also has connotations of enjoyment. Knowledge and happiness in Chinese thinking are mutually dependent. This is probably true on a practical level as well. The more knowledgeable you are about China, the easier life becomes. Business decisions will become less stressful, and relationships with Chinese partners will become less tricky. Doing business in China becomes not only profitable but enjoyable. Achieving both profit and enjoyment in your China venture is success by anyone's standards.

Part I

1   The road to Cathay

It is certain that in the course of time, and at an increasing pace, China will tend to become industrialised. There is likely to be sustained demand for capital goods and, concurrently with it, a demand for consumer goods in which the emphasis will swing in the direction of high quality specialised products as China succeeds in producing more consumer goods for herself ... In the course of time, a great and profitable trade can flow between our two countries.

(Report on the UK Board of Trade Mission
to China in 1946)

There are few remarks concerning China of which the exact opposite cannot be said with equal truth. The fact is that 'China' and the 'Chinese' are words which embrace so vast a subject that any attempt to deliberate details inevitably obscures the main features of the subject ... China, like statistics, can be made to supply apparent proof for any preconceived notion.

(Stephen King-Hall, *Western Civilization and
the Far East*, 1924)

The Board of Trade Report cited above, produced just after the end of the Second World War in Asia but while Chiang Kai-shek and Mao Zedong were still fighting over who would control China, was remarkably prophetic. It outlines a message for China hopefuls which is just as true more than 60 years later: make sure China wants you. This chapter looks at the first steps to China market entry. Topics covered include research before the first visit; options for visiting; finding business partners; using a staging post (i.e. making a first base in one of the other East or Southeast Asian countries); and the decision to enter.

Research before the first visit

Most businesses considering China have goods or services that they think would sell there, or products they are making or planning to make that might be sourced from China, or both. In other words, they are extending their current business. Strategically, the least risky option is to take a winning formula and roll it out into another market, adjusting to suit local conditions. It is unusual for a foreign entrepreneur to start his or her first business in China, although examples do exist; see the case of Sino Infrastructure later in this chapter. As one would expect, Chinese government at all levels and business are much more welcoming to those creating new exports for them than those seeking to enter their market. They are also more welcoming to those bringing goods of strategic value to China – high-technology and infrastructure, for example – than consumer brands like drinks. For our purposes, we adopt the most difficult case, market entry, leaving the reader to adapt the comments for sourcing. This book therefore assumes that an existing business is being expanded into the China market, but most of the ideas and information are relevant to China sourcing and new start-ups as well.

What sort of research does the first-time businessperson need to do? The first thing most people think of is market research. Ideally, of course, when setting up a new business with the aim of selling in China, the manager would want to know the likely demand for the firm's products and services, whether customers will pay the asking price, and whether they will do so more or less on time.

None of this can be discovered for China (or any other export market) by prior market research. It may be somewhat radical, but our view is that market research is largely useless in determining commercial opportunities – how much business there will be, or what people will buy and at what price. Research can establish *current facts*; it cannot provide hypothetical future data. Furthermore, as we shall see in Chapter 8, market research and statistics are less reliable in China than, say, Europe or North America.

Contrary to popular belief, there is never a 'gap' in the market for a new product or service. Rather, good innovations create their own 'gaps'. Research will not provide an answer. If research shows that equivalent products or services already exist, the nay-sayers will tell you that the market is already satisfied. If the equivalent does *not* exist, then they will tell you there can be no demand. In principle, China has a market for any good product, though intangible services are more difficult. There are, after all, more than 1.3 billion people in China; and while it is a dead certainty that not all of them will want your offering, some of them probably will. The questions are, how many, and where are they? And (this may be the killer) how much will they pay? Don't put too much reliance on reports of the rising Chinese middle class and their spending power. There are a lot more people with disposable income in China than before, but this does not mean they are willing to throw their money away. Chinese consumers have made their money through hard work, and are as canny and price-sensitive as any in the world.

There are, of course, benefits in doing market research before deciding on the appropriate marketing mix for the launch. A snapshot of the present puts future knowledge into perspective. Nevertheless, there can be few, if any, situations which justify commissioning new market research before the first China visit. Good first impressions require the appearance of being knowledgeable, but that can be gained from already published sources. Euromonitor is one example, or the *China Business Guide* published by *China Economic Review*. We have met managers going to China, and even taking up expatriate postings, who have read nothing at all. That is not only foolish; it is rude to the Chinese hosts.

First-time business visitors to China have this problem. They will discover most of what they need to know in China itself. Even if they had the time intensively to study beforehand, their study will make little useful impression until they have confronted the reality. Yet no businessperson, Chinese or otherwise, wants to spend time educating a novice when they could be out making money for themselves.[1] Where is the balance? Apart from the visit arrangements, this or another introductory book, together with a quick review of published market information (see below), should be enough.

Given the competing demands on most people's time, there is always a problem of how much information is enough. If one is visiting the Isle of Man from Iowa, the locals would forgive a lack of grasp of the finer points of the Manx socio-economic situation. If one is visiting Northern Ireland, on the other hand, ignorance of the fundamental political situation could create very serious trouble. China is somewhere between these two extremes: ignorance is unlikely to lead to physical risk, but it will result in loss of face. As the largest country with the longest surviving civilisation, China is, from the perspective of most of its inhabitants, the centre of the universe.

Before the first visit, then, one should therefore achieve (a) a basic understanding of the sector markets in which one is interested, and (b) some general knowledge and an understanding of social sensibilities.

Market facts

Forty years ago, getting market information for China was almost impossible; today, there is an embarrassment of data but not, unfortunately, of riches. Much of the information is unreliable and one soon learns to ask the same questions of many different people. Although there have been some improvements in data collection and analysis, accurate statistics about China remain hard to come by.

The problem of getting useful information from the World Wide Web (noted below) reflects a broader problem. Both China itself and the rest of the world publish more statistics about the Chinese economy and trade than anyone can assimilate. They may be out of date or even intentionally misleading. Disraeli famously remarked that there are lies, damned lies, and then there are statistics. Market research companies are no longer, as before, required to share their findings with the relevant ministry before they show them to clients; that regulation was repealed in 2004. Nevertheless, the suspicion remains that statistics are in some cases – not all – massaged in order to keep friends in government happy.

Some places to start include (the examples given are from the UK and the USA, but similar sources are available in most countries and now also on the Web):[2]

- specialist information providers
- home government
- home embassy in China
- home-country professionals and businesses
- dedicated trade bodies
- Chinese embassies abroad
- Chinese businesses
- the Web.

Specialist information providers

These include businesses and organisations such as the Economist Intelligence Unit (EIU) and Euromonitor. These will provide a range of special reports and databases.[3] Euromonitor's excellent

Directory and Sourcebook are a 'must' for any company entering the market.

Also, its online market research catalogue (www.marketsearch-dir.com) has around 9,000 market research reports from around the world, including a number on China. The EIU's country reports provide good background on socio-economic conditions and are updated yearly. Occasionally you will find these reports on shelf or online at a business school or institutional library. There are a range of magazines and journals covering China; many are highly academic but others such as *Far Eastern Economic Review* or *China Economic Review* can be helpful. Again, these provide background on the market, not leads into the market itself. *McKinsey Quarterly* has published useful in-house research on China over the past few years; some examples can be found in the bibliography at the end of this book.

Home government

Most governments of countries that actively trade with China will provide information and assistance to exporters. In Britain, the Department of Business, Enterprise and Regulatory Reform (DBERR), the clunky new name of the old Department of Trade and Industry, has an agency known as UK Trade and Investment, which provides support for companies wishing to explore market opportunities overseas. According to its website (www.uktradeinvest.gov.uk), the agency provides information and research reports and will also help companies join trade missions, visit trade fairs and so on (see below). As yet, we have no reports as to how effective this agency actually is. The US Department of Commerce offers similar facilities, as do trade ministries in most Western countries.

Home embassy in China

One of the jobs of embassies abroad is to help their nationals make contacts and establish relationships with clients and partners. Some embassies are better at this than others. The US Embassy in Beijing has an extensive commercial section, though the current level of political tension between China and the USA needs to be considered. The British Embassy in Peking (as they continue to call it; they do not call Rome 'Roma' either) has since the 1980s been proactive and helpful. Again, the current political situation may have a bearing.

Home-country professionals and businesses

This category includes banks, lawyers, accountants and consultants, including both specialist 'China' consultancies like Clifford Chance and A.T. Kearney and international firms with a presence in China like Accenture, PricewaterhouseCoopers (PWC), Boston Consulting Group, Bain, McKinsey and Ernst & Young. How much information they will provide before the meter starts making expensive noises depends on your existing and potential relationship with them. Many of the larger firms (including Clifford Chance, A.T. Kearney, Accenture and PWC) publish useful reports on business in China, available free or for a small fee; we mentioned *McKinsey Quarterly* above.

These organisations are also valuable in that they tend to have, on staff or as advisers, people with considerable personal experience of China. Increasingly, consultancy firms are hiring Chinese professional staff, some educated in the West, some in China. Many of these are highly intelligent and talented people, speaking excellent English, who see serving Western clients and serving China as coterminous. They can be valuable sources of insight.

Reading about China is one thing: hearing about it from someone who has already 'seen it and done it' is another. For a small fee or sometimes even just the cost of a good lunch, you can learn a lot in a short time. Finally, all the major organisations and many of the smaller ones have representative offices in China, which can usefully provide further information and make introductions during the visit. Most consultancies are now firmly established in Beijing and Shanghai, and those without a Hong Kong presence can often be found in Guangzhou. Some have opened offices in Wuhan in central China.

Dedicated trade bodies

These include both government-sponsored groups such as the US–China Business Council and the China–Britain Business Council (CBBC, previously called the China–Britain Trade Group), and private bodies such as the American Chamber of Commerce in China. These have many of the advantages of the firms we noted above, except their fees tend to be lower. The CBBC, for example, has a compact but comprehensive library (for members), of books, journals, magazines, trade reports and cuttings. Its principal function is to promote British trade through connecting

Chinese and British business partners, and to this end it organises business trips to China and helps act as a *hongniang* (go-between) to match British and Chinese firms through its offices in many major Chinese cities. Other similar bodies exist in most Western European countries.

The reciprocal to these Western bodies is the China Council for the Promotion of International Trade (CCPIT), formerly largely an export body, but now much more interested in companies seeking to invest in China. It has a good website (www.english.ccpit.org) and numerous links to local chambers of commerce, industry bodies and the like in China. The site is by no means exhaustive, but it might be a good place to get started.

Chinese embassies abroad

The Chinese Embassy is basically there to deal with the host government, not individual businesses, and still less individual managers. In particular cases, through contacts perhaps, information may be provided. Their subsidiary units may be helpful if the enquiry happens to strike a chord with a current Chinese need. The initial approach may need a contact who can arrange introductions to the right people.

Chinese businesses abroad

Chinese banks and investment groups such as the Bank of China, Construction Bank and Citic, to name just a few, are now commonly found in the financial districts of Western cities. Increasingly, they are being joined by Chinese industrial groups, airlines and other businesses seeking an international presence. To deal with any of these, you will need, first, an introduction, and second, something they want: money to invest, an innovative product or service that will grab their attention, and so on. They are not in the advice game, and will not take kindly to being approached by strangers wanting to pick their brains. But if the criteria above are met, then by all means seek out these organisations and learn as much as possible. If there are existing personal relationships or friendships with people in these organisations, then of course the matter changes; buy as many lunches or dinners as you can until you have learned what you need.

Remember, though, that these companies are by and large here to do business in the West, not in China. Increasingly, doing business with the Chinese does not necessarily mean going to China.

The Web

The virtual anarchy which we know and love as the Internet provides some good sites with up-to-date information. For every one such site there are 99 containing rubbish, out-of-date or incorrect statistics, short and fairly useless 'overviews', and rants by various groups of cranks.

Some of the organisations noted above, such as the EIU and Euromonitor, have very good websites with useful macro- and micro-level information. *Asia Business Journal* also has a good site. The following are some of the websites we have found useful and valuable, though we make no promises about any of them (not least as to whether they will still be up and running by the time this book gets onto the shelves).

- US–China Business Council (www.uschina.org)
- Canada–China Business Council (www.ccbc.com)
- China Council for the Promotion of International Trade (www.english.ccpit.org)
- Business China (www.business-china.com)
- China Business World (www.chinabusinessworld.com)
- China Business Review (www.chinabusinessreview.com)
- South China Morning Post (www.scmp.com)
- China Daily (www.chinadaily.com.cn)
- Straits Times (Singapore) (www.straitstimes.com)
- Wall Street Journal Asia (www.wsj-asia.com)
- Financial Times, Asia (www.ft.com/home/asia)

Availability of facts

What facts should be available from the above sources? The size of the market perhaps, the extent to which products sold in it are domestic or imported, and, if the latter, which countries are exporting to China. With luck, you may discover which companies now lead the market, which competitors are already in China, and how long they have been there. You may also discover which parts of China have been penetrated by the competition. This can be useful, as China is a big place: for example, presence in Guangdong may not inhibit any first-mover advantage in other provinces. Success or failure in one place may not indicate success or failure in another Chinese market.

A favourite topic of many China hands concerns the number of 'markets' there are in China, given the geographical and cultural diversity of the country. While a province-by-province separation is convenient and used by Chinese domestic marketers, even these groupings are so large as to allow many 'markets' to exist within them (see Chapter 2 for more on this, and also the case study, 'The Pine Nut King' in Chapter 7). Any cake ultimately divides into as many pieces as you care to cut it into. Realistically, each product has to consider the market characteristics necessary for its own situation (number of consumers, spending power per consumer, extent of competition, likely pricing and costs) in order to assess the minimum size of an entry market. From this starting point, one can then move on to consider how many conurbations or other regions in China have the required characteristics, that is, how many markets there are for that product. Then one can start choosing target markets, although with care, and keeping options open. The short answer is that your market should be dictated by the resources available: the fewer the resources, the smaller the territory. No matter how clear a picture you may think you have, reality may differ once you are on the ground.

What is less likely to be available? Information about consumers, retailers, pricing, packaging, distribution, availability, promotions and advertising are all unlikely to be found in your home country except very generally, unless you are able to network through to market research firms with China offices (see Chapter 8 for more on market research in China). Otherwise, you will need to visit China to see the situation for yourself.

Summary of market information sources

- specialist information providers
- home government
- home embassy in China
- home-country professionals and businesses
- dedicated trade bodies
- Chinese embassies abroad
- Chinese businesses
- the Web.

General knowledge and sensibilities

Chinese hosts would prefer (but do not necessarily expect) the visitor to have some knowledge of:

- geography, recent history and economic reform
- culture and etiquette, notably on matters of the table
- power, i.e. who is who in organisations, governments and ministries, as distinct from politics.

Readers of international media will find regular briefings on the overall political and socio-economic situation hard to avoid, but these should be treated with care. The Western press irritates the Chinese, and so media coverage provides a good list of topics to avoid. This does not just refer to government and Communist Party officials; as noted above, many ordinary Chinese find Western reportage of events in China biased. This particularly applies to Western press coverage of issues such as human rights, where many Chinese believe the Western media are particularly hypocritical (see Chapter 2 on China from a Western Perspective).[4]

Up-to-date geographies of China are hard to find, and many are fairly technical geography textbooks; but even out-of-date works will give information about landforms, climate and so on, should you need to know them.[5] Basic geographies can be found in many of the best short histories of China.[6] More detailed geographical information is available in Baedeker, which provides details including population and climate for every province, city and town of any size in China.[7]

Edwin Moise's *Modern China: A History* (1994) provides an excellent summary of recent history, while Charles Hucker's *China to 1850: A Short History* (1978) covers imperial China succinctly and intelligently (but he uses Wade–Giles rather than pinyin spellings). We also suggest Ray Huang's *A Macro History of China* (1990).

Five books to choose from

With enough time to spare, the following will give a flavour of the past:

Jonathan Spence, *God's Chinese Son* (1997). Fascinating account of the Taiping Rebellion that almost destroyed China in the nineteenth century.

T.H. White, *In Search of History* (1978). White had close personal contact with Mao Zedong, Zhou Enlai and the other leaders of the Communist revolution.

Sunzi (Sun Tzu), *The Art of War*. Classic Chinese work on strategy, available in a number of readable translations both in print and on the Web.

Robert van Gulik, *The Chinese Lake Murders* (1989; 4th edn). Fiction set in the Song dynasty, immaculately researched, full of a sense of time and place, and more fun than Pearl S. Buck.

Cao Xueqin, *Dream of the Red Chamber*. Perhaps the most famous classic Chinese novel, the tale of a wealthy Suzhou family's slide into decade and decline. Long but rewarding.

Food plays an important role in Chinese culture, and it is probably worth acquiring some familiarity with it. No restaurants in any Chinatown will prepare the visitor for food in China, though they will provide some idea of the regional variation. They will also help provide dexterity with chopsticks, which is worth acquiring if weight loss during the first visit is to be minimised.

A lot is written and said by Westerners about alcohol consumption, particularly the practice of repeated toasts during and after a meal. The more macho views on this subject can be treated with scepticism. Teetotallers will not be forced to drink, if they simply make their position clear, politely, from the outset. No one will think any the less of them.

Chinese names may seem a trivial matter for concern but names can cause embarrassment both ways around. We all know that Chinese put family names first and Westerners put them last, with the Spanish cultural variation of having the mother's family name last. But the Chinese sometimes, in an effort to be polite or to conform to expectations, reverse the order. Thus Xi Chao becomes Chao Xi. Most Chinese family names are just one character and personal names are two. This makes distinguishing the two pretty obvious. And of course when Tim Ambler goes to China, they all know his family name must be Tim.

Chinese females belonging to the elder generations (those born in the 1950s to mid-1970s) tend to have single-character personal names. Shorter names sound more 'revolutionary'. The newer generations (especially those born after the 1990s) have single-character names less often, perhaps because a longer name is more individual. A girl named ZHAO Yan, for example, may find at least 20 other Zhao Yan in her city. The move to multi-character personal names may reflect a cultural change; people now want to distinguish themselves from others. While two-character personal names remain the main form, others are being added and the record is said to be eight characters. This change is causing problems for China's bureaucracy, whose forms have limited provision for multi-naming.

This wish for individuality in names does not apply in the West, where duplications are common. There are at least two other Tim Amblers, one a musician and the other an airline pilot. Morgen Witzel may be unique, at least Google found none other. It did, however, produce this choice suggestion:

> ### Morgen Witzel
>
> www.ebay.co.uk **Morgen Witzel** on eBay for less. Feed your passion on eBay.co.uk!

In other words, names are likely to cause confusion wherever you go!

Finally, and back to business, a health warning: briefings and books like this one usually provide long lists stating how much executives must learn before visiting China, to the point of inducing total paralysis. There can never be enough time in a busy manager's schedule to learn all this stuff before departing. (In fact, having fallen into the same trap, we then removed most of our own suggestions while the first edition of this book was in draft, and in succeeding editions we have tried to pare back to the essentials.) There is no need to be over-prepared; natural courtesy will nearly always suffice. More important is to be friendly, to be alert, and above all, to keep an open mind. Some people talk of China being another world. It isn't. It is just a different part of the same world we all inhabit. There are plenty of differences between Western and Chinese people, but there are plenty of common features too.

If time is short, just browse through this book and any of the better tourist guides, such as *Lonely Planet*, which cover the essentials. It is probably more important that the first-time visitor reads *something*, rather than worrying too long over choosing the right thing to read.

Options for visiting

Broadly, there are five types of first visits:

- trade missions, led by Chambers of Commerce, trade bodies or trade associations
- cooperative missions, with perhaps 3–5 people from different companies sharing costs
- fairs, exhibitions and trade shows
- bought-in expertise
- individual.

Trade missions

These are a specialism of the dedicated trade bodies we discussed above. They offer several advantages, including both the opportunity to network like-minded businesses from your own country, and access to a wider variety of Chinese contacts than might otherwise be possible. Costs will be lower and may well be subsidised by your own government. Most of the hassle involved in setting up meetings, accommodation and travel is taken care of by the sponsoring body. More importantly, tuition about China is, in effect, provided as one goes along.

Missions have an advantage in that Chinese hosts will tend to react a bit more positively and 'push the boat out' to help delegates. An official delegation has a reassuring cohesion and substantive image, particularly if the sponsoring body has good relationships and reputation. Meeting the group's needs becomes a matter of face and, in general, more effort will be made to help with requests for meetings and introductions. Groups tend to have established seniority rankings and go-betweens. This enables the hosts to understand who is who within the group context, and to make judgements as to which members are most valuable.

Less good is the fact that time may have to be given to activities and subjects one might rather avoid. As groups are becoming more regional and specialised, the difficulty of keeping distance from direct competitors (welcomed by China of course) increases. A group always travels more slowly than an individual. This will partly depend on the balance of initiative and interest on the

Chinese and UK sides. Missions may be organised by trade sector or geographic destination(s). To minimise these problems, schedules are generally tailor-made. In the UK, the China–Britain Business Council usually meets with companies joining a trade mission for a couple of hours, well before the mission departs for China. The company's entry strategy is discussed (and perhaps challenged), and then personal appointments are made in line with that. The group travels together and meets up in the evenings, but each individual may pursue his/her own agenda.

A trade mission might best be treated more as a reconnaissance than with the expectation of finding the right partner, still less finalising a deal. On the other hand, as the mission sponsor's local offices organise the local arrangements, sensitive briefing can help to line up reasonable prospects. Trade missions are usually only a first step, but they can help open doors and establish relationships that will bloom in the future.

It is no bad thing to treat these missions as opportunities for people-watching, as distinct from business-finding. Try to develop the 'golden eye', the origins of which expression lie in the ancient story of the Monkey King. In essence, the golden eye allows you to distinguish real people from ghosts. Most bureaucracies in any country are filled with 'ghosts'. Of the huge number you will meet on a mission, only some will be 'real' and only some of those may become friends and partners. The ability to use the golden eye is far more likely to determine market entry success than any economic analysis.

As China's market economy has developed, these group missions have become less fashionable. But they do retain value for those who really have no experience of China and want to get their feet wet. The alternative is to go on your own and simply travel as a business tourist (we will come onto this in a moment), but trade missions still offer superior opportunities to make contacts, providing you can afford the time and cost.

Cooperative missions

Cooperative missions are similar to trade missions but are more tailored. This means less time spent on boring activities, but probably less access to top officials. It is unlikely that you will know compatible businesses wanting to visit China at the same time, but there are consultants who will put interested businesses together and help with the administration. Some of these specialise in working with smaller firms, and will generally do their best to help keep costs down. Again, these are becoming less common but still have a role to play.

Fairs, exhibitions and trade shows

Fairs and exhibitions are the modern equivalent of the markets along the silk road in Marco Polo's day. Handled skilfully, they are not just places to exchange goods or services for money but centres of information and the beginnings of friendships. They can also go horribly wrong; there are plenty of tales of sitting in a cavernous hall for a week, surrounded by people who don't want to know, with nothing to fill in the time except to calculate how much this experience is costing. However, a little advance spadework can avoid this fate. As one tactic, consider organising a reception (perhaps jointly to spread costs) for other compatible exhibitors and potential customers. Send out personal invitations ahead of time, using local business directories. Telephone first to try to learn personal names, rather than just inviting 'The Marketing Director'. A formal personal invitation card is highly regarded. Guests will also be favourably impressed if the attention they receive on arrival is personal, intensive and enjoyable for them. It should be like an invitation to one's own home.

In more high-tech sectors, the technical seminar has replaced the fair. Travel is simplified since, in theory, the customers come to you. Government agencies may be able to help defray some of the costs in these cases, as most Western governments are keen to support anything connected with high-tech. Another advantage of technical seminars is the involvement of the ubiquitous Chinese research institutes. These bodies are a bridge between Chinese industry and academia, and provide much of the leading thinking for Chinese commerce. Here, a successful approach in making contacts may be to stress knowledge transfer rather than commerce; this approach is more likely to succeed in getting the more senior and/or more technical brains of the institute to attend. Of course, the potential downside is that one may end up transferring knowledge without generating business for oneself.

The Guangzhou Trade Fair (www.cantonfair.org.cn) is the grandfather of them all and also the largest, with over 5,000 exhibitors. Founded in 1957, it is held twice-yearly; the 103rd session of the Fair was held in April 2008. There are national and international pavilions, the latter devoted to goods that China exports, and a recent addition is a Multinational Sourcing Service which helps overseas companies find outsourcing partners in China. Many other regional or sector-specific trade fairs have sprung up since the mid-1980s (organisations like Euromonitor provide lists of these, and some also advertise directly on the World Wide Web). Fairs can be an extremely good way of getting one's foot in the door, but as with trade missions, they do not necessarily result in immediate business.

An associated concept, not really a trade fair, is to participate in or host 'technical' lectures to explain how the products are made, tested and used. There is an insatiable thirst for knowledge, especially anything that can be seen as technology transfer.

Bought-in (or borrowed) expertise

Many larger firms prefer to buy, either directly or indirectly, the expertise they need in order to gain entry. They may prefer to avoid official and semi-official events and visits for a number of reasons. Bespoke tours may be better targeted and more relevant to the company's needs; they will probably also be more enjoyable. They are almost certainly a better use of time, but they are also likely to be the most expensive option. Bespoke visits and tours can be arranged through:

- consultants, either the major international firms or small China specialists, depending on preference
- overseas Chinese entrepreneurs with whom contact is already established
- existing businesses in Greater China contacted similarly.

This is the classic Chinese method, using one's existing network to effect new introductions; in other words, developing or using *guanxi* (relationships).[8] In many circumstances, it is the best solution. Certainly it applies the local system to the local market. However, the hazards are those of any networking solution: the intermediaries may pass on only what they want you to know. Fred's brother in Chengdu is not necessarily the best wholesaler in Chengdu. Objectivity and independence may be hard to achieve and, once the contacts have been made, it may be too late to consider alternatives. Therefore, it is very important to find the right intermediary in the first place.

Selecting the right mode of introduction largely depends on the quality, integrity and relevance of the intermediary, and the cost. McKinsey is not cheap, but then a Hong Kong Mr Five Per Cent, a 'bag company' (an entrepreneur whose only asset is his briefcase), may ultimately cost more. The expertise and contacts displayed by a sole consultant may be brilliant; they may also be ephemeral or substantive. Again, as a newcomer, it can be very difficult to tell. There is much to be said for joining forces with a compatible business, if you can find one. Be warned that some consultants will also try to sell you their own services, which may include a model for the 'best' way of doing business in China. Listen to them, but keep an open mind. Some of these people are brilliant; others are people whose own business ventures in China have gone belly-up and who are now trying to scrape a living advising others on how to make the same mistakes. (This may sound harsh, but it is also true.)

The networking approach is potentially the best, but it is also potentially the worst. Getting the right partner from the start can lead to a dream relationship; getting the wrong one can land you in a nightmare of which there are all too many examples. Get to know potential partners well before agreeing anything substantive, still less signing anything. Homework on partners is *much* more important than homework on the market. Good partners will keep the new entrant out of trouble and bad ones will land them in it, whatever the state of the market. We discuss this further in Chapters 4, 5 and 6.

Individual

A small firm may decide it cannot afford professional advice and that they have confidence in their own skills. That's fine: get on a plane and go. But it would still be wise to do some research and read a few books, like this one, before you arrive.

Solo travel in China is now easier than in many parts of the world, and the traveller to the big cities of eastern China will find that hotels and other facilities are as good or better than those at home. If all you want to do is to go and look around, a tourist visa (depending on where you come from) is the best and cheapest option. Most Western travel companies have relationships with private Chinese agents. If all else fails, the state-owned China International Travel Service will book packages and organise tourist visas for solo travellers. Solo travellers can also contact consultancies or organisations like the China–Britain Business Council whose local offices will, for a fee, organise a translator and a schedule of meetings with their contacts. This costs more, but can be very helpful for collecting knowledge.

For business visits, an official 'host' is still needed for visa purposes. You will need the host in China to issue a letter of invitation, which must accompany your visa application. Be warned that, while you are in China, the government will regard the host company or organisation as responsible for you. If the host is genuinely interested in your mission and provides substantive help, life then becomes much easier.

Finding a host to invite you, though, can sometimes be an adventure in its own right. One of the problems is that, unless you have been properly introduced by suitable intermediaries, often you simply do not exist in the minds of Chinese companies. Someone answering a ringing phone in a Chinese office will not necessarily feel any obligation to pass on a message or do a favour for an unknown voice. Letters, messages and faxes are unlikely to get any response unless contact has already been initiated. To complicate life, a letter/fax about a future event may not be deemed worth a response until immediately before that event. Silence probably means 'no'; but it may also mean that a reply is not yet necessary. At all events, make arrangements for meetings before you go to China; simply showing up on the doorstep is not appreciated, and you will probably not be invited in.

If introductions can be made from the home country and if appointments have been confirmed, then the individual visit may prove the most direct (and the most cost-effective) mode of entry. Certainly it is the most flexible. Be warned that appointments need to be reconfirmed once on Chinese soil: one materialises from being a foreign 'ghost' only in stages.

Finding business partners

It should be obvious by now that some sort of partnership arrangement is well-nigh essential in the first instance. As we will discuss later in the book, business in China functions primarily on a relationship basis, whether we are talking about customers, suppliers, joint-venture partners or even local government officials.

What about finding a partner before going to China? As we have seen, desk research and coming up with lists of potential contacts is easy; it is much harder to get a foot in the door so as to actually discuss business with them. Make use of go-betweens wherever possible, such as the China–Britain Business Council or other organisations described above. They have the local knowledge, reputation and *guanxi* to be taken seriously, whereas the visitor is just a ghost.

Ultimately, though, the job has to be done in the field. The first meetings with go-betweens, hosts and other contacts may not yield anything more than a few names. Track these down, using existing relationships to build new ones. Exploit the system: contacts lead to contacts. This will take time, and it will be hard work, but a few days in China will equate to several weeks of research at home. With these new relationships, depth matters more than quantity.

Sino Infrastructure

As an encouraging example of diving straight into the deep end, here is what one young man with a brand new MBA achieved straight off the reel.

In 1994, Geoff Mills was preparing to create a new infrastructure development business in China. On the one side, there were many British engineering and building companies and consultancies looking for work in China. On the Chinese side, infrastructure development was welcomed, provided finance could be arranged at a minimal cost. There was some dissatisfaction in the UK construction industry with the Chinese 'opportunity'. Since the advent of the open-door policy, most of the big firms had been involved in tendering, yet most of the contracts were still going to Chinese firms.

After researching the British firms involved, Mills thought he could put together an arrangement which would aid British firms in tendering. However, he faced two principal problems. British firms would only enter into a partnership with him if there was evidence of the arrangement including Chinese customers. The latter, in turn, were interested but would only come on board if British firms were already committed.

Mills needed a partner in China to help him link the two together. He was fortunate in having a well-connected friend in Hong Kong who was able to advise him on options. These were to:

- team up with a trading company such as Jardine Matheson
- team up with Chinese contractors in the hope of getting these to establish partnerships with their British rivals
- team up with 'design institutes'. These fall under the heading of GONGOs (government-operated non-government organisations) and play a central role in the project approval process; formerly, they oversaw the technical design of projects once

project approval had been given, though their role has diminished of late.
- team up with the People's Liberation Army, then a powerful and growing commercial force.

Mills himself had no China background, little or no Chinese, and few contacts outside Hong Kong. What he had was an idea which he knew would work. Through patience and persistence, he was able to establish links with some of the important design institutes. These, in turn, gave the venture the seal of approval which persuaded both Chinese clients and British contractors to come aboard. Mills's main problem then was how to manage expansion in China's booming construction and building market.

By 2008, the business now looks very different to the original model but the mission has endured unchanged and having that clarity of mission was useful to avoid the many distractions that are a constant feature of an evolving market. It has 130 staff. Their Web site (www.sipgroup.com) gives more background.

The decision to enter

The decision to enter the China market should not be made on the basis of one visit. At best, this visit will introduce key people and increase your stock of knowledge about the country. Leads need following up with further visits. Expect to make three visits before deciding whether China market entry is feasible or desirable. If one visit is all that can be risked, then do not go at all.[9]

This is not wasting time; it is building relationships. Deciding *before* understanding the calibre of relationships, however effective that may seem, is unwise. That said, if some non-committing orders can be filled, so much the better.

Establishing a base in China is not to be done overnight. It takes time to build relationships with clients, partners and others with whom mutual trust can grow. Trust is not an on/off switch. The Chinese use small matters (punctuality, for example) to test commitment. As the tests get bigger and are satisfactorily met, trust grows. The visitor's behaviour and actions on almost every level will be scrutinised by Chinese hosts in an attempt to determine trustworthiness. If suitable relationships are proving elusive, one should consider pulling back and rethinking one's approach. What is putting out the bad vibes? Get help from a Chinese expert.

First encounters with China may be more discouraging than motivating. Sometimes the reverse applies: the welcome mat conceals traps. First impressions in China tend to be even more misleading than usual; after all, this is a culture that distrusts first impressions.

Last of all, a programme of visits needs a clear and realistic set of desired outcomes. Colleagues need a shared view of the minimum conditions for entry; in other words, what results constitute 'go' and 'no go'. Benchmarks for a visit make it possible to assess whether it has been successful. On the other hand, serendipity must be given a chance. One Western firm went to China to sell cheese-making equipment (optimistic, in a non-cheese-eating society), and came back with orders for a bean curd plant, which turned out to require similar equipment. Amazing things turn up if one is alert to them. Be prepared to seize chances as they come.

China is the largest and most difficult market a business can enter (many Chinese would tell you Japan is far harder, but that is another story). If it is not also the most difficult decision, you are either very lucky, or you may be missing something. Too often in the past, the latter has been the case. The last two decades are full of tales of firms that thought they had a lucrative business deal in China sewn up, only for the whole thing to evaporate almost before the wheels of their planes had touched the ground back home.

Are we being unduly pessimistic? No, this is realism. The decision to enter the China market is fraught with risk. However, there are ways and means of laying off that risk. Success is never guaranteed, but should be more likely with the following:

- Do your homework before the visit; not market data and macroeconomic conditions, so much as researching contacts. Cultural and historical reading is good but limited by time.
- Never accept any piece of information about your own potential or prospective market at face value, especially if it comes from a Western source (that goes for this book too, by the way). Always check everything. Remember the dictum that 'Anything one cares to say about China is true; and so is the opposite'.
- Work out in advance where to go and what to achieve.
- Pick a suitable visit type, whether as part of a trade mission or larger group, or as a solo venture.
- Trivial as they may seem, worry about the diplomatic niceties. Pack samples, literature and small gifts. Your contacts will want to take something tangible from your meetings. Get your

business cards ('name cards') printed on the back in Chinese – PRC Chinese, not the traditional characters still used by overseas Chinese. Take a whole box, or two.

• Be prepared for the process to take time. Don't commit without being as certain as possible about your partners.

Inevitably, many of the details in a book like this will prove ephemeral. Names and facts change fast. At the more fundamental level, though, China does not change at all. The success of market entry depends far more on harmonising these fundamental understandings and values than any passing knowledge of current affairs.

Entering overseas Chinese markets

With some provisos, given the differing political, economic and social conditions in their host countries, much of what was said above applies also to the overseas Chinese business communities elsewhere in East Asia. Although some of these communities are hundreds of years old, all still have much in common with Chinese culture, often more than with their host culture. Conditions for the foreigner can be comparatively easy or comparatively hard, depending on the country. For British and American businesspeople, for example, Malaysia, Singapore and the Philippines offer a greater chance of English being spoken and understood by potential contacts. This can help in the initial stages, though the comments we make later in the book about the importance of translation still apply here.

Decisions about pre-market analysis and point of entry apply elsewhere in Southeast Asia, as noted above. (Note that we are talking here about dealing with the Chinese business communities in these countries only; dealings with *bumiputra* Malay or Javanese Indonesian businesses require a different set of cultural assumptions.) So too does the importance of having at least some background knowledge before you go. Finally, we would stress the importance of developing partnerships in the local community. These are still Chinese cultures, and the emphasis on relationships is at least as strong – indeed, in some cases much stronger – than in the PRC.

2   Through a glass darkly
China from a Western perspective

> To regard a nation's mentality as a fixed monolith is to run counter
> to the truth that variety is the law of nature.
>
> (Zhou Lisheng, quoted in
> *Westerners through Chinese Eyes*)[1]

> Thus, as so often when consulting Chinese sources, the historian
> is left with two divergent accounts of the same incident, in which
> the only verifiable statement of fact is palpably untrue.
>
> (Peter Fleming, *The Siege at Peking*)[2]

No matter how much you read about China,[3] ultimately you have
to go there. But on arrival, China is too vast to comprehend. Many
of the sights and experiences are too unfamiliar to grasp. Inevitably
this brings us back to the books to make sense of it all. Reading up
on China will not tell you everything you need to know, but it will
provide background and context for your own impressions. When
visiting the China offices of expatriates, look at their bookshelves.
You can assume that those without books on China will not be
staying in the country for long. Conversely, those very few you
discover to be well-read are the ones whose advice you should most
respect.

Personal experience and macro-level knowledge are complementary; one needs the other. The best learning blends personal
experience and the researches and experiences of others in a
single mix.

We will return to what is *essential* at the end of the chapter, but for
the moment, let us assume the basics outlined in the last chapter.

The Chinese, as we said, are justly proud of their long history and great culture, and expect foreigners to respect these things. Here we amplify:

- the *geography* of China (where things are)
- the *history* of China (why things are)
- the *ethnic make-up* of China (who the Chinese are)
- the *culture* of China, with reference to particularly important points such as language, food, literature and the arts
- the current government of China and the *political situation*
- the Chinese *economy* and its future prospects
- Chinese *attitudes* to the West (both official and unofficial).

Geography

China's contrasts are nowhere more visible than on the map. Virtually every extreme of terrain is present, from the rich coastal plains of the east to the barren mountains and deserts of the west. Contrary to our usual image of a teeming, crowded China, mountains and deserts predominate; much of China is a barely populated wilderness, and only about 13 per cent of its vast surface is arable land.

Geographers, economists and others seeking to segment China have approached the task in different ways. Geographers have tended to divide the country into three from north to south: north China includes the valley of the Huang He (Yellow) River and the north China plain; 'central China' is centred on the valley of the Chang Jiang (Yangtze) River and the coastal provinces around Shanghai; and 'south China', mainly mountainous but with a rich coastal plain, stretching from Guangzhou (Canton) to the Gulf of Tonkin and the Vietnamese border.

Economists also favour a tripartite division, but from east to west. First there is the relatively rich coastal region, which had the initial Special Economic Zones (SEZs) and the greatest amount of foreign direct investment. Next there is the central zone, which has been slower to develop but has now received attention, especially around cities like Wuhan. Last, there is the west, including Sichuan, which continues to lag behind in terms of investment and development, and the wilderness regions of Tibet and Xinjiang. Some of these latter are now receiving high levels of investment. For example, in Xinjiang, to counter nationalist sentiments among the ethnic Turkish and Muslim population the Chinese government is both investing directly and encouraging foreign government and companies to do so as well. The major differences between these regions concern things such as economic output and per capita income, both of which tend to be higher in the east than the west.

Although economic development zones have been set up across the country and the government is pushing hard to channel foreign investment into the centre and west, most foreign companies prefer the eastern coastal belt and the big centres of Guangzhou, Shanghai, Beijing, Tianjin and their satellites. This frankly baffles many Chinese policy-makers, who cannot understand why Westerners want to settle in the east which is more competitive, more crowded and has higher costs, when they could move further inland to find equally lucrative markets with less competition and lower labour costs. But then, Manhattanites wonder what happens in the country between them and California.

For those who want to go a little deeper, the following regions of China can be considered 'key' for business purposes (a more detailed breakdown of the regions is given in the appendix at the end of this chapter).

1   **The Beijing region**. Highly populous and relatively well-off, the centre of political power. People here are considered rather dull and serious by other Chinese.
2   **The Shanghai region**. Very populous, rich and proud of it. Motto: 'In Shanghai we make the money, in Beijing they spend it'. It is sometimes seen as money-mad, and lacking human warmth by other Chinese.
3   **The Guangdong region**. Southern, with a different language and different attitudes; considered rather brash and loud by other Chinese. Includes the first SEZs, and a long track record of foreign investment. Overcrowded infrastructure and pollution in the coastal regions mean the authorities are now looking to move beyond 'smokestack' industries.
4   **The Wuhan region**. The central heartland around the lower Chang Jiang (Yangtze) valley, well-populated and industrialised, looking forward to catching up with the better-off coastal regions.
5   **The west**. Sichuan, distinctive with its mouldering high-tech industries, sub-tropical climate and fiery cooking. Populous and eager to reap the benefits of economic reform; but many parts of the region are still waiting.

6   **Manchuria**. Often overlooked by Western investors, but rich in raw resources and industry. Shenyang and Harbin are populous and becoming prosperous.
7   **The rest**. The highlands, mountains and deserts, often empty and desolate, but with some large population centres; many non-Chinese ethnic groups inhabit these regions.

All these classifications have their utility, but for the first-time businessperson they can still be a bit daunting. After all, we are dealing with a country any one of whose provinces is the equivalent to a fair-sized European state. Sichuan has a population equivalent to France and Italy combined, or all of the states of the USA west of the Mississippi and south of New York combined.

Any one of the regions above could possibly make a useful entry point for China; all of them have markets large enough for most companies' needs, at least initially. The question is, which one do you choose?

History

A 'concise history of China' is almost an oxymoron, but useful summaries can be found in bookshops and library shelves; we recommended a few in Chapter 1. Most textbooks divide Chinese history into periods determined by the ruling dynasties. The appendix at the end of this chapter gives a brief résumé, with some notes for those too busy to read more deeply. The time frames are, of course, artificial divisions imposed by later historians, but they are widely accepted and do give an easy structure for the vastness of Chinese history.

Western businesspeople are notoriously reluctant to study history, usually citing some version of Henry Ford's dictum that 'history is bunk' (with pleasing irony, Ford himself has now become a major historical figure) and maintaining that the past is not relevant to the needs of modern managers and businesses. Even if this were true, China represents a special case. In China, history is very important indeed, and is taken seriously by almost everyone. Even more than the need to understand how China became what it is today, the Westerner needs to recognise what historian W.F. Jenner calls 'the tyranny of history', the powerful influence of the past on the Chinese national psyche.[4]

This point cannot be emphasised too strongly. In China, history is important if no other reason, *because the Chinese themselves believe it is*.

Even those Chinese that reject much of their past and want to become truly 'modern' are still influenced by history, even if only in a negative way. Recognising this is of critical importance to understanding China.

Beyond the bare framework of names and dates, however, there are some powerful themes in Chinese history, which are still alive today and which do have an indirect and often a direct bearing on the business environment. The following aspects of Chinese history should form an essential part of the businessperson's body of macro-knowledge.

The integrity of China

Many Chinese, probably the majority, believe implicitly in the territorial integrity of China. They are often rather hazier about where the boundaries should be drawn. The Han heartland of north China has been the core of Chinese and political entities for millennia, but the south and especially the southwest, with its large non-Han populations, entered the Chinese fold only later. Other areas, such as Manchuria, Taiwan, Tibet and the Turkish far west, only became attached to China in the last 500 years. Still other areas once under Chinese rule, like Vietnam, are independent today. Where, then, should the boundaries of China lie? This is a subject for some debate among the older generation of China's political leaders, and a source of concern in some quarters in the West, especially the USA. It is important to remember that the PRC's claims to, for example, Taiwan are meant seriously and are part of an emotional attachment that many Chinese feel to the integrity of their homeland. Sabre-rattling from the West will not change this view over the long term.

The threat from the outside world

Textbooks on business, politics or economics in China seldom miss a chance to point out that many Chinese dislike and mistrust foreigners, referring to them as 'barbarians' or 'foreign devils'. This point is often overstated. In fact, throughout Chinese history there has been a continuous interchange with the outside world in which not only goods but ideas were imported and found a place in some part of Chinese society. In former centuries, Buddhism, Christianity and Islam were imported along these lines. In the nineteenth century, critical Chinese saw the weakness of their country, and concluded that its best strategy was to learn from the West and became more like it (a view reinforced by the success of Japan, which did exactly this). The revolution that toppled the Qing dynasty was motivated by a desire by its leaders to make China more 'Western'. The Communists too recognised the need for contact with the West; it was Mao who opined that China should learn from the West, apply that knowledge which seemed relevant to the Chinese situation, and discard the rest. Even during the height of the Cultural Revolution, many Western companies were trading quietly with China.

Setting aside specific examples of distrust (the present Chinese government probably distrusts the US government at least as much as the latter does the former, for example), the major concern of most Chinese is not the presence of foreigners, but the impact they may have on Chinese culture and society. It is important to recognise that China's views of the outside world have been formed over centuries of often unhappy history. In the early centuries, China's primary external contacts were with Turkish, Mongol and Tibetan nomad raiders from the north and west and Japanese pirates to the east. These forces brought disorder and chaos; at times, the invaders even occupied China and ruled it. In fact, for more than half of the last thousand years, part or all of China has been ruled for a foreign power. The Manchus of the Qing dynasty adopted much of Chinese culture but remained a distinct ethnic group who controlled nearly all the political power in the country. In 1912 with the fall of the empire, there were massacres of Manchus in the south, where local Chinese took revenge for two and half centuries of foreign oppression.

More recently, contacts with the West have often been equally unhappy. The Ming dynasty restricted foreign traders to a narrow point of entry around Guangzhou, where they had to do business with local middlemen. This state of affairs lasted until a combination of opium and modern artillery blasted open the doors of China in the 1830s and 1840s, and the Western nations began to impose their authority. The damage opium did to Chinese society in the nineteenth century has never been properly assessed, but the memory of the opium trade remains vivid today. The Westerners also spread ideas, which could be just as dangerous as drugs. In the 1850s Hong Xiuquan, a young Hakka man from the south who had just failed his civil service exams, had a nervous breakdown and became convinced that he was the younger brother of the Christian God. Armed with a partial Chinese translation of the Old Testament and a series of prophetic visions, he began converting his fellows. The result was the Taiping rebellion (1853–64), which laid waste to central China and cost at least 20 million lives.

In the twentieth century, foreign meddling in China also occurred; US and other Western backing for Chiang Kai-shek and the Guomindang was bitterly resented by many Chinese. Then came the Japanese invasion with its immense destruction and loss of life. The Rape of Nanking, which may have resulted in 100,000 deaths, was but the best-publicised of many such incidents.

And yet, the foreigner going to China is nearly always treated hospitably and with great politeness. Surely the question should not be, 'Why do the Chinese distrust foreigners?' but rather, 'Why after the last thousand years, are they willing to speak to us at all?' The simple answer usually given is that we have things that China wants, such as investment capital and technology; true, of course, but far from the whole picture.

The Chinese as a nation do not hate or fear foreigners. Genuine xenophobia is very rare. Most Chinese, like most Americans, British or French, are by nature hospitable and welcoming. The Chinese are, from bitter experience, wary of the influence that foreigners bring. Contact with the outside world can bring instability and chaos, two things that most Chinese fear most of all.

The fear of chaos

China is (we'll say it again) vast and complex, but it is also fragile. The economy was, and to a large extent still is, dependent on agriculture. Foreign invasion, internal unrest and natural disaster could easily disrupt the agrarian economy, and when they did, the result was disaster. At the end of the Han dynasty period, the population of China was about 60 million. By the end of the wars of the Three Kingdoms period, 60 years later, the population had fallen by one-half. By the time the Ming dynasty took power, twelve centuries later, the population was still only 60 million; all the natural increase had been swallowed up in the bloody cycle of war, invasion, earthquake and flood. Small wonder that in classical Chinese thought, heaven is populated by a celestial bureaucracy which attempts to maintain order and keep out the demons who bring chaos.

Order is a primary social and political goal in China; it may even be the most important goal. Government policy on the economy, the reform of state enterprises, the welfare system and many other areas can look inconsistent and changeable, until you realise this simple truth: one of the government's chief policy goals is the promotion of stability. The economic reform programme began with this in mind, and economic growth and diversification continue to be focused on this. No other organisation – least of all a foreign business – whose activities seriously threaten stability will be tolerated for too long. And that still applies even now that China has joined the WTO and is expected to abide by international business regulations and norms of behaviour. The government can and does terminate the licences of those businesses that behave against the interests of the state, foreign as well as domestic.

The authority of the state

To defend against chaos, on earth as in heaven, China has erected formidable government and administrative structures. The Qin emperor, bringing order and unity to China after the chaos of the Warring States period, set the pattern followed by every ruler of China since, including the Communists: a strong, authoritarian administration and bureaucracy, pyramidal in structure, with the emperor himself at its head. In Neo-Confucian thinking (see Chapter 3), the state had a structure similar to that of the family; the emperor/father owed a duty of care to his subjects, who in turn owed him unquestioning obedience. Only through this mutual bond could order be maintained.

With some modifications, this theory has stood the test of time. Incoming dynasties, or in this century the Communist Party, usually assumed power with a great deal of moral credit, as they were perceived to have the power to clean up corruption, unite the country, oust foreign invaders and so on. Over time, of course, people start to become more cynical about their rulers and the bonds grow weaker. But criticism of rulers in China almost never means that people want to change the system by which they are governed; what they usually want is the same system but a change of ruler. Sun Yat-sen got this badly wrong in 1912 when he tried to replace the empire with a republic; the experiment lasted just a year before authoritarian rule returned under Yuan Shikai and then Chiang Kai-shek. Today, some Western observers interpret growing criticism of the Communist Party in China as a desire for democracy. This seems unlikely; what the average Chinese wants is a strong, honest leader who will guarantee stability, peace and prosperity.

The just revolutionary

Paradoxically, despite the fear of chaos and desire for stability, Chinese history is full of revolutionary movements and secret societies, from the Red Eyebrows rebel movement who overthrew the usurper Wang Mang and restored the Han dynasty in the first century AD, to the Buddhist-influenced White Lotus Society who rebelled repeatedly against the Qing in the eighteenth century. As dynasties grow weaker, such groups proliferate; the end of the nineteenth century saw hundreds of such groups springing up around China, the most famous of whom were the Boxers.

With very few exceptions – such as the special case of the Taiping, who were a religious movement apparently seeking radical change – these movements were all conservative. They did not want to change the system; they wanted to remove rulers who were perceived to be incapable of ruling. Most had roots in ancient philosophical movements such as Buddhism, Taoism and Confucian thought. There are strong similarities in ideology/theology, at least, between the White Lotus Society and the Falun Gong, a sect banned in China in mid-1999.

The most successful of the 'just revolutionaries' were, of course, the Communists. Their programme did include a radical revision of the structures by which China was governed and ruled, and they were quick to distinguish their form of authoritarian rule from that of the empire. Nevertheless, their goals were largely the same as earlier movements; to restore stability and stop the forces of anarchy. The same motivation can be glimpsed behind Deng's economic reforms.

The presence of these movements serves to remind us that although stability is desired in China, it cannot always be guaranteed. Any weakening of central power is nearly always accompanied by local unrest, the purpose of which is usually, and paradoxically, to restore order.

Ten key figures in Chinese history

1   **Duke of Zhou**. The ancient sage-king of China, widely referred to by Confucius as a fount of moral authority.
2   **Confucius**. The greatest philosopher of the East, he constructed a moral and social system which continues to serve as the foundation for Chinese society.

3   **Qin Shi Huangdi**. The first true emperor of China, he founded the Chinese bureaucracy and established its long-lasting system of government.

4   **Zhuge Liang**. A counsellor in one of the warring states of the Three Kingdoms era, he has become a legend for his cunning strategy and statecraft harnessed to a strong moral purpose and sense of the duties of the state.

5   **Zhu Xi**. One of the greatest of the later philosophers, his Neo-Confucian synthesis of earlier thought was the basis of the moral and political regeneration of China by the Song and then the Ming, and remains the basis of modern Chinese philosophy and education.

6   **Qianlong**. Probably the last truly great Chinese emperor, a warrior, poet and builder, who received the first British embassy to China in 1798.

7   **Cixi**. Imperial concubine and later dowager empress who held China together after the Taiping rebellion and in the face of Western invasions and internal unrest. Her death was the signal for the empire to collapse.

8   **Sun Yat-sen**. Chinese Christian, married to a Chinese-American wife, he admired the West and attempted to make China into a republic. Many of his followers in the Guomindang movement were descendants of Taiping rebels.

9   **Mao Zedong**. The most important figure in modern China, founder of the Chinese Communist Party and leader of it until his death in 1976. He established the modern Chinese state.

10   **Deng Xiaoping**. Mao's successor and architect of the economic reforms that began in 1979. He has been demonised by many in the West as an authoritarian and repressive ruler. On the other hand, in China his economic reforms have lifted half a billion people out of poverty. How will history judge him?

Ethnicity and language

China is dominated by the Han ethnic group, both culturally and in terms of numbers, but the country is by no means homogeneous. There are dozens of distinctive ethnic groups. Most are dispersed around the periphery of the country, though there are exceptions such as the Hakka, who still live in central and southern China. The Hakka may be descendants of the original inhabitants of south China before the Han conquest.

Another group worth mentioning are Hui, a generic name for Chinese Muslims (as distinct from the Muslim Turkish population of Xinjiang). Most of the 8 to 9 million ethnic Chinese Muslims live in the Ningxia autonomous region, but there are several hundred thousand living in their own district in southwest Beijing (you know you have entered the Muslim quarter when the butcher shops begin displaying beef instead of pork in their windows). Huo Da's novel *The Jade King* (1992) is an excellent introduction to the lives of the Beijing Muslims.

Ethnicity in China expresses itself most obviously in terms of language. There are, according to UNESCO, 205 living languages in China – more than in Europe – although admittedly some of these are only spoken by a few thousand people. Mandarin, or more correctly Pudonghua ('the people's language'), has been the standard dialect of Beijing and lower Huang He regions since the Manchu conquest. It was adopted in the late nineteenth century as the *lingua franca* for the administration and the elite. Hu, spoken in Shanghai and the eastern regions, and Yue, commonly known as Cantonese and spoken in the south, are very prevalent, but Minbei (spoken in Fujian), Xiang, Gan and Hakka are also common in some regions. Taiwan also has its own language, Minnan (a variant of Minbei), and most overseas Chinese communities speak either Minbei or Yue as their first language. Some of these languages have more in common than others. There is considerable difference between Mandarin with its four tones and Yue/Cantonese with six tones; the difference has been described as greater than that between Spanish and French.

There have been attempts to standardise spoken language. In the imperial period, *wenyan*, a very formal and ornate spoken language directly related to the written language, was used by bureaucrats and scholars, but was unintelligible to ordinary Chinese. Late in the nineteenth century *wenyan* was abandoned in favour of *baihua*, literally 'plain speech', and it was at this point that Mandarin was adopted as the *guoyu*, or national language. The use of Mandarin as a standard language was continued under the Guomindang and the Communists, and it is spoken by nearly all well-educated people. According to *China Daily* (7 September 1999), Pudonghua is spoken by 80 per cent of people in the major cities. However, it remains a second language for a large percentage of the population.

Mandarin is the language of daily use in business in China, but those with a command of a second language have an additional card in their hands. A few years ago, one of the authors of this book was at dinner with a party of businesspeople from Shanghai, in a restaurant where the waiter was from Beijing. The customers were not very impressed with the waiter, and proceeded to be rude about him in their own Shanghai dialect, which the waiter of course could not understand. This was a trivial incident, but its importance in areas such as business negotiations should be apparent. We might think our Mandarin interpreter is reporting faithfully all that the other parties are saying; but if they then break off and begin talking in their own language or dialect, then the interpreter becomes as deaf as we are.

All this refers only to spoken language. In terms of *written* language, all Chinese use almost the same characters. Thus a Pudonghua-speaker and a Yue-speaker may not be able to understand what the other is saying, but they can communicate in writing. This has obvious implications for business, particularly in areas such as advertising.

Culture

The Han Chinese culture is an ancient one, and nearly all Chinese, including many who are not themselves of Han ethnic descent, are extremely proud of it. Unlike in the West, where we see our history as marked by distinctive breaks – the fall of Rome, the Protestant Reformation, the American Declaration of Independence – the Chinese see their history as a continuous process, disrupted but never entirely interrupted by foreign occupation and conquest. The emphasis on stability means that some things such as styles of art and architecture have evolved slowly over thousands of years.

China has a scientific, artistic and literary tradition that is as old as its civilisation. Bronze working, carving of jade and ivory, silk weaving and embroidery, painting and calligraphy go back at least as far as the Zhou era, and possibly further. Chinese literary traditions span 3,000 years, from the ancient classics such as the *Yijing*, the *Daodejing*, the *Analects* of Confucius, the *Spring and Autumn Annals* and the works of Sunzi, through to the great poets and novelists of the past millennium. Luo Guanzhong's *The Three Kingdoms* (fourteenth century) is an epic tale of the fragmentation of China after the fall of the Han dynasty, focusing on the heroic figures of counsellor Zhuge Liang and his rival the great general Cao Cao. *Flowers in the Mirror*, by Li Ruzhen (nineteenth century) is a satire which compares to *Gulliver's Travels*. Other literary classics include *The Water Margin*, *Outlaws of the Marsh* and *Journey to the West* (all available in English translation). Most famous of all, the *Dream of the Red Chamber* by Cao Xueqin in the seventeenth century recounts how a great family falls into decay and declines in fortunes.[5] The book has remained popular since its inception – in the late nineteenth century, the dowager empress Cixi had several rooms in the Forbidden City decorated with scenes from it – if for no other reason than that its story has been seen as a metaphor for China's own woes.

The Chinese, or at least those in mainland China, tend to think of all Chinese, including the *huaqiao* (overseas Chinese), as being part of the same cultural family. Feelings among the *huaqiao* themselves are a little more mixed, but the majority in East and South Asia, at least, feel a strong kinship with the Chinese of the PRC, even if they may have no wish to be politically associated with it.

Yet again, reinforcing the point above, Chinese culture itself is by no means monolithic. There are regional differences, not only in the various ethnic groups but among the Han themselves. The regions are very proud of their distinctive styles of cuisine, different attitudes to life, different regional histories and so on. Different regions are perceived differently: Guangzhou people are thought of as stylish, outgoing, sometimes brash; Beijing people are perceived as sometimes dull and lacking in a sense of humour; Shanghai people are perceived as being industrious and hard-working. These perceptions are about as accurate as similar stereotypes anywhere in the world: the point is, they exist. And they may say as much about the beholders as the observed.

Interestingly, and this may be a sign of increasing confidence in the country's stability, China's leaders have shown themselves more ready to accept and even promote diversity in recent years. Tourism, widely seen as the next big growth area in China's economy, often trades on regional and ethnic differences. Museums have begun opening galleries dedicated to different ethnic minorities and their history and traditions. If at times these seem a little patronising – though not nearly as much as the galleries of Native American 'history' found in many American and Canadian museums – they are at least a step in the right direction. The most interesting signal of all may have been the presence of many delegates from the south and west of China to the Sixteenth Party Congress in late 2002, wearing their own distinctive regional costumes. During the closing ceremonies, some of these posed for the television cameras along with outgoing president Jiang Zemin.

Ethnic costume has since become more common and accepted, even featuring in television advertising. Given the overall tone of the conference, it can be suggested that China has stopped trying to suppress diversity and is now trying to co-opt it as a positive force.

Even managers have to eat

Food is an important part of Chinese culture, so much so that cuisine is sometimes called the ninth art. Eight traditional styles of Chinese cuisine survive, each named after its home region:

- **Shandong**: from the northeast, this style features seafood and emphasises stir-frying and deep-frying.
- **Guangdong**: this style, popular in the West, emphasises fresh ingredients and rapid cooking to seal in the flavours.
- **Sichuan**: this complex style uses many different pungent spices and can be very hot.
- **Jiangsu**: the cooking of the Shanghai region, it emphasises salty and sweet flavours, with many stocks, sauces and thick soups.
- **Zhejiang**: this style features seafood and is noted for its slow-cooked stews.
- **Hunan**: this style also features slow cooking, stewing or steaming, with food often heavily spiced.
- **Anhui**: this style uses plenty of oil when cooking, and deep-fried and heavy sauces.
- **Fujian**: this style features seafood and often marinates dishes in wine to achieve sour-sweet flavours.

Aficionados of cuisine point out that although Beijing does have a tradition of cooking in the Imperial Court style, it does not have a style of cuisine of its own. This is strenuously denied by our friends from Beijing!

Government and the political situation

Since 1949, China has been a one-party state, governed by the Communist Party of China. The central government is in Beijing, but under it there are 23 provinces, 4 self-governing municipalities and 5 autonomous regions (Guangxi, Nei Mongol, Ningxia, Xinjiang Uygur and Xizang (Tibet)) directly under the central government and two special administrative regions (Hong Kong and Macau). Guangxi and Ningxia were created out of former provinces in 1958, around two major ethnic groups, the Chuang (Zhuang) and the Hui, or Chinese Muslims. Below the level of the provinces there are more tiers of government, at county, township and village level in rural areas and city, district and neighbourhood levels in cities.

This organisational structure is largely the same as it has been for centuries. At the level of the provinces, there was a bit of cutting and pasting in the 1950s and 1960s: Chinese-majority areas of Mongolia were added to the Manchurian provinces, and several old provinces in the heartland were abolished. Otherwise, the hierarchy of administration is much as it has always been.

Before 1911, China was ruled centrally from its capital (most recently Beijing) by the emperor, whose will was done by the civil service bureaucracy which effectively ran China. The bureaucracy were selected through competitive examinations and were reasonably democratic, though as has been pointed out, only the wealthier families could afford the education needed to pass the exams. Only about 1 in every 2 million Chinese succeeded in joining the ranks of the bureaucracy. The short-lived republic of Sun Yat-sen attempted to create a Western-style goverment, but this collapsed in the era of warlordism. Chiang Kai-shek ran his portions of China any way he could; the Guomindang did establish a bureaucracy, but it was notoriously inefficient and even more notoriously corrupt.

The Communists swept to power, like virtually every revolutionary movement in China before them, promising to restore order, which meant effective government and administration. By and large, they did so. Most unbiased studies of China after 1949 have concluded that, except for short periods of time such as during the Cultural Revolution, China has been well run. The things that have been important to the Chinese people – peace, safety in their own homes, freedom from crime and, more recently, economic prosperity – have for the most part been delivered.

The economic reform movement has necessarily set in train events that have loosened the ties between the people and the state. Opening up the labour market, for example, has meant greater freedom of movement. The agricultural reforms of 1978 leased farmland to the farmers. The centrally planning system has been gradually replaced by the market mechanisms. There were fears from the outset that these freedoms would create the potential for disorder. Certainly there are problems in China today, such as homelessness and crime which were not noticeable two decades ago; these are often blamed on the growing populations of migrant workers in the large cities, rural people who have come to the cities in the hope of making more money. Increasing economic inequalities are also partly responsible for greater labour unrest; according to some reports, there are around 100,000 industrial disputes in China each year, and a few turn violent. More recently, rising food prices are causing growing concern, especially in poorer areas. Finally, corruption, though far from universal (and well below the levels found in some Asian countries) is on the increase.

Despite these and other signs, which many Chinese do find deeply worrying, there is at present no great call for the system to be overturned. In part, this is due to a fear that any alternative system of government might well be worse. Older Chinese remember the Guomindang era, the Second World War and the Cultural Revolution, and are willing to pay almost any price to retain stability. And, almost everyone can see across the border into Russia, and the dire consequences of a hasty and ill-thought-through reform programme. The Chinese have chosen to reform slowly and cautiously, and it is hard to blame them.

Some observers have claimed that the Chinese are fundamentally uninterested in politics. This may be true in part; there is none of the passion for politics that one finds in daily life in Italy or France, for example. To this extent the Chinese may be more like the Americans, in that most prefer politics not to intrude into their daily lives and that politicians leave them in peace. This does not mean, however, that the Chinese are incapable of taking an interest in politics; indeed, Mao was able to politicise the Chinese, especially the rural population, very effectively in the years leading up to the revolution. As Chinese history, both imperial and more recent, shows, the Chinese expect certain things of their rulers, and when the latter fail to deliver, they are more than capable of setting them aside.

Will this happen? Never say never, but at present the prospects seem unlikely. It is a bitter pill for Western neo-liberals to swallow, but the truth is that for most Chinese, in most places, most of the time, the government *is* delivering. Ask any Chinese on the street, and most will complain about corruption and government incompetence. They will also tell you that the country is richer and they themselves are better off. Housing stocks are improving, consumer goods are both plentiful and cheap. Travel and work restrictions have been greatly relaxed, and there are more personal opportunities for enrichment and growth than probably at any time in China's history. The emerging Chinese middle class is growing rapidly. So is its spending power.

And the face of government is continuing to change, though not in the way that many in the West expect or want. The legislative body, the National People's Congress, which formerly did little beyond rubber-stamping measures introduced by the executive arm of government, now examines and critiques the legislation passed before it. But most significant of all has been the gradual co-option of capitalism into the government structure. On the face of it, here is a political party trying to have its cake and eat it too. Can the Communist Party of China really create a paradigm in which capitalists will see their own interests being in line with those of the state and the people? If it can, then its own future may well be assured; if it fails, then further change is in the offing. For the time being, the debate over success and failure is largely academic. What matters most to the Western businessman operating in China is that this is the likely drift of government policy for at least the next several years. And even if one's Chinese contacts are prepared to talk politics, it is wise not to do so.

Economy

> It doesn't matter if the cat is black or white, so long as it catches mice.
>
> (Deng Xiaoping)

Most books on China devote large sections, even whole chapters, to the Chinese economy. We do not, for three basic reasons:

1   There are already plenty of sources on this subject, and for those who desperately want to know, statistics on the gross industrial output of Anhui province can almost certainly be found somewhere on the Internet, if not in print.
2   Much economic forecasting concerning China is little more than guesswork, and even Chinese economists will cheerfully tell you that the margin of error in their figures could be anything up to 10 per cent.
3   China may not be changing fundamentally, but the economy is changing really fast. If commentaries, and especially Western economic commentaries, were initially accurate, they soon may not be.

The businessperson with limited time to research China should not waste it on what the Chinese economy has done/is doing/will do, even if he could identify the right sources. Some broad macro-economic and financial market data *are* useful in terms of identifying trends, and it is well to keep an eye on things like the inflation figures, especially locally. Really, though, the Chinese economy can be summed up as follows:

- it is big
- it is getting bigger.

Business interests in the economic situation mostly concern price, or inflation, the strength of demand, currency exchange rates and the impact that government economic policy has for firms at the micro level. In terms of the former, the Chinese market has seen price deflation over the turn of the millennium as the rush to found new manufacturing enterprises in the mid-1990s resulted in a glut of products on the market. White goods, air-conditioning machines and clothing were among the most overstocked, but most consumer goods were affected. Meanwhile, wages were rising, and by the mid-2000s the ranks of the middle classes had grown substantially, with more and more people enjoying a disposable income. In Beijing, the average dwelling space per person had increased from 7 square metres in 1998 to 27 square metres in 2008. All that space had to be filled with something, and consumer spending started rising again, pushing inflation up and Chinese economic growth overall back into the double-digit range.

The Maoist approach to economic management was to plan *everything*. Setting quotas and measuring production allowed state planners to allocate resources with a view to matching food production with population requirements. Industrial investment was planned in exacting detail, with resources often dictated by the requirements of military strategy. Key industries were often dispersed over many provinces, so that should some parts of the country be overrun by an invader, China would still have an industrial capability. The railway network was rebuilt with a view to moving troops and material quickly from one threatened frontier to another.

Again, by and large, this system worked. China experienced rapid economic growth in the 1950s and early 1960s, which faltered during the Great Leap Forward, and then went backwards during the Cultural Revolution disaster – but that was ideological, not economic. However, there were problems. Though food production increased, it could not keep pace with the rising population, and by the early 1970s China was importing food. Food could only be paid for if China had something to export, but many of its traditional export industries such as textiles were in dire need of modernisation. Also, largely isolated as it was from the West, China did not have access to much of the technology that its industry and its army needed.

By the end of the Cultural Revolution it had become apparent to many of China's leaders and planners that the planned economy was increasingly unable to meet the needs of the state. So, quite pragmatically, the decision was taken to experiment with market reforms, initially in the tightly defined Special Economic Zones (SEZs) along the coast, then in the coastal areas more generally, and finally on a nationwide basis. It was quickly seen that the market system could deliver more than the centrally planned system. Almost immediately after land reform gave the farmers ownership of their fields and the right to sell their crops for cash, agricultural output doubled. Private industrial enterprises were soon seen to be far more efficient and productive than most (state) firms, and the open-door policy allowed foreign investment and technology to provide a further stimulus to the economy.

Deng's statement quoted at the head of this section is often cited as evidence that he was a pragmatist rather than an ideologue. Well aware of the dangers inherent in the free market, he was convinced that the benefits outweighed the risks. (In similar vein, when asked about the prospect of foreign business influences leading to corruption, Deng responded, 'When one opens the door, one must expect that a few flies will get in'.)

The importance for the businessperson is this: China's long-term goals have not really changed. The aim is still to create a strong, self-sufficient, prosperous, independent state. The free market is encouraged because it delivers these things. If it were to show signs of failing to do so, or if the costs started to outweigh the benefits, China's leaders might well be tempted to dump the free market as unceremoniously as they dumped the planned economy. The problems, as noted in the introduction, are corruption and the disparity in incomes. New Socialism in China faces the same ideological compromises as New Labour in Britain.

Over the short term, the government of China faces a number of difficulties. How it deals with them will impact directly on the business environment.

The problem of managing and stimulating growth

The Chinese government faces the same problem that most governments face: how to get enough economic growth without having either too much or too little. In this case, however, the pressures and forces at work are slightly different. In the initial reform stages, there was an attempt to control growth very tightly, by limiting many activities to the SEZs and restricting the numbers and location of these. By the mid-1980s, however, it was seen that the advantages of faster growth outweighed the disadvantages and risks, and many controls on foreign investment and internal entrepreneurship were lifted or reduced. But this move, as the government itself later admitted, went too far in the other direction, and the result was serious overheating in 1993 and 1994, with rapid inflation hitting many people in rural areas in particular. Even before the Asia Crisis broke, the central government was putting the brakes on.

Then came the Asia Crisis, and the problem then was how to sustain growth and not see the Chinese economy falter in the same way that the Tiger economies had. China actually came through the crisis relatively unscathed, but now finds its economy in a peculiar position. Rates of growth are good, but that growth is heavily dependent on exports. There is a need to stimulate the domestic economy and encourage more consumer spending. But structural and infrastructural factors mean many options are limited. Encouraging people to spend money on cars would be an option – except China does not have enough roads for them to run on, as witnessed by the horrendous traffic problems in nearly every major city. Nor is there enough fuel to run them all: the problem here is one of distribution, not production, for until early 2002 Shanghai, a city of (conservatively) 10 million people, had 70 petrol stations. Plans are now in hand to double the number.

Government came hard up against these limitations in 2001, when it hit upon the idea of stimulating spending in the domestic economy by promoting tourism. New public holidays were created, local and regional governments were encouraged to develop and advertise their tourist attractions, and television stations began making travel programmes about the beauties of different regions of China. On the first public holiday, government forecasters predicted that 4 million people would travel from China's cities to the country. The real figure was closer to 40 million, and the railway and road infrastructure proved totally unable to cope. There was widespread public anger – which was reported in the Chinese domestic media – and the government was forced to create more holidays so as to spread the demand around, and to invest more heavily in the neglected railway system.

More recently, as we noted above, there has been no need for demand to be stimulated; demand has been roaring away on its own. By mid-2007 Chinese policy-makers were considering measures to slow things down, and some limited food price controls were indeed introduced in 2008. It is promised that these will only be temporary and will be removed once inflation eases. But it looks as if the West has come to China's rescue. The sub-prime mortgage fiasco and the global credit crunch that has followed has braked the whole world economy, and in China property prices in particular have slowed down, if not levelled out. With the prospect of economic growth coming down from 11 per cent in 2007 to 7 or 8 per cent in 2008 and 2009, policy-makers are breathing a little easier.

The Chinese have discovered that economic management in free markets is largely crisis management. Getting the economy on an even keel has been difficult, and keeping it there will be even more so.

The problem of regulation

The Chinese government wishes to keep control of the pace of economic reform, to ensure that there is no corresponding social breakdown or unrest. Foreign (and domestic) companies investing in China wish to earn profits. Not surprisingly, the two objectives collide on a regular basis. Equally unsurprisingly, the Chinese authorities use regulation as the principal tool to control the economy. On a single day in 1996, over 140 joint ventures were abruptly terminated by the authorities in the city of Tianjin, for a variety of reasons ranging from lack of profitability, to incompatibility between partners, to fraud. There was another set of closures early in 2002.

The problems of regulation will be discussed in more detail in Chapter 5, but for the moment it is important to remember that 'regulation' in China is a somewhat fuzzy concept. On the face of it, China's business and economic regulations have been brought into line with those of the international business world more generally in order to comply with WTO requirements. But what the regulations say and how they are interpreted are two different things. Also, China was allowed a number of significant opt-outs in areas such as financial services. Look before you leap; don't assume every WTO condition applies automatically, and check to see what the Chinese version of the relevant regulations says. And be aware that the local interpretation of regulations may vary.

The problem of reforming state industries

Economic planning in Mao's China involved the centralisation and concentration of many industries. Ball-bearings were concentrated in the Nei Mongol, while defence industries went to Sichuan. Most of these heavy industries were designed to produce goods for internal consumption only. Most were also hopelessly inefficient. The remaining industrial sectors, those depending on agriculture, remain as affected as ever by the vagaries of the weather. Of the heavy and light industries, there were in 1990 over 11,000 large and medium state enterprises in China. Many have since been closed or merged, but there are still several thousand in existence, mainly in heavy industries such as coal and steel. Most are still making losses, and it is believed that the majority are technically insolvent. But closing them down would put many hundreds of thousands of people out of work, add to the welfare burdens of the state, and risk popular unrest. Leaving them to operate is seen as the cheaper and safer option; subsidy costs less than welfare and is less politically risky.

This does not mean that attempts at reform are not made, but they are gradual and subtle. Early in the present decade, the central government suggested that the big four Chinese banks should take over 600 state-owned enterprises (SOEs) through their affiliated asset management companies. The asset management companies would then restructure these enterprises, cancelling some debts and swapping others for equity. The banks, despite being state-owned themselves, were understandably reluctant to undertake this, suspecting (rightly) that the management problems of these white elephants were being sloughed off onto them. There were some successes, however, and many of the firms taken over have at least reduced their losses to manageable levels while job cuts have been kept as low as possible.

More recently, reforms have been targeted at a widely recognised problem; that is, the lack of a responsible agency that can effectively monitor state enterprises and their managers. State enterprises were never short of 'mothers-in-law' (government agencies that claimed authorities over the affairs of state firms). There were simply too many of them. 'Five dragons govern the water' is a vivid term used to describe the situation: these dragons – powerful government agencies – fought for their sectional interests and seldom bothered to fulfil their regulatory responsibilities. This leaves opportunistic managers to actively divert enterprise funds for their own use and engage in asset-stripping. The central government created in 2003 the State-owned Assets Supervision and Administration Commission (SASAC), which is supposed to represent the government in its role as the owner of state enterprises. SASAC and its local branches are now the regulators that oversee the operation of state enterprises under their jurisdiction. They have the authority to decide whether or not to sell stakes in state enterprises to foreign investors, to whom, and on what terms.

Some of the leading business schools, such as Beijing University, have special MBA programmes for SOE managers. In September 1996, Rolls-Royce led a consortium of British businesses to create the China–Britain Industrial Consortium (CBIC). This went on to develop a number of successful training programmes including:

- an annual prestige seminar on, for example, change management
- a three-week course in the UK divided equally between the Cranfield School of Management, the City of London and visiting consortium companies
- MBA and similar scholarships
- three- to six-month placements in UK companies for middle managers
- experts from consortium members acting as consultants for a week on specific problems in SOEs.

The PRC government actively encourages these sorts of schemes by foreign investors, and regards them as valuable and positive partnerships.

The problem of reforming the agricultural sector

The agricultural sector, as mentioned, remains dominant in China, and the Chinese economy stands or falls on agricultural prosperity. The agricultural sector remains responsible for over 30 per cent of total output. Wages are low and conditions for workers are extremely hard. The recent rise in food prices has hit agricultural communities particularly hard; this may seem surprising, but historically food price inflation has always hit farmers hard, in the West as well as in China. Part of the reform of the agricultural sector involves reducing the economy's dependence on it. Progress is being made in this direction, but is still slow.

The problem of reducing regional disparities

This is part of the developing wealth disparity issue. The economic boom in China has been largely centred on two regions: the mouth of the Pearl River and the Chang Jiang river delta around Shanghai, with other concentrations around Beijing and Tianjin. More generally, the whole of the coastal belt has prospered when the inland regions have been slower to grow. Some inland centres like Wuhan are now beginning to grow rapidly, but others are stagnating. Despite steady migration to the cities, rural unemployment is rising faster than urban unemployment. Standards of living are lower in the west of China than in the east, and both sides of the country are well aware of this divide. The disparity between eastern and western China continues to cause concern to policy-makers, and is perhaps the area where the least headway has been made over the last ten years.

Chinese attitudes to the West

In 1988 a television series called *Yellow River Elegy* was shown on Chinese national television. Widely perceived as an attack on China's ancient culture and history, *Yellow River Elegy* used a series of images to contrast China's past and its future. The past was shown in brown earth tones, using images of the Huang He (Yellow River), the Great Wall and so on; the future was shown in blue, using images of the open Pacific Ocean, representing freedom and contact with the outside world. The film's message was that China could only progress by jettisoning its own past and merging its future with that of the wider world.

Needless to say, the film generated a ferocious backlash, and several politicians made their careers by criticising it. Proponents of closer relations with the West and those who favour an arm's-length distance became known as the Blues and the Browns. The two factions were sometimes defined as modernisers and conservatives, but this was too simplistic. The Blues, generally speaking, were those who believed that China's future lies in opening up to the outside world, taking a step away from its purely Chinese heritage, culture, history and so on, and deliberately becoming more like the West. The Browns were those who believed that China's heritage must be maintained, as it is the country's primary source of strength, and that China must be strong but independent.

In these two factions and their attitudes, one can see much of the Chinese ambivalence about the West. In the attitudes of the Blues, one can see much of the same sense of inferiority to the West, and the desire to reduce that inferiority by imitating the West and becoming more like it, that one saw in the Guomindang and the liberal reformers of the early twentieth century. In the views of the Browns, we can see the remembrance of things past, the Opium Wars, warlordism, the Japanese invasion, and the fear that what happened once can happen again.

Since the late 1990s positions on both sides have softened considerably. Few educated Chinese believe that China has any option but to integrate into the family of nations, but few believe that China's ancient history and traditions should be thrown on the scrapheap. In part, this is thanks to a burgeoning confidence by Chinese in their country and its capabilities. Reform and development have a long way to go, but China no longer needs to feel economically inferior to the West.

The rapid and successful growth has in some ways vindicated Chinese culture and traditions in the eyes of many. Chinese symbols and scenes are returning to the forefront in advertising, Chinese ethnic costume is making a comeback, and Chinese are being encouraged to travel, see and admire their own country. This new confidence has in turn strengthened China's hand when dealing with the West. When crises arise, such as the American spy plane incident of 1988, the bombing of the Chinese embassy in Belgrade during the Kosovo war, or Chinese rejection of the American position over Iraq, the Chinese government makes its position known firmly but without the paranoid rhetoric of the Maoist years. The ordinary person on the street will also make their feelings known, without in any way lessening the politeness and hospitality with which most foreigners are received. This is a country that feels it no longer has to worry about what Westerners think of it – if, indeed, it ever did.

This new confidence was most notable during the credit crisis of 2007–8, especially in January 2008 when stock markets around the world began to tumble. Shanghai, Shenzhen and Hong Kong were all affected but many Chinese policy-makers and academics – along with many in Singapore and India – began rather pointedly asking why. China's economy is strong, generating huge surpluses. Why should the Chinese economy catch a cold just because feeble Wall Street had sneezed? There was talk of 'decoupling', of the Chinese and other Asian economies simply going their own way, no longer affected by the economic woes of America or Europe. Such talk was largely fantasy – given the dependence of the Chinese economy on exports, few really believe that such decoupling is possible – but the fact that decoupling is being talked about is a strong indicator of China's new economic confidence. Business-people are likely to find that confidence reflected in the attitudes of their own partners and prospective partners during meetings.

Why all this matters

We come back to the question posed at the beginning of the chapter. What does the business person of today need to know about China? Will an understanding of culture and history be of any assistance when doing business? Will a knowledge of the works of Confucius or Mao's *Little Red Book* be useful when negotiating a joint venture?

The answer, as with most knowledge, is that it depends on how it is used. Culture is not an exact science; it is a set of frameworks, which are often intuitive and emotional, within which people operate. As we discuss in the next chapter, we are affected by culture without being aware of it. Our attitudes to hierarchy, the way we make decisions (including purchasing decisions), our attitudes to others, ethics and personal tastes are all to some extent shaped by our inheritance.

This does not mean that culture is a predictor. Within the parameters of a given culture, vast allowances must be made for variations in the behaviour of individuals. With 1.3 billion people in the PRC and another 55 million overseas Chinese, the variations are very numerous indeed.

A study of culture as an environmental factor makes sound economic sense. Some firms seem to approach the world as if all humanity were universally the same. That is soon modified. The next level of simplification is racial, or national, stereotypes. Politically correct commentators are appalled by this but, for most international travellers, they are useful first approximations. The Chinese use them when they meet people from other parts of China. Marketers the world over are trying to get through these superficialities to understand the real people behind them.

Western and Chinese businesspeople routinely misunderstand each other. In these circumstances one can retreat to fixed positions or try to empathise with the other person's frame of mind. Of course, the other person may be trying to rob you, but that cannot be assumed of everyone. More than anything this book is about comparing how Westerners and Chinese see the world, so that robbers can be distinguished and friends can come to terms. It is about risk assessment. Understanding the underlying forces gives better preparation.

Finally, and perhaps most critical, is the appreciation of the differences between other cultures and one's own. By looking at Chinese culture and asking how it differs from our own, we are forced to start looking at our own culture in more depth. Why do *we* think and behave as we do? Are there any lessons to be learned from this? We can, if we are careful, use China as a mirror. Although, as Sir Percy Cradock says, we are looking through a glass darkly, we can nonetheless see something of our own reflection.

Appendix

(a) The regions of China

1 **The north**, including Beijing and Tianjin cities and Hebei, Shandong and part of Henan provinces. Population: *c.* 250 million. This is the second most densely populated area of China and contains several major cities (including the capital), much rich agricultural land and a lot of heavy and light industry. The climate is temperate, though winters can be cold and harsh.

2 **The Huang He valley and the northwest**, including Shanxi, Shaanxi and part of Henan provinces, the eastern part of Gansu province and the Ningxia autonomous region. Population: *c.* 138 million. This is the ancient heartland of China, including in its bounds the 'yellow earth' country where the first Chinese civilisation emerged. The western part of this area has some minority Turkish ethnic groups, and Ningxia is home to a large proportion of China's Hui (Muslim) people. Climate consists of cold harsh winters and hot dry summers.

3 **The east coast**, including the city of Shanghai – China's largest – and Jiangsu and northern Zhejiang provinces.

Population: *c.* 132 million. This is the most densely populated area of the country, with some its richest agricultural land, particularly in the delta of the Chang Jiang (Yangtze) river. Apart from Shanghai, there are also a number of large urban manufacturing centres, including Nanjing, Wuxi, Suzhou and Hangzhou. The cities are growing rapidly, encroaching on the agricultural land as they do so. Climate is generally moderate, though winters can be very wet.

4   **The Dongting Hu and the lower Chang Jiang valley**, including Anhui, Hubei, Jiangxi and Hunan provinces. Population: *c.* 156 million people. This is rich agricultural land studded with industrial centres, the largest of which is Wuhan. This area was largely overlooked in the first wave of economic growth, but is now receiving increasing levels of investment. The climate is comparatively moderate.

5   **The upper Chang Jiang**, including the province of Sichuan. Population: *c.* 130 million. Cut off from the lower valley by the Daba Shan mountains, Sichuan was once rich and prosperous but has fallen behind in recent years. Current Chinese government efforts are targeted at reviving Sichuan's economy. Sichuan has a distinctive subculture, history and cuisine of its own.

6   **The southeast coast**, including Fujian and southern Zhejiang. Population: *c.* 58 million. This heavily mountainous region faces the sea, and until fairly recently was almost entirely dependent on shipping and fishing. It too has its own regional subculture. Some of the first Special Economic Zones (SEZs) were located here, giving a considerable boost to the local economy. Parts of the region are also heavily militarised as Taiwan continues to occupy several islands just offshore.

7   **The far south**, including Guangdong and Hainan provinces and the eastern part of the Guangxi autonomous region. Population: *c.* 110 million. This area, almost cut off from the rest of China by the Nan Shan (Southern Mountains), is sometimes referred to collectively as Lingnan (South of the Mountains). Population densities are much lower than in the north. The economy is booming, thanks in large part to the presence of Hong Kong and some early SEZs like Shenzhen,

Shantou and Hainan. Guangdong is the centre of the Yue
(Cantonese) language region and has its own subculture and
cuisine. Guangxi is the home of the Zhuang ethnic group.
The climate is sub-tropical with heavy rains in the monsoon
season.

8 **The far southwest**, including western Guangxi and the
provinces of Guizhou and Yunnan. Population: *c*. 104 million.
This region is very mountainous, ranging from the lower
mountains along the Vietnamese border south of Nanning
to the high ranges bordering Tibet to the west. Timber and
mining are major industries but agriculture is also important
in the deep valleys around Guiyang and Kunming. The area
has considerable strategic importance in Chinese military
planning. The population includes about 50 different ethnic
groups. The climate is sub-tropical in the valleys, harsh in the
high mountains.

9 **Manchuria** (the northeast), including Liaoning, Jilin and
Heilongjiang provinces. Population: *c*. 124 million. An industrial powerhouse, Manchuria has China's largest oilfields and
a number of major manufacturing centres including Harbin,
Jilin, Changchun, Shenyang, Fushun, Anshan and Dalian. The
Manchu and Han Chinese ethnic groups are effectively inter-
mingled, but there are Mongolian groups in the west and several
hundred thousand Russians, descended from White Russian
refugees, around Harbin; these retain their own language,
restaurants and even vodka distilleries. The climate is harsh
and cold in winter, dry in summer.

10 **Mongolia**, encompassed by the Nei Mongol autonomous
region. Population: *c*. 22 million. The major centre is the capital,
Hohhot; elsewhere, there are scattered towns and mining, but
most of the area is given over to pastoral herding, much as it has
always done. There is a Han Chinese majority, most of whom are
comparatively recent emigrants; the rest are of Mongol descent.
Hot dry summers give way to bitterly cold winters.

11 **Turkestan**, as the West still sometimes calls it, including most
of Qinghai and Gansu provinces and the Xinjiang Uigur
autonomous region. Population: *c*. 45 million. As in Mongolia,
the majority of the population are now Han Chinese, but these

66   *Doing business in China*

are concentrated in cities such as Urumqi. The rural population are largely Turkish. Much of this vast area is almost entirely uninhabited, such as the Tarim Basin and the Takla Makan desert. Again, the climate ranges from hot dry summers to cold hard winters.

12 **Tibet**, including the Xizang autonomous region and part of Qinghai province. Population: *c.* 3 million. High mountains, bleak and largely uninhabited. Tibet has its own culture and history, and was largely independent until occupied by China in the 1950s; its status continues to be the subject of dispute and protest both inside Tibet and internationally.

(b) Chinese history in a nutshell

- **Ancient period**. Chinese civilisation was established along the Yellow River; the legendary king Huangdi (Yellow Emperor) probably flourished around the 25th century BC.
- **Xia dynasty**, *c.* 21st–*c.*16th centuries BC. The first Chinese state of note.
- **Shang dynasty**, *c.*16th–11th centuries BC. Bronze working and horse-drawn chariots were introduced.
- **Western Zhou dynasty**, *c.* 11th century–770 BC. This is the era of the fabled sage-kings of ancient China who so influenced Confucius, King Wen and the Duke of Zhou. This period laid the groundwork for much of later Chinese culture and society.
- **Spring and Autumn period**, 770–481 BC. This period saw China politically divided but culturally rich, with many competing artistic and philosophical schools. Confucius, Mengzi (Mencius), Laozi (Lao Tzu) and Xunzi (Guan Tzu) all were active, and many classics of Chinese literature date from this time.
- **Warring States period**, 403–221 BC. The rich and powerful states of north China fought each other for supremacy almost continuously for two centuries. The master strategist Sunzi (Sun Tzu) was active in this period.
- **Qin dynasty**, 221–207 BC. The civil wars ended with the unification of China by its first true emperor, the powerful Qin Shi Huangdi, who suppressed dissent, reformed society, expanded imperial rule into southern China and began works such as the Great Wall. He has been described by some

historians as a bloodthirsty tyrant, but modern China still shows many influences of his rule.

- **Western Han dynasty**, 206 BC–24 AD. Qin's heirs were not able to keep the throne, and the strong monarch of the Han dynasty consolidated the empire. This was a period of economic prosperity and cultural greatness.
- **Eastern Han dynasty**, 25–220 AD. After the brief usurpation of Wang Mang, the Han resumed their rule, but their power was much weakened. Ultimately the empire slid into chaos and broke apart.
- **Three Kingdoms period**, 220–265. As in the earlier Warring States period, the country was fragmented and several states fought each other for control.
- **Jin dynasty**, 265–420. China was briefly reunited under the dynasty of Western Jin (265–316) before breaking apart again under the Eastern Jin dynasty.
- **Southern and Northern dynasties**, 420–589. Several emperors built their dynasties, but could not last. China was fragmented, with much conflict and many smaller states attempting to break away.
- **Sui dynasty**, 581–618. This dynasty reunited China, but collapsed when the Emperor Wen was defeated by the Koreans and the Turks.
- **Tang dynasty**, 618–907. Picking up the pieces after the Sui, the Tang dynasty restored order and its emperors expanded China's power and prestige.
- **Five Dynasties and Ten Kingdoms**, 907–79. When the Tang dynasty collapsed, China fragmented into more warring states. Foreign invaders, mainly Turkish and Mongol tribes from the north, increased the pressure.
- **Song dynasty**, 960–1279. The Song were able to reunite China for a time, but the pressure from the northern invaders was becoming intense, and the Jurchen tribe ultimately drove the Song into the south in 1127. China was divided once more.
- **Yuan dynasty**, 1271–1368. Kubilai Khan's Mongols conquered all of China and united it. This was actually a time of some prosperity, with China opened up to foreign trade.
- **Ming dynasty**, 1368–1644. After the Mongol empire disintegrated, the Ming dynasty took control and swiftly reunited China. Culturally and economically, China reached a high level during the Ming dynasty.

- **Qing dynasty**, 1644–1911. The Ming Dynasty gradually decayed and was replaced by the Manchu tribes from the northeast, who conquered all of China in a series of military campaigns lasting about 20 years. The Manchu emperors Kangxi and his grandson Qianlong were great figures who between them ruled China for 135 years (1661–1796). Kangxi was a warrior and conqueror, and under his rule China reached its greatest extent, occupying its ancient enemies in Mongolia, Turkestan and Tibet. The Tibetans were singled out as they had been allies of the Mongols and remained implacable enemies of China. Qianglong was poet, artist and builder; in Beijing, many of the buildings in the Forbidden City and the Bei Hai park were built to his direction.
- **Republic of China**, 1912–49. Established by Sun Yat-sen, it quickly collapsed into feuding provinces ruled by warlords, until Chiang Kai-shek was able to impose a form of unity in the late 1920s. The Japanese invasion (1933–45) then tore much of the country apart. After the success of the Communist revolution of 1949, the government of the Republic of China went into exile on Taiwan.
- **People's Republic of China**, 1949–. Established by Mao Zedong and the victorious Communists in 1949, the PRC has undergone many changes, including the Cultural Revolution of the 1960s and 1970s, and the economic reform process, which began in 1978.

3   The furniture of the mind

The average Chinese has long been and still is an animist, a Buddhist, a Confucianist and a Taoist with no sense of incongruity or inconsistency.

(Kenneth Latourette, *The Chinese*, 1934)

Once more I recollect the past, and wrongs of former days.
Let others stoop to gain some win, but I'll not change my ways.
Such men as change to win some gain, I always have despised,
But hold the Principles of Old, the rules we used to prize.

(Qu Yuan, *Thoughts before Drowning*, 3rd century BC)

A comprehensive coverage of the roots of contemporary Chinese business thinking would take a thousand scholars a thousand days. Here, we seek merely to open the door into a room, one that is full of furniture that the occupants of the room themselves have, for much of the time, long ceased to notice. The 'room', i.e. the Chinese mind, is dimly lit. When the Westerner enters it, some pieces seem the same as at home; some are strange, some are old, inherited from ancestors long dead, and some are new. Some may not be noticed in the half light and blundered into, perhaps causing damage.

The Western mind has its own furniture that we likewise rarely notice. The way we think is inherited from Greek, Jewish and Christian patterns of analysis dating back two thousand years or more. Whether we now go to church or synagogue is no reflection of their influence on our thinking today. With more powerful means of mass communication and a missionary zeal for which there is no apparent explanation, patterns of Western thinking have been more exposed to the Chinese than theirs to us. The lighting, in this metaphor, is thus brighter for the Chinese entrant.

The first focus of this chapter is on philosophies and how they affect the psychology of today's businessperson. Whether the inheritor of the culture is in PRC, Singapore or the USA matters about as much as whether the inheritor of European culture is in Europe, Argentina or Australia. Location does make a difference and younger generations feel, as they always have, that they are very different from their parents' age group. Latourette's comment (to which can now be added Communism and, according to some, capitalism) illustrates that point. Why, if every generation is so different, do ways of thinking survive for centuries?

The line between philosophy and school of thought and religion is not as clear as in the West. Confucianism is not a religion in the sense of believing in supernatural powers or beings that should be obeyed. Buddhism is not strictly a religion either, but the ancestor cult may be. Frankly, their classification is immaterial; we are concerned with their impact on modern thinking. This leads to a review of values.

From philosophy and values, we go on to discuss strategy. Sunzi, or Sun Tzu as he is more familiarly known in the West, could be called the greatest strategist of all time. His book *The Art of War* has had a profound effect on military thinking, especially guerrilla warfare. (*The Art of War* as we know it today was heavily rewritten in the third century AD by the general Cao Cao, one of the key figures of the Three Kingdoms period, who adopted it as a manual of strategy for his own officers. The end result is no less valid for all that.) Today, the 13 chapters provide guidance to businesspeople and generals alike and are too well known to need more than the briefest of recaps here. Another famous text, *The Thirty-Six Stratagems*, has also had much influence, as has the novel *Romance of the Three Kingdoms* which chronicles the struggle between the master strategist Zhuge Liang and his rival Cao Cao.

Philosophy

In broadly chronological order, let us look at:

- Ancestor cult
- Daoism (or Taoism)
- Confucianism
- Confucian disciples
- Legalism
- Buddhism

- Neo-Confucianism
- Christianity
- Communism.

Chronology is not necessarily the most accurate way of looking at these concepts, since they moved in and out of fashion in no particular order. Confucius may have lived before and/or after the early Daoist philosophers but their thinking seems to have preceded his. Confucianism, however, did not dominate until Han times 300 years or so later, and was followed by Daoism's resurgence.

These schools have supplied much of the furniture of the Chinese mind, but as the pieces have passed from one generation to another, so the distinctions have become blurred. In any case, they have much in common. It is curious that so much philosophy originated in a relatively brief period around 400 BC, right across the world from Greece to China: 'The Pre-Socratic Greek (Thales and Anaximander of Miletus), Confucianism, Mohism, Upanisadic Hinduism, Jainism, Taoism, Buddhism, Zoroastrianism, and Biblical Judaism' all flowered at about the same time.[1] Daoism and Indian Yoga (Sufism) are not just contemporary but very similar. Whether some of these philosophies inspired each other, or they were inspired separately by some common source, is not known.

Ancestor cult

This is both the oldest belief system and the core of Chinese religious observance. For perhaps 4,000 years, all classes of society from emperors to serfs, intelligentsia to peasants, have swept out tombs and left food, drink and lights for their fathers and forefathers, particularly at the Qing Ming Festival (5 April) which is dedicated to this purpose. The beliefs seem to be traceable to Shang times (16th to 11th centuries BC). At that time, the worship of royal ancestors was central to maintenance of the dynasty. Certain ancestors were worshipped on certain days, and the pattern of associations of days and observances built up.

The same period seems to have seen the birth of many of the Chinese equivalents of Western superstitions concerning numbers (such as Friday the 13th) and practices (such as walking under ladders), though the origins of these may be far older. Whether such things are rational is beside the point; they deeply affect doing business in Greater China today. Eight and scarlet are still 'lucky'. There are right times to do things, such as start a business, or buildings to face. Fortune-telling is strong, just as the West has an undiminished appetite for astrology. *Feng shui* is taken seriously by many: the series of fatal accidents that attended the construction of the Jinmao Building in Shanghai were attributed by senior project managers not to shoddy construction methods, but to the fact that 'the building is too high and too aggressive. It disturbs the dragons in the clouds' (Tang and Ward 2003: 26). Popular beliefs of whatever type often exercise more influence over popular culture than does formal religion.

Daoism (c. 500 BC)

'Dao' ('Tao' in older texts) is usually translated as 'The Way', although there are many other connotations as well. Daoism is not a religion as such (though there are religious movements based on Daoist principles) but suggests a way of thinking that will bring harmony and wisdom through respecting 'the all-pervading, self existent, eternal cosmic unity from which all created things emanate and to which they all return'.[2] The instigator was Laozi (*Lao* = old, *zi* = master; older Western texts refer to him as Lao Tzu), who is supposedly the author of the immortal classic *Daodejing* (in fact, modern scholarship has cast doubt on whether Laozi existed at all). The title *Daodejing* was applied to the work subsequently; the title has been translated as 'the classic book of integrity and the way' (the middle word, *de*, means integrity or virtue). It began possibly as a collection of oral stories developed over the great period for Chinese philosophy between 600 and 300 BC. Zhuangzi, the greatest of the Daoist writers whose existence can be verified, lived towards the end of that period.

We cannot overstress the importance of Daoist thinking in 'pairs of opposites'. On both sides of every argument, there must be right and wrong. Paradox and ambiguity flow directly from this concept of balance. So does 'and' thinking, as distinct from Western 'or' thinking (either A is right *or* the opposite of A). To a Daoist, the fact that A is right probably means the opposite of A is right too. And both are wrong. This kind of thinking has been referred to as 'the unity of opposites'.[3] The Chinese search for such solutions in negotiation baffles Westerners.

For those unfamiliar with the *Daodejing*, it is worth at least dipping into to get the flavour; it can be very enjoyable. Daoism has been accused of being at the root of fatalism in China. If what will be, will be, there is no need to do anything to prevent it.

While people will rationalise in all kinds of ways, the charge is unfair. At the certainty of massive over-simplification, Daoism actually encourages people to do what they can do, but not then worry about the results. This calm in the face of adversity may give the *appearance* of fatalism, but is an unfair reading of the situation. Of course it also leads many people too quickly to disengage and to assume that they have done what they can. Therein lies the danger.

We have looked here at Daoism before turning to Confucianism, whatever the precise chronology, because it provides many of underpinnings of Chinese thinking which so differentiate it from the West. Specifically, there are the concepts of balance and paradox: for example, 'Heavy is the root of light; calm is the ruler of haste'.[4] The *dao* is the 'non-being' (*wu*) within which any 'being' (*you*) exists, and vice versa. The *dao* is the source of all being and non-being, so to speak, the natural laws of the universe from which we spring, to which we return and with which we should be in harmony in the meantime. *Yang* and *yin* are essential Daoist concepts which we define later. They are not polar opposites so much as complementary halves of the same whole. Even, for example, the selection of a balanced meal uses these two powerful concepts. Food and drink are functional such as red wine (*yang*) being perceived as good for the blood (which it probably is) whereas white wine (*yin*) is more gentle and romantic (no comment). Thus choosing the dinner wine can have unintended overtones.

One of the most important concepts in Daoism is *wu-wei*. This translates literally as 'non-action', but should not be thought to imply 'inaction'. Rather, *wu-wei* is the process by which a leader causes things to happen by providing an essential state of harmony wherein action happens spontaneously or naturally. This concept found its way to the West in the eighteenth century via the Jesuit missionaries in China, who were rather taken with Daoism and thought they glimpsed similarities with Christianity. A number of Daoist texts were translated into French and were widely read by French philosophers and intellectuals of the period. One of these, the economist François Quesnay, translated the term as *laissez-faire* and used it to justify free markets and non-intervention by the state in the economy, on the grounds that unregulated markets would function naturally to produce the greatest possible good. So, the cornerstone of modern capitalism, which the West is trying to export to China, actually comes from China in the first place.

Confucianism (551–479 BC)

This period when philosophy flowered was also marked by continuous warfare around much of the globe, notably the period of Warring States in China (475–221 BC). Perhaps this was responsible for the intellectual search for a route to harmony. Certainly Laozi regarded war as a last resort: 'the killing of masses of human beings, we bewail with sorrow and grief; victory in battle we commemorate with mourning ritual'. Interstate rivalry changed the selection of senior advisers from hereditary to the most (intellectually) competent, albeit from within the *shi* (gentleman) class. As a result there was considerable social and intellectual movement. It was also a time of rich cultural flowering, when the Hundred Schools of philosophy debated amongst one another. Only a few of these, including Daoism, survived; others like the Mohists were later suppressed, and of some, such as the Agriculturalists and the Story Tellers, only their names survive; we have little idea as to what their beliefs were.

While Confucius, a member of the *shi* class and a senior civil servant, was certainly affected by the war-ravaged times in which he lived, his philosophy did not become official orthodoxy for China until about 300 years later, during the Han dynasty. The following traditional Chinese story is used to introduce a discussion of Confucian social philosophy, which is central to efforts to explain and predict Chinese social interaction.[5]

The protagonist, Xue Ren-gui, is an accomplished soldier who left his pregnant wife 18 years earlier to fight a distant campaign for the emperor. Returning home, he notices a young man shooting wild geese with great skill. Provoked, he challenges the youth to a test of marksmanship. The rival readily accepts, whereupon Xue immediately puts an arrow through his heart, saying 'a soldier like me could not let another live if he was a superior in marksmanship with the weapons in which I excel'.

Of course, it turns out the youth is Xue's son, whom he had never seen. The remorse of the father is tempered by the fact that the son has violated two cultural imperatives. First, he did not recognise his father: so strong are the bonds of family and the imperatives of filial piety that a son should know his father regardless of any factors that may disguise his identity. Second, the son has committed the cardinal sin in the Chinese tradition: he has challenged his father and thereby affronted social order. In the words of a Chinese proverb, 'In a family of a thousand, only one is the master'. A threat to the family is a threat to the body politic and a violation of heaven's mandate. It must therefore be ruthlessly put down.

Confucianism has been guiding the behaviour of people of all classes since the Han dynasty, irrespective of the criticisms. Under Mao, Confucianism was officially out of favour even though Confucian thought patterns were too well entrenched to be much affected (and he himself was imbued with them). In 1985, a special institute was founded in Beijing for the study of Confucian thought. Today, interest in Confucianism is increasing, and the works of Confucius and his school are being studied in the light of today's social and economic problems.

In the time of Confucius, the great problems were how to govern, how to maintain order in society and how to guarantee happiness and prosperity for the people (*plus ça change*). Confucius's solution was that both the rulers and the ruled should be educated. Governing is in the first place education and training, and the ruler should first educate himself and then govern with the help of 'virtues', meaning something close to the Daoist 'integrity' (the word does not have quite the overtones morality that it has in the West).

In this sense, there are 'Five Constant Virtues': humanity, righteousness, propriety, wisdom and faithfulness. These virtues are expressed in 'Five Cardinal Relations': sovereign and subject, parent and child, elder and younger brothers, husband and wife, and friend and friend. Of these five relationships, the first two are the most important in Confucianism but the last, faithfulness, is still seen as necessary, especially in business. Constancy is, as we shall see, a key part of *guanxi* (relationships).

Confucius held that all men were alike in nature. He suggested that good and capable people should be appointed to official posts, a proposal that was contrary to the prevailing hereditary rule. Yet he also defended the hierarchy of the nobility. He advocated the elevation of good and capable people, but never opposed the hereditary system and advised people to accept their lot. Confucius saw a world in which harmony could best be achieved by everyone recognising his or her place in the world. Confucius thus legitimised the strong hierarchical order which dominated the family and the society of his time and throughout much of Chinese history. This is in interesting contrast to Western thinking, where liberation of slaves, for example, is associated with the overthrow of the current governance.

Confucius distinguished two kinds of individuals: *jun zi* (Gentleman, Prince, Great Man or Proper Man) and *xiao ren* (literally Petty Man or Small Man):

- Great Man, being universal in his outlook, is impartial; Petty Man, being partial, is not universal in outlook (Confucius, Book 2).
- He (Great Man) sets the good examples, then he invites others to follow it (Confucius, Book 2).
- Great Man cherishes excellence; Petty Man, his own comfort. Great Man cherishes the rules and regulations; Petty Man, special favour (Confucius, Book 4).
- Great Man is conscious only of justice; Petty Man only of self-interest (Confucius, Book 4).

Leadership belonged to Great Man; he need not be of noble birth, but should have the Five Constant Virtues.

Confucius defined filial duty as:

> While his father lives, observe a man's purposes; when the father dies, observe his actions. If for three years (of mourning) a man does not change from the ways of his father, he may be called filial.
>
> (Confucius, Book 1)

Both the subject and filial relationships lead to a predominantly vertical structure of relationships. In modern business, a paternalistic management style is thought by some to be a direct consequence in both China and Japan.[6]

According to Bond and Hwang,

> the essential aspects of Confucianism in constructing a Chinese social psychology are the following: (a) man exists through, and is defined by, his relationships to others; (b) these relationships are structured hierarchically; (c) social order is ensured through each party's honouring the requirements in the role relationship.[7]

The Confucian scholar A.S. Cua defines Confucian philosophy as 'primarily a set of ethical ideas oriented towards practice', found on the threefold principles of benevolence, righteousness and propriety.[8] In essence, Confucianism sets out a framework for interpersonal relationships of all kinds.

Confucian disciples (Mozi, 5th century BC; Mencius, c. 371–289 BC; Xunzi, c. 298–238 BC)

Confucian thinking was the standard against which others pitted their wits. Mohism advocated universal love, which was an extension of the idea of humanity. Mozi, the movement's leading thinker, believed that people with 'virtue' and ability should be elevated and was opposed to inherited wealth or nobility.

Mencius developed a theory of government by benevolence, believing that man was born with goodness. In his view, man possessed inherent qualities of benevolence, righteousness, propriety and wisdom which some people were able to preserve and others not. In Mencius's view, every sovereign was able to rule by a policy of benevolence and every citizen was able to accept it.

Xunzi thought that man was born with evil, but education could change man's nature. Further, he emphasised self-improvement and self-fulfilment. As he says, 'If an ethically superior person studies widely and daily engages in self-examination, his intellect will become enlightened and his conduct will be without fault' (quoted in Cua 1998). This view, that study can lead to self-improvement, remains current. The educationalist Clive Dimmock, reporting on surveys of attitudes among Hong Kong high-school students, noted that the prevalent belief was that by studying hard, one could improve one's abilities. This was precisely the opposite of the view current among American students at the same time, where studying hard was seen as a way of compensating for *lack* of ability; if you had ability you did not need to study, and studying was unlikely to make you any better.[9]

Legalism (c. 220 BC)

Legalists believed, quite simply, in law and order. Furthermore, they believed that the law possessed a virtue that set it above any other human principle; everyone had to obey the law in every circumstance. This was law applied exactly, without exception. The Legalists believed that man is amoral and is guided purely by self-interest and the future, not by tradition: he must therefore be coerced by law into doing right. Otherwise, man had to be punished. Thus the Legalists are more or less opposed to the Confucians even though the first Legalist philosophers drew heavily on Confucian teachings.

Han Feizi, the most prominent exponent of Legalism, rejected the Confucian notion that most men tend towards the good and can be relied upon to behave ethically through a social system that exerts pressure on people to conform. For him, the only way to achieve conformity was through the rule of law. His system of thought was based on three important principles. The first of these was *fa*, meaning roughly 'prescriptive standards', but also with connotations of law and punishment. People should comply with *fa* so that their behaviour conforms with the public good, or be punished as a result. The second was *shi*, meaning 'authority' or 'power'. The exercise of *shi* is necessary to ensure compliance with *fa*; but conversely, *shi* should also be governed by the dictates of *fa* to prevent abuses of power. The third was *shu*, the technique of controlling the bureaucracy by comparing 'word' with 'deed' (or more generally, potential performance with the actuality). Han's views were adopted by the emperor Qin Shi Huangdi, and became the guiding force behind the Qin empire.

Apart from being a convenient doctrine for powerful leaders, this concept never gained much ground, and when the Qin dynasty was replaced by the Han dynasty, Confucian thinking became the norm and Legalism was consigned to the scrapheap. Some elements of Legalism can still be seen in Chinese thinking, particularly on the authority of the state over the individual, and certainly influences of Legalism can be found in some of Mao's writings. But these are influences, not whole systems. Modern commerce, therefore, exists in an environment where Legalism did *not* prevail over Confucian thinking.

Buddhism (c. 4th century AD)

By the third century AD, Confucianism was discarded by the then governing class, just as the Han dynasty also began to fail. Social elites were looking for something new, and as in most cases in China, this meant that they turned to the past to resurrect older, purer forms of thinking. Daoism enjoyed a resurgence. At the same time, Buddhism arrived from India.

Buddhism's official arrival dates to about 70 AD when the Han emperor Ming Ti had a dream of a golden flying deity. Why the Chinese were suddenly so open to a foreign religion is not very clear, but it may be that Buddhism and Daoism have enough shared ground to allow the Chinese to see it as meshing with previous belief systems. Certainly Chinese Buddhism quickly evolved away from many of its Indian roots. Although Indian classics like the

Awakening of Faith in Mahayana were widely read and studied, within a few generations Chinese Buddhist scholars like Fazang and Linji were establishing 'Buddhism with Chinese characteristics'. Perhaps the most famous Chinese Buddhist school was that of Chan, which later took hold also in Japan (where it is known as Zen). The masters of one particular branch of Chan had some unusual ways of teaching. One used to belabour students with sticks during lessons; another would interrupt speakers by shouting at them, 'If you meet the Buddha on the road: kill him!' Needless to say, this was not mainstream, but it does illustrate one of the essences of Chan, namely stretching the mind to think the unthinkable.

By the sixth century the monasteries, largely thanks to imperial patronage, had obtained substantial economic power. Inevitably, excess power led to corruption, and in 845 the Tang emperor Wuzong began a persecution, destroying monasteries, works of art and scholarship. Over 250,000 monks and nuns returned to the laity. Later, the Cheng brothers and Zhu Xi built many elements of Buddhist thinking into their Neo-Confucian synthesis (see below). Today, Chinese Buddhism is so intertwined with Confucianism and Daoism that it is difficult to tell the consequences of the three apart. Buddhism was largely suppressed after 1949 and many temples closed. In the 1990s they reopened both as tourist centres and for their traditional purposes.

Neo-Confucianism

Neo-Confucianism appears in the period of imperial revival in the Sung and Tang dynasties. Like many reform movements in China, it sought to make China strong again by ridding the country of foreign and corrupt influences and adopting a purely Chinese philosophy. A group of scholars set out to resolve the apparent contradictions between Confucianism, Daoism and Buddhism and create a unified system of thought. Much of the early work was done by the brothers Cheng Hao and Cheng Yi; the exposition of the final product was the work of the most important late Chinese philosopher, Zhu Xi.

By building a single thought-system which took in all the different aspects of Chinese philosophy and thinking, the Neo-Confucians (the name is a later tag) set a framework for thinking in China. Highly conservative, looking back to the masters (Confucius, Laozi *et al.*), the Neo-Confucians reinforced views on education, self-development and interpersonal relations along largely Confucian lines. This system has persisted to this day.

Christianity (1583 AD)

Exactly when Christianity arrived in China is not known, but there was a Nestorian Christian community in the west of China from at least the eighth century, and in 1289–90 a Chinese Christian called Rabban Sauma visited England and France as an envoy of one of the Mongol rulers. He must have caused a sensation.

Franciscan missionaries followed (or maybe preceded) Marco Polo into China; an archdiocese of Beijing was created, but converts never numbered more than a few hundred. Matteo Ricci pioneered a Jesuit presence in 1583, even though the Ming emperors had closed China to foreigners. He was well trained in language and Confucian thinking, by Chinese in Europe. With modern echoes, the Jesuits' market entry strategy was to make themselves valuable to the Ming emperors through technology transfer (including cannon manufacture) and thus earn import rights for Christianity. Ricci determined that the ancestor cult and Confucianism were 'social' rites, and could thus be incorporated within Christianity, just as Saturnalia had become Christmas.

Initially the strategy worked well, and by the end of the Ming dynasty a substantial foothold, and converts, had been achieved in Beijing and some cities further south. In the eighteenth century, however, other Catholic orders, perhaps jealous of the Jesuits' Chinese exclusivity, challenged Ricci's acceptance of ancestor cult and Confucianism. One thing led to another, the missionaries were forced to leave and Christians were persecuted.

As the Qing dynasty weakened in the nineteenth century, fresh waves of missionaries of all denominations appeared. Undoubtedly heroic, they made various contributions to health and education at local levels and achieved many converts. Nevertheless the impact on China, and Chinese thinking, overall was minimal, apart from the unintended disaster of the Taiping rebellion (1853–60) (see Chapter 2). This counterfeit Christianity (intellectual property rights have always been a problem) must have damaged the real thing. During the conservative Boxer Rebellion in 1900, many missionaries were killed by the rebels. Today there are perhaps 2 million Christians in China; they have little or no influence, certainly less than the 8 million or more Muslims.

Communism (c. 1920s)

The history of Communism in China has been well covered in a variety of other books, and does not need repetition here.[10] As a *philosophy*, Communism never really put down roots in China. Mao ruled in much the same way that the emperors had, and so did Deng. Today it operates as ruling *party*, which is a good enough reason to join, but Communist ideology has adjusted to market pragmatism. The cynical might think that acceptance of the ideology was convenient in providing a rationale for revolution and to get support from Russia. That would be unfair. Mao and his contemporaries had a genuine desire to reform China, and to distribute wealth from the rich to the poor. Corruption and the abuse of power in the 30 years either side of 1900 had advanced to the point where some puritanical doctrine was essential to clean the stables. Confucianism, which respected inherited order, was banned; yet many of the precepts of the two systems (such as the idea that government is for the benefit of the people) coincide, and Confucian ideas continued to infuse practice. Mao's doctrines on education and (early) concepts of government owe more to Confucius than to Marx.

However disastrous it proved and however badly history now judges it, the Cultural Revolution was, at least in part, an attempt to bring the furniture of Communism permanently into the Chinese mind alongside, or in place of, earlier philosophies. Mao noted that, whilst the means of production, both industrial, commercial and agricultural, had wholly been transformed from private family ownership to the state, the same old civil servants still seemed to be running the place. The Big Idea was to unleash young idealists, brandishing his thoughts in Little Red Books in order to democratise authority. Government would be by the masses, for the masses.

With hindsight, it is hard to conceive a more crass notion. Barring one, perhaps: after the Japanese, Civil and Korean Wars, Mao told the Chinese to restock the population, resulting in the overpopulation that now causes China, and the rest of the world, so many worries. Anyway, nothing brings Communism down faster than implementing it.

While Communism, a Western creed in any case, has been rejected, Maoism is still there. Walk in any park and witness the respect accorded to his poetry and literature. We are too close to events to be sure, but we would not be surprised if 'Maozi' comes to be read alongside Zhuangzi a thousand years from now.

Eight key concepts in Chinese thinking

- *Dao*: The Way.
- *De*: Virtue. A key Daoist concept which guides people to correct behaviour and away from narrow self-interest.
- *Li*: Rituals or rites. Sets out the correct form of behaviour in a given situation, so as to preserve harmony and face.
- *Mianzi*: Face, including one's self-respect and public dignity. Preserving *mianzi* is a key goal in most interpersonal relations. Having a 'thick face' means that one is impervious to face issues, i.e. thick-skinned in English, probably because public respect is already eroded.
- *Ren*: Literally 'benevolence'; but in fact covers the traditional ethical code of how one should treat other people. Not to be confused with the same (pinyin but not Chinese) word for a person.
- *Yi*: Rightness or righteousness; the knowledge of what is correct in any given situation.
- *Yin-yang*: The two halves of a whole, often in reference to *dao*. Treated as complementary, rather than polar opposites, *yang* and *yin* describe two halves of the same whole; they are, so to speak, the sunny and shady sides of the same mountain, but one needs to be careful with analogies. *Yang*, which also means the sun, is associated with positiveness and masculinity; *yin* (the moon) is negative and feminine.
- *Zhi*: Knowing or knowledge but procedural rather than factual. In other words, knowing *how*, not knowing *what*.

Values

A discussion of values in Chinese society deserves a book in its own right. Here we focus on a few of the most important, including:

- age, hierarchy and authority, which are strongly linked
- wealth
- face
- cultural dimensions.

Despite the caution introduced with the Latourette quote at the beginning of this chapter, one must recognise that younger managers do not necessarily share the values of their elders. As is also true in Japan, Europe and elsewhere, the younger are more international, more prepared to experiment, more looking to have fun and less dedicated to family, or any other, ties.

Age, hierarchy and authority

Respect for tradition, ancestors and age, stemming from Confucius, was among the main values of people in old China. The respect for age was manifested especially in family life, which had a profound effect upon other parts of social life. The hierarchical relations of a Chinese family were determined by age. The names of sisters and brothers follow the age-order of the family members. For example, an older brother is addressed as 'older brother' (*gege*) and a younger sister likewise (*meimei*). Only parents call their children by their given names.

Similarly, industrial workers in old China did not typically question higher authority or seek authority themselves, thus reinforcing the subordinates, subservience and dependence on superiors. Authority in industry and business was viewed as an absolute right of owners and the managers in control. Superior–subordinate relationships were typically personal, subjective and viewed as father–son or master–servant relationships. No two persons were equal in relation to each other. An older person had more authority than a younger one, and a man had more than a woman.

The Qin dynasty (221–207 BC) held the family responsible for the public acts of its members as part of their social pressure on each individual, inculcating obedience to the government and to the social order through the family. This still operates. The one-child rule, for example, is enforced more through family and local community pressures than any legal system. Today the one-child rule is slowly being relaxed; families who wish to have more than one child and who have the money to do so can pay a fee to the authorities in order to obtain permission. This practice is more widespread in some parts of the country than others; more conservative and poorer parts of China tend to stick to the rules.

Wealth

The need for self-sufficiency traditionally bred a savings mentality. Money should be hoarded: if times were good now, they were likely to be bad later. The culture required even the rich to pretend to be poor. *Inside* the PRC, the first-class cabin is likely to contain only the occasional Western businessperson. But there is a paradox here. Whether it was Shanghai in the 1930s or Hong Kong more recently, the opposite view was that money attracts money. It should be flaunted. *Outside* the PRC, first-class air travel is taken by some who cannot afford it but must be seen to do it. Here is another warning: do not be taken in by appearances. Old money is more likely to be hidden, new money more likely to be flashed. That does not make one, necessarily, better than the other (nor is it so different from New York, San Francisco, Paris or London).

Face (miànzi)

The pervasive Chinese concept of gaining, giving or losing 'face' focuses on questions of prestige and dignity, and reflects surprising vulnerability in self-esteem. The Chinese are acutely sensitive to the regard in which they are held by others or the light in which they appear. Causing someone to lose face can have severe consequences: at the very least, cooperation will cease and retaliation may ensue.

Losing and saving face are well understood in the West. Less so is the concept of giving face; that is, doing something to enhance someone else's reputation or prestige. The heavy use of shame as a social control mechanism from the time of early childhood tends to cause feelings of dependency and anxieties about self-esteem, which produce self-consciousness about most social relationships. As a result, a great deal can be gained by helping the Chinese to win face and a great deal will be lost by any affront or slight, no matter how unintended, especially for older and/or more senior people.

The Chinese concept of sincerity is the opposite of the Anglo-American, in that the Chinese believe that they can manifest sincerity only by adhering carefully to prescribed etiquette, whereas Westerners believe that etiquette obscures truth.[11] In a sense the Chinese are saying, 'I will show my sincerity in my relations with you by going to the trouble to be so absolutely correct towards you that you will be untroubled about any matters of face'. Again, the form of the interchange is as important as the content, as is laid down by *li*.

Giving face is also closely connected with *guanxi* (see Chapter 4). We are more likely to establish good relationships with those who always give us face, and vice versa. That accumulates. If *guanxi* already exists, then giving face increases the opportunity for rewards. Flattery, in short, will get you anywhere.

Cultural dimensions

Geert Hofstede has referred to culture as the software of the mind.[12] In research which is very widely cited on differences between Eastern and Western business cultures, Hofstede uses four dimensions from Western research and found that a fifth was required when the work was re-run in Hong Kong. They are: power distance (hierarchic respect), individualism v. collectivism, assertiveness, uncertainty avoidance and, later, long-termism. Since he was measuring IBM managers, the PRC was not included and it is dangerous to make inferences from Singapore, Hong Kong and Taiwan. Nevertheless, it is reasonable that the overseas Chinese rated as highly on hierarchy and low on individualism, and as middle of the road on assertiveness/masculinity. Taiwan felt much more threatened by uncertainty than Hong Kong (which was then a British colony, not part of China), and Singapore was most confident of all. The PRC *was* included on the long-term orientation scale, and rated highest of all.

For many people familiar with both China and the overseas Chinese, however, Hofstede's conclusions do not match their own experience. The Hofstede research is not reliable in an oriental context because it falls into the either/or trap. Hofstede is a prisoner of his own (Dutch) culture and, frankly, this type of research is hocus-pocus. The Chinese are not *either* individualist *or* collective but both at the same time. In 1992, Li Huaizu and his colleagues provided what we feel is a more insightful and elegant perspective on Chinese tradition and Western decision-making theory. The authors identified five groups of differences between Chinese tradition and features of Western decision theory: motivation and consequence, unity and diversity, circle and sequence, harmony and self-interest, and certainty and uncertainty. Other writers have commented on a number of elements from Chinese culture that impact on decision-making, including face, the individual–collective dichotomy, hierarchy, equality, self and social role, and personal modesty.

Motivation and consequence

According to Western theory, the manager assembles the possible outcomes from alternative actions, judges the probability of each outcome, and then chooses the action most likely to have favourable consequences. In contrast, the Confucianist evaluates the motives and intention of the manager, taking ethical or moral principles as the criteria. The consequences examined are those that arose in the past, facts about past decisions and not estimates about the future. In other words, if the principles worked before, continue with them and do not speculate about the future.

Examples illustrating this are found in classic Chinese doctrines such as 'The gentleman makes much of ethics; the villain of gains and losses' and 'The person who worries about outcomes is no gentleman'. Thus while governments go in for elaborate economic (i.e. Western philosophy) planning, Chinese businesses tend not to have any *financial* plans at all. They do, however, think strategically (see below).

In the 1920s, Li Zongwu's *The Theory of Thickness and Blackness* became an overnight sensation in China. Li argued that successful decision-makers in China are not those who adhere to the Confucian ideals and aim to preserve face and maintain good relationships. Instead, they are those who possess the qualities 'thickness' or 'thick face' (that is, they do not care what others think of them) and 'blackness' or 'black-heartedness' (that is, those who are able to act in their own self-interest without guilt). In traditional style, Li illustrated his work with examples from the Three Kingdoms period. But then, no one would assume that all Chinese act in a purely Confucian (or Daoist, or whatever) spirit all the time.

Unity and diversity

Chinese tradition emphasises synthesis and unitary principle, from which problem-solving attributes are deduced, while the Western approach is to focus on the specific characteristics of the problem, permitting a variety of objectives. An example of this thinking is found in the ancient Chinese classic, the *Yijing* [*The Book of Changes*], which deals with knowledge of the universe as a whole. Minor principles can be deduced from a few major ones, instead of working Western-style from the observation of reality. Having said that, Chinese thinking, obviously, includes the observation of reality as well.

Circle and sequence

Chinese think of nature in terms of closed, spiral or circular systems of interrelated elements, whereas Western decision theory is sequential (for example, with linear, exponential or repeated patterns such as economic cycles). In traditional Chinese thinking, consequence is from many interrelated factors. A circular network is used to highlight the effects as a whole. The more linear Western approach can be presented as a sequence of decisions, such as a 'decision tree', each analysing the problem more narrowly.

Harmony and self-interest

When determining the optimal decision, Chinese tradition is to emphasise harmony and the group, but Western decision theory presumes that the decision-maker will optimise self-interest (maximise subjective expected utility). There are many Chinese sayings which reinforce the idea that a person who stands out from the group will be criticised and may be prevented from reaching his/her goal: 'The tree growing high above the others will be blown down by the wind' and 'The gun fires at the first bird in the flock'. Similarly, the Confucian Doctrine of the Mean is, 'Take the mean of the two, remain neutral without bias' and the Daoist doctrine is, 'Strive for no fault rather than merit, retreat for the purpose of advancing'. Of course business people, in search of first-mover advantage, will quite often seek to be first. A Chinese businessperson may well be embarrassed by being innovative, whereas a similar partner in the West would be proud of it. Being first in China has profound cultural and social difficulties. Imitation, however, gives face.

Certainty and uncertainty

Chinese tradition is oriented towards certainty, not the evaluation of uncertainty that is emphasised in Western decision theory. In their struggle for existence against numerous dangers and disasters, the Chinese felt that the future was very hard to face. As luck and misfortune came from the supernatural, divination was appropriate for decisions. The Chinese value past experiences more highly, depending on these for future action; again, note the importance of history and historical thinking. Past experiences are the guarantee and premise for success (just as they are for many Wall Street analysts, come to that). This view is reflected in sayings like, 'The old finger is hottest', and 'One will pay for it if one does not follow an old man's words'.

Economics

Ancient Chinese contained no word for 'economics'; the modern term, *jing ji*, is a Japanese loan word and does not appear until the end of the nineteenth century. There is, however, a very ancient term, 'administering wealth', which appears in the Daoist text the *Yijing*, and this gives some clues as to how the Chinese approached and continue to approach the concept of economics. Unlike rationalist Western theories, Confucian thinking sees human agency as an essential feature of economics. Chen Huan-chang, a Chinese mandarin who later studied Western political economy, argued in his *The Economic Principles of Confucius and His School* that Confucian writings mention three factors of production: land, capital and the virtuous man. Of these three, it is the latter that is by far the most important.

Moreover, the administering of wealth is not an end in itself; it is done for a purpose. In Confucian thought, wealth is inseparable from ethical and social considerations. Chen sums this approach with a quote from the *Great Learning* (p. 293):

> The superior man must be careful about his virtue first. Having virtue, there will be the man. Having the man, there will be the land. Having the land, there will be wealth. Having the wealth, there will be its use. Virtue is the root, and wealth is its only outcome.

In order to remain virtuous, economic activity must be managed and controlled. Doing this is the task of sages and kings, whom Confucius advises to remain above or outside the economic system and act as external agents. He often calls for those in positions of power to avoid personal enrichment. Most notably, whereas Western economic theory often focuses on increasing supply in order to match demand, Confucius favoured curbing demand so as to meet supply. He proposed not only economic controls (such as sumptuary laws to inhibit demand for luxuries) but also the curbing of human wants through moral and social education.

This idea is, of course, in sharp contrast to the Daoist idea of *wu-wei* noted above, and it conflicts too with the Han Fei–Legalist notion of centralising all power and activity in the hands of the state. Three different and apparently competing ideologies helped shape Chinese economic development down through the centuries, and influences of all three can be seen today. Regulation of demand continues to be seen as very important in China, even if at present the main emphasis is on stimulus rather than curbing demand. *Laissez-faire* is accepted as a tool through which economic benefits can be delivered, but a check to its excesses is provided in the form of a Confucian and Legalist-inspired bureaucracy, the tool through which the state attempts to compel a balance between competing forces. This sounds to us very much like a paradox. To the Chinese government, at least, it seems a perfectly logical way to look at economics.

Strategy

'Strategy', as most business school students learn at some point, means almost anything anyone wants it to mean. In chess, it refers to broad principles of attack and defence, to parts of the board on which attack will be focused; it does *not* mean the identification of a series of moves that anticipate competitive reaction. Even chess-playing computers can only look a few moves deep. Any decent strategy expects the unexpected. In business (schools), the word is confused with planning and with marketing. In China, the idea that one can lay out strategic moves, step by step, in some pre-planned sequence is even more unlikely than elsewhere. One is not even a player surveying the chessboard, just one of the pawns. But does that mean that Chinese businesses do not think strategically? Quite the reverse. For reasons of space, we will touch here on just two aspects: strategy as warfare, and cleverness or trickery.

Business strategy as warfare

As mentioned above, the period of Warring States (475–221 BC) provided plenty of material for strategist theorists, chief amongst whom was Sunzi. As the people who led the army during war and the government administration during peace were frequently the same people or drawn from the same circle, the same strategic management principles were applied in peace and war. According to Sunzi, the supreme aim of war was 'not to win one hundred victories in one hundred battles' but to 'subdue the enemy without fighting'. In competition either in politics or business, strategy should be aimed at disposing one's resources in such an overwhelming fashion that the outcome of the contest is determined before it gets started.

According to Sunzi:[13]

Strategy is the great work of the organisation.
In situations of life or death, it is the Tao of survival or extinction.
Its study cannot be neglected.

Therefore calculate a plan with Five Working Fundamentals,
And examine the condition of each.
The first is Tao.
The second is Nature.
The third is Situation.
The fourth is Leadership.
The fifth is Art.

Or in another translation (Chang 1976: 74) version,[14] the Five
Working Fundamentals are listed as government, the environment,
the terrain, the command and the doctrine. In modern marketing
terms, the equivalent would be:

* what kind of business are we/should we be in?
* analysis of the competitive environment
* competitive positioning
* motivational factors
* implementation.

In short, Sunzi describes, in subtle language, the modern marketing plan.

Strategists study these five factors to assess the chances of success
and calculate their strengths and weaknesses *vis-à-vis* that of their
opponents. Deception, speed and concentration of forces are the
rules of war. Norman Dixon, whose hilarious account of military
disasters *On the Psychology of Military Incompetence* is a must-read,
summarises the same principles into focus of firepower (small time
and place) and the quality of information which probably extends
to disinformation – a Chinese speciality.[15]

Of the various military metaphors, guerrilla warfare is the most
appealing both because marketers usually have too few resources
for the task and because it is not just Army A versus Army
B: the surrounding population (i.e. end consumers) is usually
decisive. Guerrilla warfare, if successful, proceeds through three
phases: invisibility, evasion and concentration. In the first, the
guerrillas maintain the lowest possible profile and set up their
infrastructure and relationships with the surrounding population.
In the second, battles/skirmishes are fought only to increase
resources at the enemy's expense. The third stage is akin to classic
warfare.

Whether it is in the small wins early or the pitched battles later,
all writers point to the importance of focusing energy onto the

point of contact so that, in that place and at that time, the enemy is outnumbered, encircled and suppressed. Failing that, at least ensure your positioning occupies 'the high ground', whatever that may be in consumer terms. It may well be as simple as a higher price. As far as Mao was concerned, only now could resources be spent, only now could losses be justified by gains. Mao's formula for deciding on attack is reproduced here:

> We should in general secure at least two of the following conditions before we can consider the situation as being favourable to us and unfavourable to the enemy and before we can go over to the counter-offensive. These conditions are:
>
> i   The population actively supports the Red Army.
> ii The terrain is favourable for operations.
> iii All the main forces of the Red Army are concentrated.
> iv The enemy's weak spots have been located.
> v   The enemy has been reduced to a tired and demoralised state.
> vi The enemy has been induced to make mistakes.
>
> (Mao 1954 [1938])

Mao was also fond of saying that his main two mistakes were over-estimating and under-estimating the enemy. That this recent Chinese history echoes Sunzi is no surprise. Mao was a scholar. He was not just a master general but a master guerrilla and, in another time, would have been a master marketer or business executive. Brand names and business reputations in China live as long, perhaps longer, than anywhere else. In this long-term game, the Chinese players will have learned from these histories and the application of military game-playing to business is both a major and conscious part of their planning.

Shanghai Volkswagen

When people think of joint ventures (JVs) in China, they often think first of Shanghai Volkswagen. It is one of the oldest JVs by a Western company in China, having been established in 1985;

the Chinese partner was the Shanghai Automotive International Company (SAIC). A second JV was established with First Automotive Works in 1987, in the city of Changchun. Between them, these two JVs gave Shanghai Volkswagen a powerful presence in the market. Growth was slow at first, as there were few roads, few petrol stations and few people with the disposable income to buy a private car.

Instead, Shanghai VW's managers concentrated on two markets; government car fleets and taxis. They were highly successful in both cases. The red Volkswagen Santana became a feature of Shanghai's streets, and there were sales in other cities too. In 2000 the Santanas were replaced by Passats, a European design but made locally in China by the joint ventures. In 2000, Shanghai VW manufactured 53 per cent of all the cars sold in China.

However, its very success in these fields became Shanghai VW's undoing. The newly affluent middle classes in China could now afford private cars, and they did not want a brand that had associations with either taxis or the cars used by civil servants. It was estimated that by 2004 there were 60 million people in China with the means to buy and run a private car, and they were not buying Volkswagens. Other competitors were crowding in. General Motors launched a joint venture in Shanghai in 1997, and its Buick brand became popular almost at once. Honda, Toyota and Peugeot were also on the scene with joint ventures or subsidiaries of their own.

More critically, the domestic car industry was surging, and local brands like Chery, Lifan and Geely were cheaper than cars made by the joint ventures. Chery's QQ micro-car, costing the equivalent of around $4,000, saw sales increase by 130 per cent in 2006. Altogether, the Chinese brands had taken 28 per cent of the market by 2006, and Japanese imports another 27 per cent. Meanwhile, Shanghai VW had seen its market share slide from over 50 per cent in 2000 to just 15 per cent in 2005.

In October 2005 Shanghai VW announced a programme aimed at recovering its old dominant position. The plan was to roll out at least ten new models, aimed specifically at Chinese consumers, with the first to go on show by the opening of the Beijing Olympics in 2008. At the same time there would be a radical shake-up of its cost structures and supply-chain operations, including re-negotiating the two JV contracts to reflect the realities of the new situation. In particular, Shanghai VW wanted its two JV partners to collaborate more closely with each other in order to achieve 'synergy'. This was a very ambitious programme, and not all observers believed Shanghai VW could achieve its goals in the short time it had allowed itself.[16]

Trickery/cleverness

We have a semantic problem here: no one, including the Chinese, likes a word like 'trickery', loaded as it is with negative connotations. At the same time cleverness (better) does not quite convey the legitimate role of disinformation. Context affects meaning: we like to be tricked by a magician at a party, but are angry if we are tricked out of our money by a fraudster. In this section, we refer to business practices that are legitimate but likely to mislead, and thereby outwit, other players. We are not talking about cheating.

We will call it 'cleverness' to avoid offence. The Chinese tolerance of cleverness in this sense is greater than that in the West. As ever, it is limited by relationships (you do not outwit your own father) and it is also reciprocal (the West is *expected* to be devious even when it is not). The cunning entrepreneur, the crafty businessman who is 'eight sides all wide and slippery', is an admired figure in many circles.

The view of cleverness or trickery is invariably one-sided. Here is a Chinese view of Western business people, written in a handbook for Chinese managers in 1990:

> We have to know the tactics needed for the struggle, know the opponents and ourselves, and be able to see through their tricks. The foreign capitalists will always try to cheat money out of us by using every possible means including deception.

In China, as elsewhere, cock-up is far more frequent than conspiracy. The papers that the other side left on the table when they took a quick break from the meeting may be valuable information, intentional disinformation, or completely irrelevant and really left by mistake. The odds on the papers being a plant (especially if they are in English) are probably somewhat higher, but no more than that. This all contributes to the absolute rule for old China hands that no one source of information is reliable. When three independent sources provide the same information, one can begin to take it seriously.

The overseas Chinese

Most of this chapter will apply to the overseas Chinese communities too, though with some exceptions. Most importantly, although most overseas Chinese communities had some Maoist sympathisers, especially in the 1950s and 1960s, Maoism was never put into practice in these countries and therefore this philosophy does not really figure strongly in their furniture of the mind. There has also been greater penetration of Western ideas in many cases; there are far larger numbers of Chinese Christians overseas than in China, for example. Finally, through education and the media, many overseas Chinese have accepted some Western modes of thinking along with their own Chinese modes. (This is one of the reasons why many mainland Chinese regard the overseas Chinese with some reserve).

Be prepared for variations. Many overseas Chinese have become acculturated and even 'Westernised'. Others are strongly conservative in social and mental terms, and can be 'more Chinese than the Chinese'. See Chapter 10 for more on this phenomenon.

Conclusions

The purpose of this chapter has been to explore, and to some extent compare, mental furniture. No single individual, still less 1.3 billion people, think exactly alike, nor would anyone expect that. For the purpose of contrasting differences, we have tended to compare China with the West and ignored other parts of the world. Obviously, the closer the cultural and historical links – for example, with Japan, Korea and Vietnam – the more furniture is shared or similar; yet it does not do to ignore the great differences between modes of thinking in these countries as well.

4 Relationships and regulations

The rules are fixed; the people are flexible.

(Chinese proverb)

We are not sure this proverb is still entirely true. Rules only seem to be fixed for the moment; they may have been promulgated but overtaken before officials get around to implementing them. If anything, though, this makes the need for relationships all the greater. Researchers in many parts of the world have noted how, in the absence of a formal structure of laws and regulations, personal relationships become the framework through which connections are made, trust established and business done. China, as we shall see in the next chapter, is in the throes of large-scale legal reform, but that does not mean relationships are becoming less important. Indeed, in many ways they are becoming *more* important.

Foreign businesses in China need local partners in just the same way that they do in any world market. Relationships have to be cultivated with distributors, suppliers, customers, local government and administration, and the community in general. Relationships are more important in China than in many other countries, however, for three reasons. First, government plays a much more direct role in the economy in China that it does in most Western countries or even in many developing economies. As we noted in Chapter 2, in China the economy is seen as being at the service of the state, and the state does not hesitate to intervene when it thinks the economy is going in undesirable directions. This applies to local as well as central government in the People's Republic of China, and to a greater or lesser degree it applies to every government in the region. Cultivating good relationships with government is therefore often a critical factor in assuring the success of a venture.

Second, there are sharply differing attitudes to law, particularly to its aims and purposes, in China than in the West. In the latter (for better or for worse), we tend to see the law as the essential set of rules of conduct governing our society, and also as our primary form of redress when things go wrong. Quite different traditions exist in China; here the 'rules of conduct' are the ethics and standards of behaviour required in a Confucian society. Social pressures rather than legal instruments are used to ensure compliance. Of course this does not mean that there are no laws in China, but the laws are used in different ways. As we discuss below, many of the issues that Westerners tend to think of as legal are better seen in China as relationship issues.

Third, and related to the above, there is the fact that much of Chinese society – including its businesses – is and always has been organised on relationship principles. There are three key principles which can be added to the box in the last previous chapter:

- *Qingmian*, or 'human feelings'; respect for the feelings of others is of great importance, particularly in relationship management.
- *He*, or 'harmony', a very powerful concept which stresses the smooth running of a group or a society. Harmony is seen as good, conflict as bad. *He* also means gentleness or friendliness.
- *Guanxi*, which is usually translated simply as 'relationships' or 'connections'. It is no exaggeration to say that relationships are the *modus operandi* of Chinese business. They are how things get done.

After looking more closely at this last concept, this chapter and the next apply it in three contexts – government, legal/contractual and commercial. In all three, relationships are essential for doing business in China and around the region. They need to be considered and developed *simultaneously*. Some types of relationships will, in given circumstances, be more important than others; but over the long term, all three will be necessary and cannot be turned on and off like taps.

Guanxi

There are almost as many definitions of *guanxi* as there are people who have observed and written about it. 'A network of interpersonal relationships and exchanges of favours established for the purpose of conducting business activities', is how one recent article describes it, and that is probably as good a definition as any.[1] The idea of favours is particularly important. Implicit in the concept of *guanxi* is the expectation that, at some time, favours will be returned.

Nevertheless, *guanxi* is not some form of bank account where net favour indebtedness can be measured. The whole system, *guanxiwang*, is a web of subtle, and not so subtle, obligations, not rights. *Guanxi* has both good and bad meanings. In this chapter we intend the good. (*Guanxi* and corruption will be discussed in the 'Ethical Interlude' which follows Chapter 5.) Some businesspeople, especially younger ones, dismiss *guanxi* as old fashioned and to be replaced by modern Western methods. That is unwise; the two will co-exist. *Guanxi* is a comparatively new word, entering the vocabulary only in the twentieth century, but the practice goes back to antiquity. *Guan*, from which it derives, means a customs house, gate or barrier. Thus, without *guanxi* the door to business is firmly barred.

Westerners have difficulty with the concept of obligations unmatched by rights. Conversely, the Chinese had no word for (and thus concept of) 'rights' until they had to import *quan li*, via Japan, for Western translation purposes. *Guanxi* is rooted in Confucianism. Family and social context defines the individual as distinct from the Western view in which the individual defines his context. 'In other words, self-individualisation is possible only through a process of engagement with others within the context of one's social roles and relationships ... the self is always a relational self, a relational being ...'[2] Mayfair Yang traces the influence of *guanxi* through all forms of social and commercial life in China.[3] Kevin Bucknall describes it as:

> Something like a valuable bank account of favors owed and owing, and people with bigger networks tend to do better. However, the bank account is not unlimited so after receiving, say, two or three favors in a row, people must repay when approached, even if it might disadvantage them in some way.[4]

The bank account metaphor is, however, very crude. *Guanxi* is not an accounting concept but a description of affect, or feelings, in which a very small favour may mean a lot and a big one count for very little. Feelings are not subject to double-entry book-keeping. The concept is also pragmatic: if doing a favour, whether in reciprocation or not, can fit in with what one plans to do anyway, so much the better. But it may not be presented to the recipient in those terms! Business in China, however much influenced by Western theory and practice, can be expected to depend on relationships.

The Chinese classify *guanxi* capital (*ziben*) according to its efficacy (*ling*). The key features are:

- Durability (*naiyong*), meaning unconditionality. Thus the more certain you are that support will be reciprocated, the longer it can be deferred.
- Hardness (*ying*) *guanxi* refers to the relative importance of the other party: the more senior the 'harder'.
- Connectivity (*lianhuo*) refers to the onward *guanxi* in relevant networks. However strong the relationship may be with some one who is a dead end, he is still a dead end.

The last idiom seems to be somewhere between consanguinity and the degree of obligation. The sub-components are 'endowed' (*tianzi*) by birth, whether immediate family (*zhixi qinshu*) or father's relations (*nanfang*). The weaker non-birth varieties are seen as personal savings (*jilei*) which may be utilised (*laguolai*) for business. Feelings (*ganqing*) built up from shared experience accumulate: the longer (ideally since childhood), the better. Relationships formed within the family are, for the purpose of business, the weakest and seen, to some extent, as instrumental (*liyong*), self-interest (*liyi*) and money (*jinqian*) *guanxi*.

Durability is similar perhaps to trust, and connectivity to identity (of interest). This shared identification is sometimes called the *guanxi* base. Each of us is an amalgam of nature (genes) and nurture (experience) and this last idiom directly mirrors that with *tianzi* and *ganqing*. It is interesting, but not surprising, that expatriate Chinese are more likely to deal with other expatriates originating in the same part of China.

It is important to note that not all *guanxi* relationships are equal, and two people having a *guanxi* relationship does not imply an absolute bond between them. Either or both may have still stronger *guanxi* relationships with others, perhaps depending on the degree of kinship, as noted above. The Chinese scholars Zhang Yi and Zhang Zhigang, whom we quoted above, describe *guanxi* as existing in concentric circles around each person. First there are *guanxi* relationships with members of one's own family and kin-group. These they describe as 'obligatory' relationships.

Kinship means obligation, and this is the strongest form of *guanxi* because, in theory, you must perform any favour asked of you. The second, middle circle they term 'reciprocal' relationships. There are lasting, long-term relationships with old friends, classmates, close colleagues and peers. People exchange favours here as a matter of course, but there is always a sense of balance; you must not ask too much of someone, or at least, not unless you are prepared to give an equal or greater amount back at a future date. The outer ring the authors term 'utilitarian' relationships. These relationships are with people one knows through association but perhaps not well. At the same time, they are not exactly strangers, and so if person A needs something, he might well think of approaching person B and asking for a favour. The favour might or might not be granted; there is no necessity for person B to do so. Nor will person B necessarily want the favour returned, though person A should be prepared for the request in any case.

Westerners have these relationships as well, of course, though they do not classify them. The family, the home, the office, the golf club or sailing club or cricket club, one's own village or neighbourhood, all contain people with whom we have relationships. Psychologists, sociologists and historians, tell us that Westerners have become less good at recognising and managing these relationships over time; hence former UK prime minister Margaret Thatcher is attributed with saying 'there is no such thing as society'. What she actually said was much closer to the Chinese point of view, namely people should acknowledge their own individual responsibility before looking to society. For the vast majority, society and relationships give them their context, show them where they belong, and are used to help their personal and business ventures flourish.

Guanxi is a mechanism for dealing with risk. The Chinese may be gamblers but, without *guanxi*, they prefer to miss the opportunity for gaining £1 million. On the other hand, they may prefer to risk losing £100 in order to build *guanxi* for the future. We should not risk what we cannot afford. This is why the Chinese build trust progressively by introducing more and more risk and seeing how it works out. They are looking backwards, not forwards.

These components need to be seen in a competitive environment in which they act on two levels: a strong enough relationship gains entry to the consideration set and then the relative *guanxi* affects the probability of doing business. The bigger the risk, the stronger the *guanxi* will need to be. For example, tendering for large contracts in China is rarely the free-market auction Westerners expect. The supplier will be determined by *guanxi*; only the terms of that business are determined by the tenders.

We are not alone in seeing *guanxi* as an alternative to contract law; no less a figure than Singapore's Lee Kuan Yew has made the same observation. One could argue that it is also a great deal cheaper, but the US, for example, and Chinese systems are not easily compared in financial terms.

Guanxi and business

For the Western manager coming to work in China, an understanding of *guanxi* is critical. It can also be a very difficult concept to get one's head around, especially for someone coming from a highly individualistic society (America springs to mind, but there are others). Academic research tells us that many Western businesspeople are bad at building and maintaining relationships, so that means that in China, these managers will automatically start out with one hand tied behind their back.

Researchers have tried to help matters along by classifying *guanxi* into various types. At first this idea seems rather futile. So ubiquitous is *guanxi* that you might as well try to classify the types of air that businesspeople breathe. But there is one way of classifying *guanxi* that some might find helpful: not by its type or nature, but by its effect. What does *guanxi* actually do?

Once again, there are many different opinions and views, as one might expect from the study of such a nebulous subject. However, there does seem to be some consensus on the purposes that *guanxi* can be put to and the effects it has. These effects can be seen both outside and inside the firm.

Guanxi *substitutes for institutional frameworks*

It is this aspect of *guanxi* that most people think of, and to Western businesspeople it is often the aspect that is most apparent to them. Following economic reform, China for a long time had what is described as a 'weak institutional framework'. Central and local governments clearly played a key role in the economy, but there was no *coherent* body of laws and regulations. In the somewhat chaotic atmosphere, businesses turned to building personal relationships with key government officials as a substitute. Friendly officials could give advance notice of new development plans, tell which projects had government support and which did not, get access to other officials, help arrange permits and licences, help with planning permission and a whole host of other highly necessary things – all perfectly legally, it should be added. It was not just businesses that benefited. Government departments and agencies, themselves floundering as they tried to bring about a new economic order, were grateful for these relationships too. A word in the right ear could see a vital new power plant or highway built, without having to go through cumbersome tendering and approval processes.

Today the situation is changing, as we shall see below and in Chapter 5, but *guanxi* with government remains of primary importance for any businessperson, Western or Chinese. Observers are unanimous on this point: *guanxi* with government officials plays a much more critical role in business growth and profitability than does *guanxi* with other managers.

Guanxi *builds strong organisations*

Another point which is often made is that *guanxi* is the property of individuals, not organisations. Businesses do not have *guanxi*; the people within them do. The point is that unless the people within the business are prepared to use their *guanxi* on behalf of the business, nothing will happen.

Therefore, the argument goes, it is necessary to build strong *guanxi* within the business as well as outside of it. Chinese businesses, except for very large ones, seldom have organisational flowcharts or diagrams showing who is responsible for what. And in those large organisations, particularly the old state-owned enterprises (SOEs), the value of these flowcharts is questionable. Things get done because people know, often at an unspoken or even subconscious level, whom to go to. If a purchasing order needs to be filled quickly, do not submit a memo to the head of purchasing, go instead to Ms Li the under-manager who was a classmate at university and who can be trusted to do the job as required. It might sound chaotic, and sometimes it is, but the evidence from Chinese businesses is that it works. Chinese managers, when they want something, are far more likely to pick up the phone than write a memo or an email. There is no question of 'it's not what you know, but who you know'. Chinese managers realise that both are equally important.

The role of *guanxi* in building what we would call organisational commitment, teamwork and so on cannot be overstated.

Poor internal relationships can result in such problems as high staff turnover, difficulty in recruiting skilled staff and so on. We shall discuss this further in Chapter 9.

There are more specific uses of *guanxi*, of course. Good *guanxi* with external partners, especially government, can give access to scarce resources: land, raw materials, distribution networks, markets, labour, money. Strong *guanxi* within the organisation not only helps pull people together and enables leaders to function effectively, but it also leads to shared knowledge and ideas. Again, it has been remarked in recent research that Chinese companies are much better at pooling ideas than are Western firms. There are clear benefits for innovation and R&D for example. All these are strengths that a manager can use to advantage, provided he or she is able to build *guanxi* in the first place.

Government

Since economic reform began in 1978, the government of China has consciously orchestrated legal and commercial changes so as to maximise China's economic interest, both domestically and globally. Relaxation of rules on foreign ownership and investment, reforming state ownership ('privatisation' is not accepted as a word) and liberalisation of the economy generally are only pragmatic tools. The government sees the free market as a means to its own ends, not as an ideological principle. The rules will change whenever it is perceived that there is a need to do so. To this extent, looking back to the previous chapter, the government of China is behaving in a Confucian way; *laissez-faire* capitalism is used to generate wealth, but it is the responsibility of the state to ensure that the resulting wealth is used for the most appropriate ends.

It is worth cautioning the reader again about the rate of change in China, particularly in government. New rules on foreign investment are announced nearly every year, and more minor regulatory changes more often than that. Government itself is in a perpetual state of flux: Premier Zhu Rongji abolished five entire ministries in 1998 and drastically reduced the numbers of employees in many others. The late 1990s also saw the beginning of a trend towards devolution of powers, and of tax collection, to regional and local governments. This has been more a devolution of responsibility than of power, as Beijing still retains the right of oversight in most fields and decisions that are made at local levels can be reversed on appeal to higher levels. But this does not mean that local authorities have no freedom of action. Consequently, one of the principal rules of dealing with government in China is to recognise that several different departments at several different levels may have – or think they have – the right to interfere in your business. And, they may each be working to entirely different agendas.

The paragraphs that follow, therefore, are tinged with envy rather than criticism. The PRC bureaucratic process works remarkably well, from their point of view. They invented the concept of mandarins, after all, and had centuries of managing the country with very few, but highly intelligent, civil servants.

Government in China has considerable powers. It can deny approval for proposed projects and can withdraw licences from existing ones. On a single day in 1996, the government of Tianjin withdrew licences for over a hundred joint ventures, for reasons ranging from disputes between partners to lack of profitability. The government also has great authority. As distinct from power, this means that the government in China often gets its own way without having to invoke its formal powers, by 'suggesting' that companies or individuals should pursue a certain course of action (remember the Daoist concept of *wu-wei* from the earlier chapter). This is very much in line with the Chinese avoidance of confrontation and preference for arriving at mutually agreed solutions (even if in this case, one party tells the others what they are agreeing to).

It follows that if you have good relationships with the relevant branches of government, you are more likely to get what you need, be it permission to build, develop, sell goods, set up a factory, form a joint venture or whatever. Good relations with government can make the wheels of bureaucracy turn faster, even allowing you to 'jump the queue' and get approval more quickly than you might expect. Poor relationships or none at all, conversely, can put ventures at risk. One notorious example remains that of McDonald's in Beijing in the 1990s. Having been granted permission to establish a restaurant in a prime location on the south side of Tiananmen Square (ironically enough, almost opposite Mao's mausoleum), a few months later the company discovered the permission had been revoked and the site had been given to a Hong Kong-based developer. After three years of wrangling, McDonald's finally recovered the site. Less lucky was Starbucks, kicked out of its prime site inside the Forbidden City in Beijing after people complained that the presence of an American coffee bar was not appropriate in the middle of one of the landmarks of Chinese culture. Starbucks was told without ceremony to pack its bags.

Outside the PRC, governments are also interventionist to some extent. Democracies like Taiwan have more restrictions on the powers of government and more give and take between government and business. In Singapore, Thailand and Indonesia, on the other hand, government is every bit as omnipresent as in China. (The governments of Taiwan, Indonesia, Thailand, Malaysia, Singapore and several other countries are described briefly in Chapter 9; the rest of this section looks specifically at the PRC.)

Bureaucracy

Sally Stewart suggested that:

> It would perhaps be sensible, when introducing a paper on so controversial and complex a subject as the loci of power in the People's Republic of China, to issue a disclaimer to the effect that anyone (the author included) who imagines that he comprehends all the complexities of the situation is probably deluding himself. Nevertheless, it is important for all those engaged in business with the PRC to have some feel for the general nature of the decision-making process; even though the complexity and size of the organisational chain, and the intervention of influential personalities, lobbies or local authorities and the like, may lead to there being endless exceptions to the rule.[5]

Bureaucracy has been a feature of China for millennia. Under the Qin and Han dynasties, strong centralised bureaucracies were developed first as a counterweight to and later as a replacement for the land-owning nobility. They became the elite of Chinese society. Selection was by examination, after a course of study comprised mainly of studying the classics of literature. Bureaucrats were steeped in Confucian traditions and were intensely loyal to the state. The 1949 revolution brought some changes, mainly in the nature of education and the way in which bureaucrats were selected; the ideology changed, but the bureaucracy remained.

Any Western business going into China will encounter the bureaucracy, probably sooner rather than later. Again, it is a mistake to think of the bureaucracy as being homogeneous. Stewart lists ten branches of government that participated in 'a relatively low technology project'. This was not unusual, but, as discussed below, bureaucracy is being cut down. Westerners marvel at how decisions can ever be made through so many authorities. Travellers' tales abound of decisions being made by silent bureaucrats who seemed too lowly to take part in the proceedings, or who never appeared at all. (In the 1970s, a joke business card circulated among the Western community in Beijing. Printed in Chinese and English, it bore no name or title, but simply the legend: THE RELEVANT OFFICIAL FROM THE DEPARTMENT CONCERNED.)

Bureaucracy can intervene anywhere it wants but money is increasingly a reason for doing so (China's economic benefit) and for not doing so (cost to the PRC government of getting involved). Decisions are intended to be made by consensus and the extent of lateral communication can be remarkable. Normally, the decision process begins with reports from subordinates, which are sent upwards to superiors. Decisions then come downwards from supervising authorities, after substantial consultation both up and down the hierarchy and across different functions and ministries. Individual responsibilities are not as clear as in the West but, since the goal is consensus, they do not need to be. There is much informal reporting and personal relationships play a key role.

Every department or agency has its own area of responsibility, but frequently these areas overlap; and, since every department also jealously guards its own privileges and responsibilities (just like in the West), disputes are frequent. One Western firm trying to set up a plant in Lanzhou ultimately gave up in frustration after securing approval from Beijing but then being persistently blocked by local government. We repeat: it is not enough to cultivate relationships with one level of government only; you need to look at doing so on several levels.

This problem is further compounded by the fact that bureaucrats can hold many different positions simultaneously, including some in the private sector. Ian Rae recounts a meeting with a Chinese official and being given three business cards: according to one, the Chinese official was the deputy head of a government department, a second listed him as the vice-president of a construction company, while the third named him as consultant to an investment bank.[6] Such people are of course well-connected and make valuable contacts, but they do rather transcend Western thinking about the need for separation between business and government.

As with civil servants the world over, initiative-taking is to be avoided. The aim is to reduce the in-tray by whatever means necessary, and react only when one has to. You can never go wrong or be criticised for doing nothing; you are only blamed when you demonstrate initiative. Thus even the most minor matters are referred up the chain of command, and the highest-ranking bureaucrats are inundated with minutiae. This does happen, but it would be wrong to suggest it happens all the time. In fact, decisions get passed all around the organisation – up, down and sideways – but not for reasons of insecurity. Rather, the factor at work here is the Chinese dislike of confrontation. Any decision which could result in confrontation (with its possibility of loss of face) is bypassed; either it is handed on to someone else, or it is simply ignored. When faced with a problem, Westerners typically feel the urge to resolve it; Easterners do not. Indeed, forcing a Chinese person to make a decision where consensus cannot be achieved may put the latter under real personal stress. (For example, Chinese managers can be very reluctant to fire workers.)

Bureaucrats, like Margaret Thatcher, prefer solutions to problems. And most like the sort of solutions everyone else will like. Persisting in confrontation can delay the decision for ever as they do not like saying 'no' either. One important point to recognise is that authority is used differently. In the West, a bureaucrat usually has the authority to say 'yes', whereas in China authority more usually extends only to saying 'no' if the interests of their part of government are threatened. In order to overcome this tendency, businesspeople work out, in advance, the interests of each participating (and possibly competing) branch of government.

Our advice is to start with a map of the network (*guanxiwang*) involved. Then, for each network node, list the interests of those involved and see the situation from their point of view. Shape your plans with these interests and viewpoints in mind.

Beijing Air Catering Company

Beijing Air Catering Company, China's oldest foreign-funded joint venture, was set up in 1979 to provide in-flight meals for airlines flying out of Beijing International Airport. At the start, BACC serviced only three airlines, but a decade later this had grown to 20 clients. By then, its staff were preparing up to 12,000 meals a day on antiquated equipment with a theoretical capacity of 4,000.

In 1987, the company decided to embark on a second stage of development. The Chinese investor, the Beijing Management Department of the Civil Aviation Administration of China (CAAC), and its foreign partner, the Hong Kong Chinese Food Company, injected more capital to build a second production line which was supposed to be ready for the Eleventh Asian Games in Beijing in September 1990. Eighteen months after the games ended and despite more than 100 stamps of approval from various higher authorities, work had still not begun. Difference between the various government departments, including disputes over the complicated procedures required for the import of much-needed new equipment and other facilities, were the main reasons for the delay. The company was regulated not only by the Beijing Civil Aviation Administration but also by the Beijing Municipal Finance Department, Personnel Department and several others.

Better analysis of the *guanxiwang* would have avoided many of these problems.

Branches of government

At the top of the pyramid is the legislature, the National People's Congress (NPC), whose responsibilities include approval of national economic plans, state budgets and state accounts. The Standing Committee of the NPC interprets the Constitution and the laws, enacts decrees and has the power to annul or change the decisions of lower organs. The NPC used to be something of a rubber-stamp body, but the representatives have recently begun flexing their muscles. The NPC as a body has not yet dared to veto measures approved by the State Council, but the number of representatives voting against unpopular measures has begun to rise.

In theory, the State Council, the executive body, which is chaired by Premier Wen Jiabao, is subordinate to the NPC. In practice, like any executive group and wide council, effective power rests with the Council. The premier, his vice-premiers and state councillors administer China through roughly 100 organisations under State Council supervision.

The courts, of which the highest is the Supreme People's Court, settle civil disputes, including commercial cases, and punish criminals. More will be said on this later. There is no separation of powers between the executive and legislative branches, although there is an ongoing discussion as to whether there should be.

Provincial and municipal governments mirror the structure of the central government. The chain of command among government units has, as noted above, given rise to a Byzantine system of multiple reporting. For example, a drug factory located in Shanghai might report to both the Shanghai Pharmaceuticals Bureau – a unit of the local government – and to the state Pharmaceutical Administration, part of the central government in Beijing. Various other agencies – the local labour bureau, the local environmental bureau, and so on – would have a say in certain activities of the factory. Also important to consider in the relationship matrix are the industry associations and commissions (known as 'mothers') that sit above the immediate partners, and other authorities such as taxation departments, who are known as 'mothers-in-law'. 'Too many mothers-in-law' is a frequent complaint by Chinese managers overwhelmed by bureaucracy.

Of course in China, government is not only active as a regulator; it is also an active player, owning and controlling thousands of businesses. One result of the reform programme has been to relax control over individual businesses, either by assigning autonomy to their managers or by selling them altogether. But in some sectors and regions, government is reluctant to cede control, and sometimes a relaxation of control by one level of government is replaced by another. WTO rules are changing this slowly, but the process will take time.

Although government is less involved in running businesses, it is still very much involved in ownership; not only centrally, as in the case of the much discussed and much abused state enterprises, but also locally through forms such as township enterprises. As for those enterprises under collective ownership, there is no clear separation between state and private ownership, with a lot of hybrid forms in between.[7] Change is constant and ongoing, but does not always point in the same direction; the government is quite capable of backtracking and reasserting control over sectors that are not performing as required.

Regulatory problems in China are almost a given. Ian Rae comments that not only do regulations and their implementation differ from place to place, but many regulations are not actually written down (see Chapter 5 also).[8] Regulations vary from province to province, but having the right Chinese partner can ensure that some regulatory problems simply vanish. Companies working with

CITIC, for example, report that regulatory barriers are much lower than when working with smaller regional businesses or institutions.

That kind of intervention can be very valuable because to the outsider, Chinese business and economic regulation and planning can be bewildering, particularly when the effect of local government intervention is added to national law. Some superficially good projects might be vetoed by the Chinese local government because they do not fit with current economic planning. The reasons for the veto will make perfect sense to the Chinese authorities but may be completely mysterious to the Western firm that has been rejected.

In addition, the government of China is far from the monolith it is often portrayed as being. Some municipal and provincial authorities can be very strong-minded and take their own approaches to business. Shanghai has a reputation for being cooperative and helpful, Guangdong may be less helpful but is more easy-going, Beijing municipality tends to be bureaucratic and insist on the letter of the regulation being adhered to. However, there are plenty of exceptions in these three centres, and plenty of other variations in other provinces and cities. Much depends on the attitudes of local government, which can range from old-style Marxist (still to be found in parts of the west of China, for example) to go-ahead neo-capitalist (more common in the east and Manchuria).

The Communist Party

Little needs to be said about the Communist Party (Party) beyond the fact that it remains a powerful force in China, with more members today than it had at the height of the Cultural Revolution. It continues to operate as a parallel structure to the government, with considerable overlap; most bureaucrats are also Party members. As noted in the introduction, the Party continues to play a central role in Chinese economic planning, and the recent attempt to co-opt leading capitalists into the Party may give it a new and different role as a networking body rather than an enforcement agency.

Formerly, the Party had an important role in the workplace, with enterprises managed by a triumvirate of the commercial manager, the senior trade union official and the senior Party official. The Party official was the top decision-maker. Since reform, the Party has begun scaling back its involvement. It is no longer mandatory for a Party cadre to be present in each workplace, though most state enterprises still have one. The cadre is mainly in charge of ideology and some important personnel, instead of business administration as in the past. But the influence is still there.

Many join the Party less out of a sense of ideological commitment than out of a desire to gain access to privileges and take advantage of the networking opportunities. As networks go, the Party is excellent, with access to key players at every level of government and industry. Outsiders should consider these advantages as well; establishing contacts within the Party can mean opportunities for getting around some of the bureaucratic roadblocks. Today it should be seen as an elite club driven less by ideology than its ability to select the most talented applicants from each generation. Faced by a choice of hires, other things equal, the Party member is probably the better bet because of the stronger *guanxi* he or she will bring.

Commercial relationships

The opening section may have seemed intimidating but it is all quite normal. We all develop *guanxi*-type relations throughout our lives, and we all have our *guanxiwang* (network of relationships) with family, friends and so on. What is different in China is that this same pattern of relationships gets transferred into the business world, on a quite explicit and open basis. Business associates within a network are referred to as being *zi jia ren* (one's own family). In a Confucian society, *guanxi* represents a natural blurring of the line between the professional and the personal.

Guanxi is a powerful social force in all Chinese cultures. People's sense of themselves, their self-perception and their self-worth, is determined mostly by their relationships with others. It is important not to confuse *guanxi* with the 'groupist' traits noted in Japanese society. Chinese do not identify solely or even primarily with the group to which they belong; the self is, and always has been, a very important concept. The distinction is subtle but there is a difference between the individual defining the network (US) and the individual being defined by the network (China). The Chinese are both individualist *and* group oriented, and the relationships between group and individual are complex and deep-rooted. Thus personal (and business) relationships are always formed on two levels; with the person as an individual, and the person as a member of a reference group.

So important is *guanxi* that some observers (such as Seligman 1990) maintain that you cannot get anything done in China without it, even simple things like buying a train ticket. That is no longer true, but in a commercial sense at least, establishing *guanxi* with partners, suppliers and even customers is an essential prerequisite. Virtually every major success story involving foreign companies in China involves the building of *guanxiwang* before proceeding with business. Companies like IBM China and Shanghai Volkswagen have devoted literally years to this process.

Getting on the inside has been, and remains, Asea Brown Boveri's (ABB) corporate strategy. The Swiss–Swedish power engineering giant is seeing its payoff. ABB is part of the consortium for the 1,980MW Shajiao C coal-fired power station in the Pearl River delta and provided the steam turbine and plant in the $34.5 million Fushun power plant in China's northeastern Liaoning province. ABB's business strategy aims for solid vertical penetration, each step increasing its understanding of, and interdependence with, the China market. Becoming an 'insider' required ABB to:

1   enter first as a technology seller; China most wants foreign investment and technology
2   licensing and transfer of technology
3   build market understanding and sales through opening representative offices and entering pilot joint ventures
4   establish a network joint venture that will absorb the representative offices. ABB's conception of being an insider in China also envisages it setting up a training centre in Beijing and targeting R&D to China's needs.[9]

Guanxi takes time to develop. Relationships, once created, are hard to break; the obligations you accept when you enter into *guanxi* are not easily avoided. Most Chinese are therefore cautious and proceed gradually step by step. Beware the Chinese contact who says shortly after meeting, 'now we are friends': this is either insincere flattery or mischief. The first steps in relationship building, however small, are critical: as one Chinese friend says, 'a satisfied beginning is equal to half the success'.

On the whole, Westerners have tended to be suspicious of *guanxi*. We like to think that in our societies, everything is done openly and fairly and everyone has access to the same opportunities and the same information. Indeed, we tend to regard instances where people do favours for friends in business as bordering on corruption, if not actually stepping over the line. The equation of *guanxi* with corruption is common, as for example in the following guidebook for managers:

> With the right connections, there is a window of opportunity for coming in via a side entrance, a fast track which will allow you to open a business at a fraction of the prevailing costs and the minimum of frustration. All you need is cash and a good Chinese partner, with the right connections – who did they go to school with or who did their father go to school with or serve in the army with? – and anything is possible.[10]

In China, state employees earn very little and can exert a great deal of power over private concerns. Small salaries but large fringe benefits (such as housing) encourage them to stay in their posts but to earn cash on the side. Despite several well-publicised anti-corruption drives, the situation looks set to continue. As one businessman remarked:

> Here you have all these very powerful state-run organisations looking for a way to make a bit of money. The official who has got the golden chop to give you that licence you need to operate your business is now ready to listen to your proposal. That's bribery, of course, but it's always been part of the system – *guanxi*.[11]

We do not regard *guanxi*, in its true sense, as bribery at all but it does have its dark side which we review following Chapter 5.

Sunrise Lamps

Sunrise Lamps was founded in 2002 as a collaborative venture between four Hong Kong-based entrepreneurs. It began with one factory near Shenzhen, and has now expanded to three locations, employing around 1,600 people in total. The business makes ornamental glass lamps for export under a variety of brand names, and deals with wholesalers in the USA, Britain and Germany. The end customers are either department stores or specialist lighting shops. The business has been growing steadily, and recently a major Scandinavian customer expressed an interest in placing orders.

However, over the past few years several problems have arisen. Labour costs in Shenzhen are going up sharply, and these are eroding the company's cost base. The local electricity grid is under severe strain, as more factories and homes are being built than the infrastructure can stand. Blackouts and brownouts cause severe problems for a business like Sunrise; on one occasion, a blackout caused damage to equipment and the loss of almost an entire production batch of lamps, when the glass for making them failed to heat to the required temperature and then cooled inside the injection system.

More recently, the government of Guangdong has announced a policy of 'encouraging' local businesses to either move up the value chain or migrate to another, less developed part of the province, or out of the province altogether. By switching the emphasis to services and high-technology businesses, the government hopes to reduce the pollution caused by 'smokestack' industries, to cap rising energy consumption, and to generate more wealth through these higher value-added activities. When Sunrise's owners complained about the electricity failures, they met with a cool reception.

Sunrise Lamps thus faces a dilemma. Is it better to stay put and negotiate with the government, perhaps pointing out that theirs is not a particularly 'dirty' industry, even though the owners have little *guanxi* with the government? Or should they consider moving to another location? But here again they will have no *guanxi* and no way of tapping into local networks. Would relocation mean jumping out of the frying pan and into the fire?

Conclusions

Government, the law and *guanxi* all interweave and are hard to separate. No one 'connection', however good, is adequate. In cultivating multiple connections, we have to remind ourselves that they are reciprocal: favours received are credits against future favours expected. Be cautious about the favours you accept.

To the Chinese and others in the Pacific Region, cultivating and using relationships is second nature, a natural part of the environment and doing business. Westerners, however, need to plan and track such networks consciously and with great care. We need to build our networks carefully and patiently.

The overseas Chinese

As we have already noted, most of the remarks on relationships apply to the overseas Chinese communities every bit as much – if not more so – than in the PRC. Some mainland Chinese even complain about the strength of family-oriented *guanxi* in overseas China, seeing it as more restrictive and less 'open' than their own networks which may instead be built around professional associations or groups of university classmates.

In terms of law, we concentrated here on the legal and governmental situation in the PRC. Overseas Chinese communities operate in a variety of different legal and governmental environments. Chapter 10 discusses these briefly, but readers are strongly advised to familiarise themselves with these issues at an early stage by reading up on their target country, as suggested in Chapter 1. This kind of pre-research takes little time, and can help avoid a number of traps.

5   Business and the law

Over the past quarter century, the PRC has been engaged in the
most concerted program of legal construction in world history.
(William Alford, testimony before the US
Congressional-Executive Commission on
the People's Republic of China, 2002)

Forty years ago or so, at the height of the Cultural Revolution,
the *People's Daily*, the mouthpiece of the Chinese Communist
Party, published an editorial entitled 'In Praise of Lawlessness',
denouncing law as the protector of bourgeois social order. In that
decade of political turmoil, laws were replaced by Party policies and,
sometimes, by Mao's words. Courts were sidelined, and lawyers
were outlawed. Forty years later, China has emerged as a major
economic power but the impression that China has been trapped in
the state of 'legal nihilism' seems to remain with many Westerners,
still influenced by what they have seen and heard in the media about
the Cultural Revolution or copyright piracy.

This impression clearly is a myth, one among many myths about
the legal system in China. As Steven Dickinson rightly cautions in
a November 2007 issue of *Business Week*, these myths can lead
businesspeople to make costly mistakes when doing business in
China.

In this chapter, we look at some key aspects of the Chinese legal
infrastructure that distinguish it from the legal systems in the West,
especially in the UK and the US. The focus of our analysis is on how
the features of the Chinese legal system bear on business operation
in China. We begin by looking at the process of law-making, which is
proceeding at a rapid pace in China. Indeed, so rapid that conflicts
between pieces of legislation are creating both loopholes for those
who wish to turn the law to their own advantage, and difficulties

for Western businesspeople seeking to determine which particular conflicting law applies to them. The answer is that, as we will see below, even Chinese judges do not always have a ready answer. In theory, when two laws conflict, the superior law prevails. But the inferior law may remain valid and still affect investors, even though it does not, strictly speaking, apply to them.

China has traditionally had a strong preference for the resolution of disputes through mediation, with litigation being the last resort. However, the last two decades have witnessed an explosion of litigation in Chinese society, and the court has emerged as a primary forum for resolving commercial disputes. Foreign investors should understand the alternatives. They can use the court system, which might seem more familiar but is full of potential problems (for both sides, of course). Or they can go down the more traditional route of mediation, which may seem more unfamiliar but probably offers the better chance of a soft landing; alternatively, they can try arbitration which is unfamiliar, and therefore unpredictable, in China. This chapter discusses these options.

With this evolutionary process in mind, this chapter looks at the following:

- law-making and the legislative process
- courts and judges - who are they and how are they appointed?
- lawyers and the rise of the legal profession
- contracts and contract law
- arbitration and mediation as ways of resolving disputes
- intellectual property

Law-making

Broadly speaking, in terms of law-making authority, there is a hierarchy of four levels of legislative bodies. The National People's Congress (NPC) is China's highest legislative body. The NPC and its Standing Committee are vested with the authority to enact, amend and interpret the Constitution and national laws. The State Council is the next highest authority in law-making, and it makes administrative regulations. The third level in the hierarchy consists of the people's congresses of provinces, autonomous regions and municipalities directly under the central government and some major cities[1] (the local legislatures) and their standing committees. They make local regulations. At the bottom of the hierarchy are the departments of the State Council, provincial governments and the governments of the major cities. The legal rules they make are referred to as ministerial rules and local administrative rules, respectively.

Most local authorities and government agencies lower than the provincial level – including county-level governments and various departments of the provincial-level government – are outside of the legislative hierarchy, and thus do not have formal law-making power. They do however issue rules, which they do often. These rules are referred to as 'normative documents' which are, strictly speaking, not legally binding and Chinese courts are not supposed to enforce them. However, it would be wrong to suppose that they do not affect the local operation of businesses. Investors may run into trouble with a government agency if they disregard the normative documents it makes. Thus investors are advised to comply with them, to the extent that these documents do not conflict with valid and enforceable laws, regulations and rules.

In the interests of catching up, Chinese law-making bodies have in recent times created a huge amount of legislation, covering virtually every area of business and personal life in China. According to official statistics, from the end of 1979 to April 2003, the NPC had made 438 national laws and decisions on law, the State Council had made 942 administrative regulations, while 31 provinces, autonomous regions and municipalities under the central government had made over 8,000 regulations and rules. As Professor William Alford at the Harvard Law School commented 'the PRC has been engaged in the most concerted program of legal construction in world history'. To put the figures in context, the UK enacts about 100 new laws each year, and around 3,000 Statutory Instruments or pieces of secondary legislation. About 300 of these are laws, or regulations, that affect business. Comparisons are difficult because law-making structures and terminology differ. The EU, which is perhaps a better comparison than the UK, approves about 100 Directives per annum (requiring member states to pass equivalent laws) and 2,000 'Regulations' which do not need to be duplicated by member states but 97.5 per cent are not laws; they are just Administrative Orders.[2]

Starting with virtually no laws, after three decades of legal reform, China now is seen by some as having too many laws or perhaps too much law that has not been properly refined and worked through. The real problem is that these laws are not always consistent and coherent. This problem needs to be understood in light of a key feature of Chinese law-making: excessive generality and vagueness. Like EU Directives, laws enacted by the NPC and its Standing Committee are general, broadly drafted and sometimes vague. Thus, before laws can be properly enforced, they often need to be supplemented by more specific regulations and rules that adapt the statements of general principles in laws to local conditions. Given the vast regional differences in China, this approach to legislation may be desirable as it allows flexibility. It also, however, gives the local authorities the ability to interpret and implement laws in a way that best advances local interests – sometimes to the extent of contradicting the laws themselves. If local authorities don't like new laws handed down from on high, they are likely to twist them to suit their own agenda. Examples of contradictions and inconsistencies in law are abundant. For example, the *New York Times* on 28 November 2005 reported a case (the 'Seed Case') in which the local court found that a provincial seed regulation conflicted with the national Seed Law.

The central authorities have made various attempts to resolve inconsistencies between different legislation – with the 2000 Legislation Law being a milestone – but with limited success. The Seed Case highlights the need for further reforms. In this case, the local court held that the provincial seed regulation was 'spontaneously invalid' because it contradicted the national Seed Law. This decision, however, almost cost the responsible judge her position when the local legislature condemned her for overstepping the court's authority. Under Chinese law, judges do not have the power to invalidate provincial regulations; such power rests with the NPC Standing Committee (NPCSC). It was not until recently that the NPCSC started to lay down formal procedures (many feel these are excessively onerous) and build up institutional capacity to review inconsistent legislation. The NPCSC has reportedly never invalidated conflicting regulations. Lacking the power to invalidate legislation, Chinese courts have worked out their own solution: they apply the superior law and refrain from touching the inferior law that conflicts with it. This solution is problematic for investors, as the inferior law remains intact and continues to bear on the business.

Inaccessibility of laws is another issue that has concerned foreign investors. This concern has to a large extent been alleviated with respect to trade-related laws. As part of China's WTO accession protocol, China has committed to make public all trade-related laws, regulations and measures, and enforce only those laws that have been actually published. Most trade-related laws and regulations are now published in the *China Foreign Trade and Economic Cooperation Gazette*. Some have been translated into English and are available at www.fdi.gov.cn. Anecdotal evidence suggests, however, that there still exist some 'internal' regulations, whose contents and even whose existence may not be divulged to foreigners.

Overall it is perhaps unsurprising that so many laws conflict with each other and that sometimes laws, once enacted, need to be changed; this happens in the West as well. In Britain and elsewhere, however, there are established procedures for doing these things. In China, hasty law-making by inexperienced law-makers sometimes leads to problems, and few mechanisms have been put in place to effectively solve these.

Courts and judges

There are four levels of court in China: the Supreme People's Court (SPC) at the central level, the Higher People's Courts at the provincial level, and the Intermediate People's Courts and the Basic People's Courts at the local level.

In the UK, judges are chosen from lawyers who have had distinguished careers as private practitioners. By contrast, Chinese judges are, like their counterparts in Germany and France, almost invariably career civil servants who expect to rise through the ranks by diligent effort in their job. The overall level of competence of the Chinese judiciary was once startlingly low. Until 1995 – when China enacted its first law on judges – there were virtually no requirements or qualifications to be a judge. Judges were often drawn from the ranks of military officers, who received little legal education but tended to be more obedient and loyal to the state. In 2001, China amended the law to impose higher standards for judges. Now, new judges must possess at least a bachelor's degree, plus at least two years of experience in law. In addition, they must pass a unified national judicial examination (with a pass rate as low as 10 per cent). The percentage of judges with a bachelor's degree rose from 6.9 per cent in 1995 to 51.6 per cent in 2005 across China. The percentage is generally higher in the court divisions that handle commercial disputes and in economically more developed regions. Training for sitting judges is also moving up China's legal reform agenda. All judges are required to undergo regular training, and many have received training in leading overseas law schools.

While the Chinese authorities are encouraging the development of more professional and competent judges, they firmly reject 'Western-style' judicial independence. The Chinese judiciary is not intended to be an independent branch of government. Judicial independence, though recognised by the PRC Constitution, is limited, both in theory and in practice. Three particular sources of external influence bear on the court's decision-making. Constitutionally, courts are responsible to the people's congresses (legislature) that create them. Politically, and more importantly, courts are subject to the influence and control of the Party. Courts are also financially dependent on the local governments. In commercial cases, undue influence of these sources can be overwhelming, when key local interests are at stake. Courts may be pressured in making a decision that unfairly favours the local parties.

Lawyers

For almost every aspect of their business operation, foreign investors need professional legal help on an ongoing basis. And this is so even if their *guanxi* with the authorities is a strong one; local governments themselves turn, from time to time, to lawyers for help. Some 15 or 20 years ago, it was difficult to find an English-speaking Chinese lawyer. This is no longer a problem; the problem is indeed the other way around. Many younger-generation Chinese lawyers are able to communicate in English. And, annoyingly, almost every Chinese lawyer who speaks English claims expertise in foreign investment issues. Then how to find a good lawyer who can deliver results in a manner that foreign investors want?

Many investors find it comfortable to work with representative offices opened by international law firms in China, because these offices generally have a deeper understanding of foreign clients' needs and interests than most Chinese law firms. By September 2006, 149 such offices had been authorised to operate in China. Professional services offered by these offices are not inexpensive, though many believe they offer value for money. Some offices are willing to lower their fees for new clients, hoping to generate repeat business. Investors may be surprised to know that, under Chinese law, these foreign representative offices are prohibited from undertaking PRC legal services. But people on the ground report that many foreign offices do not follow the law in this respect, and routinely provide clients with advice on Chinese law. It was rumoured at some point in 2006 that the Chinese authorities were going to crack down on some foreign offices because of their unauthorised practice of Chinese law. The feared crackdown has not as yet happened.

There are a handful of Chinese local firms that have been competing head-to-head with foreign law offices for lucrative foreign investment business. Jun He Law Offices and King & Wood are two big names among them. These firms' profound local knowledge, in tandem with their natural ties with Chinese authorities, gives them a competitive edge. Sometimes they are able to deliver results in a way that their foreign competitors envy. In addition, most senior lawyers in these firms have extensive experience in serving foreign clients, and they know their clients well. The rates of these lawyers, however, may not be significantly lower than their counterparts in the leading foreign law offices operating in China. Some commercial publications, such as Legal 500's *Asia Pacific Legal 500* (www.legal500.com), and Chambers & Partners' *Chambers Asia* (www.chambersandpartners.com/Asia), provide useful information about leading firms and lawyers, both foreign and local, practising in various areas of law in China.

If the deals are smaller in size or less sophisticated in nature, then it can be more cost-effective to use smaller but specialised local firms. Some regional law firms have developed extensive connections with local authorities and can get the necessary approval or licence in a matter of days, rather than weeks or months. Many of these firms are now informally associated with foreign firms that have no presence in China. Foreign investors may either check with lawyers in their home countries, if they have associated Chinese local firms, or consult international networks of law firms (for example, Advoc (www.advoc.org) and Lawyers Associated Worldwide (www.lawyersworldwide.com)) for information.

In China, there is no divide between barristers and solicitors. Lawyers are licensed to engage in both litigation and non-litigation business. The English 'loser-pays' costs system that makes the losing party in the litigation pay some or all of the winning party's legal expenses does not exist in China. Chinese courts generally leave each side responsible for its own lawyers' fees, regardless of who wins. Contingency fee arrangements have operated unofficially in China for many years. Chinese lawyers charge clients on a 'speculative' basis in a growing variety of cases, ranging from industrial injury compensation to recovery of non-performing bank loans. The range of the contingency fee percentage is reportedly from 10 per cent to 40 per cent of the recovery, though a new regulation promulgated in 2006 sets a cap of 30 per cent.

Contracts

Contracts have a different place in Chinese negotiations. In the West, it is not unknown to begin with draft contracts and use them as working documents until agreement is reached. China is getting used to Western ways, but historically such a move would have seemed like bad faith. Other countries in the region, with longer exposure to the West, tend to be more attuned to the needs of Western businesses.

Contracts should be drafted in Chinese as well as the language of the foreign investor, ensuring of course that they are identical in all material respects. Some China hands recommend having important documents translated twice by independent translators, and then comparing the two versions. Back-translation is also recommended: have an English document translated into Chinese, then ask a second translator to translate from Chinese back into English and look for discrepancies. Checking translations is vital to ensure that the wording of the contract is unambiguous. One European firm found itself committed to a technology transfer deal whereby the Chinese partner was not obliged to pay any royalties until they were capable of producing a 'first-class product'. Needless to say, they never did so; but they did manage to produce and sell profitably a great deal of 'second-class products' without paying a penny to the technology supplier.

Under Chinese law, contracts that must be approved by Chinese government authorities do not become legally binding upon signature, but only when the approval certificate is issued (this is standard procedure in the West as well). Central government ministries and subordinate provincial or municipal agencies are responsible for issuing approvals. The level of approval depends on the amount of investment involved and the nature of the project. More than one Western firm has been caught out this way.

Approval by the relevant ministry secures the operating licence, but is not the end. Separate applications must be made to the tax authorities, foreign exchange authorities and customs administration. Furthermore, the consent and active support of local authorities must be obtained for a host of matters under local jurisdiction such as assuring the supply of utilities, materials and labour, the plans and costs for the construction of buildings and compliance with environmental regulations. Consultants advise that, when possible, these approvals and commitments should have been ensured before signing the contract; failing that, make the contract conditional on their satisfactory resolution.

Arbitration and mediation

Mediation and arbitration are not the same thing. Mediation, seen in China as good, is the process of facilitating agreement between two parties. Arbitration, seen as a poor solution, is the process of finding some fair compromise. Most Westerners do not notice the difference, even though this is an important distinction in China. Not surprisingly, there are many mediators in China (about 5 million), but few arbitrators. The courts and tribunals encourage mediation between the parties even after litigation proceedings have commenced. As arbitration is so ingrained in Western business thinking, however, China is learning to accommodate it.

China has used mediation for centuries, and its methods stem from the teachings of Confucius. Essentially, mediation seeks to resolve disputes in a way acceptable to all parties, without loss of face; it is primarily a method for defusing or dispelling confrontations. Much mediation concerns family and social issues, not commercial, and is also informal. The Chinese are encouraged to solve their disputes on their own initiative through mediation committees or mediation groups in their neighbourhood or workplace. Mediators are chosen within the neighbourhood, and no formal training is required to qualify. There has been a significantly increased emphasis on using judicial mediation to resolve disputes in recent years. One outcome is the promulgation of an SPC normative document in March 2007,[3] which instructs local courts to mediate civil litigation suits whenever possible. Some 60 per cent of first-instance civil cases have been solved by mediation in China. Mediation was also not disrupted by the Cultural Revolution in the same manner as the legal system.

Arbitration is much more formal. Where both parties to a dispute are Chinese entities (for this purpose, joint ventures and wholly foreign-owned enterprises (WFOEs) are Chinese entities), arbitration would normally take place within China. Where one of the parties is foreign, a foreign venue may be selected. Sweden, for reasons going back to the eighteenth century, is a preferred venue for arbitration involving joint-venture disputes in China. The dispute between PepsiCo Investment (China) and the Chinese partner of its Sichuan joint venture was solved in a Stockholm arbitration in 2005. The high-profile Danone–Wahaha arbitration is, at the time of writing, taking place in Stockholm.

Sichuan Pepsi

Sichuan Pepsi was established in 1993 as a joint venture (JV) between Pepsi China, the Chinese subsidiary of PepsiCo, and the Sichuan Administration of Film, Radio and Television (later Sichuan Yunlu), with the latter holding 78 per cent of the venture and Pepsi China the remainder. Pepsi China was thus a minority stakeholder, but this did not trouble the company unduly; it often took minority positions in local JVs. And Sichuan Pepsi was initially among the most successful of Pepsi's 30 JVs in China. It captured more than 50 per cent of the carbonated soft drinks market in the province.

However, problems soon emerged. There were disputes with local bottlers, but even more critically, the Chinese partner began to complain that Pepsi China, the minority stakeholder, was exercising too much control. For its part, Pepsi China complained that the management of the joint venture was failing to report its financial position accurately, and there were allegations of financial irregularities. Matters came to a head when the Chinese managers appointed by Sichuan Yunlu decided to branch out into making other soft drinks and launch their own brands, which would effectively compete with Pepsi. Early in 2002 Pepsi China demanded that the management of Sichuan Pepsi be replaced, but the managers refused to go, responding: 'For years Pepsi China has been acting like a god and forcing its opinion on us. Two Pepsi China executives played behind-the-curtain tricks by cheating and misleading us.' The relationship had now broken down entirely, and Pepsi China had effectively lost control.

Pepsi China took legal action to close down the joint venture. The two parties agreed in the JV contract to arbitration: Sichuan Yunlu wanted this to take place in China, but it was finally decided that the arbitration would take place in Stockholm but with Chinese arbitrators. In 2005 the arbitrators found in favour of Pepsi China. Sichuan Pepsi was ordered to be dissolved. It seems that, however, the arbitration awards have not been enforced by Chinese courts, although the joint venture was in effect dissolved.

Intellectual property

As is well known, intellectual property is the largest legal minefield in commercial international relations with China, and is probably the most difficult legal issue to resolve. Part of the problem is that there was no sustained tradition of protecting patents or copyright in imperial China. This does *not* mean, as some journalists have written, that the Chinese do not see anything wrong with piracy. Piracy is wrong, and it is illegal in China. However, enforcing anti-piracy laws is taxing the powers of the legal and enforcement system to the limit.

In 2004, industry estimates put US trade losses due to piracy in China at $2.54 billion a year.[4] The United States Trade Representative claimed that 85 to 93 per cent of all copyrighted products sold in China in 2006 were pirated. And according to a February 2005 issue of *Business Week*, China accounts for nearly two-thirds of the estimated $512 billion worldwide counterfeit market. The US government has been pressing China to reduce its intellectual property rights (IPR) infringement levels. American efforts culminated in its request in April 2007 for formal WTO consultations on China IPR enforcement issues and, subsequently, the establishment of a panel in September 2007.

To be fair, China's legal framework of IPR protection has been improving. China amended its Patent Law, Trademark Law and Copyright Law in 2000 and 2001, and has periodically issued new IPR regulations and rules since 2002. An Action Plan was announced in 2007 in an attempt to better protect IPR. Many Chinese courts have set up a special division to hear intellectual property-related cases. But even with these new laws and institutions, foreign companies do not feel secure from IPR infringements.

Starbucks

Starbucks Corporation (Starbucks Co.) registered its 'Starbucks' trademarks in 1996 in China, and registered in 1999 the transliteration of Starbucks in Chinese characters – 'Xing Ba Ke' (in Chinese, *'xing'* means star, and *'ba ke'* sounds like bucks). When Starbucks Co. decided to expand its business in Shanghai in 2000, it found that a Shanghai local company set up in 2000 – Shanghai Xing Ba Ke Coffee Shop Ltd (Shanghai Xing Ba Ke) – had already started using a variation of the green Starbucks logo and the name Xing Ba Ke.

Starbucks Co. brought an action in December 2003 against Shanghai Xing Ba Ke. Shanghai No. 2 Intermediation People's Court decided in December 2005 in favour of Starbucks Co., ruling that Starbucks and its Chinese name Xing Ba Ke are 'well-known marks' and thus deserve special protection under Chinese law. Shanghai Xing Ba Ke was ordered to pay Starbucks Co. compensation of 500,000 yuan, and was prohibited from using Xing Ba Ke marks. After the ruling, Shanghai Xing Ba Ke appealed. Shanghai Higher People's Court in January 2007 upheld the first-instance decision.

Well-known trademarks are protected by law in China, even if they are not registered or the trademark owner registers the mark late. However, Chinese law gives the court the discretion to determine whether or not a mark is a well-known one. Despite the Starbucks case, there is uncertainty involved. Pfizer has lost its legal battle to register the Chinese transliteration of 'Viagra', because a Guangzhou local company had already registered it. More recently, a Chinese court reportedly ruled that a businessman in Wuhan could legally sell products bearing the transliteration of 'Louis Vuitton' in Chinese characters, since the lawful owner of the LV brand had not registered the brand's Chinese name in China.[5]

A few simple precautions can make it easier to locate violators and obtain compliance:

1   Prepare an intellectual property inventory.
2   Appoint an intellectual property manager responsible for keeping the inventory current and scouting the China market for infringements.
3   Register everything as quickly possible *in both English and Chinese in China*, in order to avoid the prohibitively high costs of litigation, both in terms of fees and time (consider the Starbucks case).
4   Conduct regular market surveys to determine if trademarks, patents or copyrights are being violated.
5   Go to court even if redress is not seriously expected, because the authorities will not take the matter seriously until the matter reaches the courts.

The problem of intellectual property infringement is by no means unique to China, and it can be argued that China is doing more than some countries to deal with it. Taiwan is also home to many software and music pirates (strangely, the US government gets far less exercised about these than it does about those in mainland China), and Indonesia, Malaysia and Thailand all have their pirate kings. And never mentioned, of course, is the scale of routine, everyday software piracy that goes on in many homes and offices in the West.

Conclusions

To sum up, the legal system in China is becoming steadily more complex, and this has implications for businesspeople. On the one hand, there is more legal protection for businesses, including Western businesses, now than probably at any time in China's history. At the same time, going to law is a complex and risky option, not least because the legal system is still in a state of evolution and flux.

Twenty years ago, few businesses operating in China would have seen the need to hire a Chinese lawyer, even if they could find one. Now, hiring a lawyer to check contracts and advise on national and local business law makes sense. We think local Chinese law firms probably offer better value, having more local knowledge and better *guanxi* with government. That said, China is still a long way from becoming a Western system where the court is the primary vehicle for resolving disputes. Arbitration and mediation remain important. If or when a dispute breaks out, choose the route most likely to give satisfaction in China, not the one that worked best back in the home country.

And remember: important though the law is, it is no substitute for *guanxi*. The two systems, legal framework and relationships, operate in parallel, often in tandem.

An ethical interlude

Two main consumer rights are universal: the right not to buy again and the right to inform others about the product. Repurchase rates and word of mouth are powerful marketing forces which may apply in China with *relatively* more importance in the absence of other rights Westerners take for granted. This section pauses to reflect on the general question of 'rights' and the dark side of *guanxi*, namely corruption.

The interlude is arranged as follows:

- **Development.** Centuries ago, both societies were more concerned with responsibilities than rights. Here we mean rights of all kinds, human as well as political and economic. The assertion of rights has grown faster in the West than in China. This, like democracy, has both advantages and disadvantages. We see no *higher authority* grounds for asserting one orthodoxy over another but do see *evolutionary* benefits in going with the flow. Each set of ethics simply reflects the way that culture polices its people. As global cultures fuse, we are evolving toward a universal view of rights and ethics. But it is not so simple, as we are seeing both globalisation and localisation happening at the same time. The Balkans provide an example.

- **Contract law.** Business practices in the West are backed up by contract law and in China by *guanxi*. Legal processes carried to excess are as corrupt as *guanxi* carried to excess, but the corruption lies in the excess, not in the product itself. Determining where healthy business practices degenerate into corruption depends on the culture concerned. Some Chinese practices would be corrupt in the USA but, conversely, some US practices would be corrupt in China. The issue turns on whether they reduce the public good in that context, not whether they have intrinsic merit. This is, of course, the relativist position.

- **If marketers act responsibly, do rights take care of themselves?** We conclude with pragmatic advice, offered without warranty.

The development of rights and responsibilities

The need for harmony between rights and responsibilities has long been noted in East and West but they are not a zero-sum game. Having fewer rights does not imply having more or fewer responsibilities; the concepts are linked but independent. From the earliest times, the individual's place in the community has been described by responsibilities, e.g. Confucius. The idea of rights is more recent; in the West it mostly hails from the Age of Enlightenment 300 years ago. You will not find much, if anything, about rights in the Christian Bible. The New Testament drills home the need to be responsible to God and then your neighbour. The Old Testament is even more obligation-heavy.

Probably Descartes, with his focus on identity, helped develop the idea that, if others have responsibility to me, then that gives me some rights, or at least expectations. If the husband should be faithful to his wife, then the wife may expect faithfulness from the husband. 'Rights', in the sense of human or consumer entitlement, were given eighteenth-century support as a matter of fairness. Given a choice between having rights or no rights, I would rather have rights. And, given that, why should I have them if others do not? There was a recognition of reciprocity. Slaves had no, or not many, rights and it was not until recently that the human race had a problem with that. 'Rights' etymologically come from the word 'straight', like the Greek 'ortho' in orthodox. It is reasonable to recognise that others have similar rights to those one expects for oneself.

What is important here is that rights grew from responsibilities and the demands for rights have been increasing. How far should that go? The increase of one does not necessarily imply a decrease of the other. However, if everyone demands their rights and no one exercises their responsibilities, society will fall apart. Eastern commentators like Singapore's Lee Kuan Yew have pointed to the moral degradation of the West meaning just that: responsibilities to others buried by demands for one's own rights. Human, and consumer, rights are important but may not have much value unless others exercise their responsibilities. The world has seen ever more small countries demand, as a democratic right, to have full independence. At the same time, the EU, a vociferous supporter of universal human rights, creates a new treaty for itself without allowing its citizens a vote on the matter (because, of course, they would lose the vote). And Americans lock prisoners up in Guantanamo Bay for years on end with little if any regard for their human rights. The Chinese have some justification for cynicism.

Second, for whatever reasons, the creation of rights from responsibilities happened far more slowly in China than in the West. That may be because, as we suggested in the last chapter, settled communities could manage well enough with reciprocal responsibilities and had no need of rights or contract law. Wang Gungwu, Vice Chancellor of Hong Kong University, once remarked that, 'The ancient Chinese only knew of duties but had no notion of rights.'[1] Whatever may be the position in the PRC, it is clear that overseas Chinese have latterly adopted the notion of rights with enthusiasm.

Third, whilst the concepts of rights and responsibilities are universal, the particular selection of what they are varies from culture to culture and from era to era. They are evolving. Today Britain attributes rights to animals too. As computers become more intelligent, we can expect computer rights at some point in the future. We see no evidence of any of this being God-given: rights and responsibilities are what different societies decide them to be.

While the Western media harp continually on human, or civil, rights, these are only part of a continuum of rights, including economic rights. The introduction of the free market in the PRC has undoubtedly had a dramatic effect on the latter and some commentators suggest that PRC consumers are far more interested in economic than civil rights. We are now witnessing globalisation forcing cultures to accommodate each other's standards for rights and responsibilities. That does not make any one set either correct or universal, as some of our American friends seem to believe. Indeed the Iraq invasion of 2003 has encouraged the view that America thinks that universal human rights are whatever America says they are.

The reality is that a shrinking globe is forcing the world to share their cultural evolution. The imposition of ethical standards by one culture on another is ethical fascism, in the original sense of 'fascism'. On the other hand, as we are going to have to live together, it would reduce conflict and misunderstanding if we allowed our standards to co-evolve. This in turn requires each culture to respect the de facto ethics of the other, at least in the sense of seeking to understand their philosophic and historic roots. Asserting one's own standards as universal is both arrogant and unhelpful. It used to be called colonialism.

Western linear thinkers are puzzled by the Chinese ability to hold on to a mass of apparently contrary philosophies at the same time – ancestor cult, Daoism, Confucianism, Legalism, Buddhism, Christianity and Communism to name but a few. The Westerner tends to *replace* one set of beliefs by the next, whereas the Easterner tends to *add* them. This may be due to the Daoist tradition itself.

Be that as it may, in Confucianism the individual is defined by his relationships with others, whereas in the West our relationships are defined by our self-identity. This overstates the distinction in order to make the point. The virtuous person only acquires rights to the extent to which he gives them to others: do as you would be done by. Descartes' *cogito, ergo sum* (I think, therefore I am) owes nothing to anyone else. As we noted in the last chapter, the Chinese did not even have a word for 'rights' until recently: 'they borrowed from Japan a term, *chuan-li*, manufactured for translating Western political thought about a century ago'.[2]

Contract law versus *guanxi*

The divergent cultures of the law in the US and *guanxi* in China may have arisen from the essential difference between cowboy and farmer communities. *Guanxi*, personal connections, implies reciprocal altruism. There is just a responsibility when a favour is accepted that one day, when it is needed, the favour will be returned. But this implies that the two parties can expect to be in the same community for long enough for that to happen. For many centuries, the vast majority of Chinese citizens lived all their lives in their home villages. The shift to the cities is very recent. Conversely, America was formed by immigrants constantly on the move. And there was little point in expecting favours from people who would not be there next week.

Contract law was never a big deal in Europe until the nineteenth century, when citizens began to move about. A man's word was his bond and if he failed to honour it, society shunned him. It is mere speculation but we think that the shift to contract law takes place where the reciprocation has to be clearly stated and it is enforceable.

Contrary to some Westerners' beliefs, *guanxi* cannot be purchased. In that sense it is priceless and explains why in China one builds friendship before seeking to do business, whereas in the US the order is reversed. In the West we feel vaguely uncomfortable doing business with friends, whereas in China, one would be uncomfortable if they were *not* friends.

So passing money in red envelopes may or may not be corrupt, but it is not *guanxi*. If you define doing business with friends as corrupt, then the 'corruption' arises from your definition. Others may regard *not* doing business with friends as unethical because it offends the expectations of that society. Who is to say which is right?

Thus it is a question of context: ethical Chinese practices may be corrupt in the US and – now this is controversial – ethical US practices may be corrupt in China. Where *guanxi* is the norm, behaving in a non-*guanxi* way will degrade (corrupt) business. The importation of some Western business practices into China today is doing just that. The 1999 Disney negotiations between Shanghai and Hong Kong, while probably fair competition in a US context, can be seen as corruptive in China.

In the largely settled, rural communities that made up China until very recently, relationships between individuals and between families were very long, and *guanxi*, with endless chains of gift-giving, is the very foundation of their relationships. The main reason, in our view, for the importance of improving legal processes in China has less to do with importing Western business practices than with finding new enforcement rules where people are moving in huge numbers from one part of the country to another.

Corruption is, of course, a major issue in China. Since economic reform, it has become one of the biggest problems facing the Chinese economy and has deeply distressed many ordinary Chinese. It played no small part in the protests of 1989. It has also led to a growing number of officials receiving a bullet in the back of the head from the official executioner. The Chinese are fearful of it for the same reason that Germans fear inflation: they remember the damage it did in their past.

But this merely reinforces the point that *guanxi* and corruption are *not* the same thing, any more than drink is the same as drunkenness. One can enjoy the one and still avoid the other. One Chinese term for corruption, *zou houmen*, or 'going through the back door' can be applied to relatively innocuous practices such as the giving of a *hongbao*,[3] a red envelope containing a small amount of money. But in context it certainly is not. Gift-giving is a long and honourable tradition in most parts of the world.

Christmas presents between businesspeople are less prevalent in the UK than they used to be, but that probably has more to do with accountants than morality. Accountants plead morality just as the UK Chancellor claims to be improving the nation's health when he raises duties on alcohol, cigarettes and petrol.

The line between corrupt and harmless practices is not easy to draw. The US Foreign Corrupt Practices Act specifically excludes 'grease payments' and tipping, i.e. money given to encourage officials to do what they should do anyway. Some governments regard those as necessary salary adjuncts, i.e. they save money for the taxpayer. Corruption, i.e. bribery, involves paying someone to do what he should not do.

But it is not as simple as that either. A British Chief Financial Officer of a pharmaceutical multinational in China was recently surprised to receive an envelope from the taxman with a substantial amount of cash. He was told it was a thank-you for handing over the PAYE collections from the payroll so promptly – clearly an unusual event. He decided it was wrong to rock the boat and credited the money in the company's books. He was not personally corrupt and it is not immediately obvious that the taxman was. But was he wise? What happens when the taxman needs a favour? This is not *guanxi*, which cannot be bought, but it may be starting a chain that should not be followed.

Many businesspeople think that corruption is an acceptable and necessary part of doing business in China. Or at least getting started. It is all very well for IBM and Johnson & Johnson (or Janssen Xian) to act high and mighty, but the newcomer without brand equity is under pressure to go through the back door if he cannot get through the front.

Bribery is expensive, tends rapidly to get more so, damages reputations, and leads to pseudo-*guanxi* with the wrong people. There is also the risk of substantial legal penalties in China and at home. Yet it is difficult to be too whiter-than-white about it. The entire alcoholic drinks distribution infrastructure in the US is founded on illegal and corrupt (by any standards) relationships built during prohibition. And it has stood for over 60 years.

If marketers exercise their responsibilities, will consumer rights take care of themselves?

This chapter has represented the idea that rights are a recent, not wholly desirable, outgrowth from responsibilities. This is a step back from the fashionable notion that rights are a universal human entitlement. Indeed, there is some inconsistency in the secular age that has rejected God and higher authority claiming such rights. By whom are these rights given?

A more consistent idea, which can be drawn from biology, is that social groups do better with reciprocal altruism, i.e. rights balanced with responsibilities. So they are not God-given but just part of a useful strategy for beneficial development. Rights, in short, are only as moral as the responsibilities that underpin them. We should worry more about responsibilities than on rights: if marketers behave responsibly, consumer rights will take care of themselves. Furthermore, in China it is not enough to do the right things; they have to be done in the right way (*li*). Bombing the Chinese embassy in Belgrade during the Kosovo conflict was clearly the wrong thing, and the American and British problems thereafter were compounded by a failure to observe the correct form. A quick and apparently insincere apology made things worse. Genuine contrition required a proper investigation and explanation. Thus marketers should not only act responsibly but do so according to the conventions of the local market.

It would appear that the Chinese have a very hazy view of both sides of this marketing coin relative to established foreign markets. Consumers are quite happy buying goods known to be counterfeit on the grounds that they are similar but cheaper. They do not expect any consumer protection and, as yet, show little sign of wanting it. Retailers develop amnesia when faulty goods are returned. As marketing develops, so will both rights and responsibilities because reliable products and strong branding are in the commercial interests of both sides. Consumers should behave responsibly in their own long-term interest because merchants will respect them more and not, for example, dismiss complaints because the motives are suspect.

The idea that we should focus more on marketer responsibilities than on consumer rights is perhaps more Chinese than American. Yet this is supported in the West by the declining profile given to consumerism since the 1970s. *Which?* magazine, the journal of the UK Consumers' Association, is struggling to keep afloat. One cause is probably the greater dominance of brands. With so much investment in these assets, their owners *have* to act responsibly and the need to protect consumer rights thereby diminishes.

Few China market entrants will be concerned with the theoretical and long-term implications of branding. They want to know whether to pay off Mr Li. All official advice will be to avoid doing so but ours is more complex. Whether everyone else is doing so is relevant but everyone else may not own up. Bribery (paying people to do what they should not do) is definitely a bad idea. Not only is it illegal; it damages the reputation of firms that do it. Grease payments are the problem.

Grease payments fall into two categories: tips and service payments where the amounts are minor compared to possible costs, and extortion. It has long been the custom, for example, to leave Y100 notes in envelopes under the plates of senior people invited for lunch and a business presentation. The money is ostensibly to pay for travel expenses. Clearly that $10 or so is not going to make much difference to anyone. The practice is being replaced by small gifts like ties and pens and only the most petty-minded would regard it as unethical.

Extortion, where quite a large sum is involved before something happens (unloading cargo for example), is another matter. Here it is tempting to regard the payer as the victim and the payee as corrupt but it is a brave, and probably foolish, foreigner who blows the whistle.

International businesspeople have long got around the difficulty by hiring consultants at rather larger fees than they might otherwise expect so that they can take care of these matters. This 'monkey's paw' approach is less good in China than West Africa because of the negative effect it can have on long-term *guanxi*. This really is the issue. If the business is too small or too under-funded to survive without the grease payment *and* the longer-term effects are not damaging to true *guanxi*, then it is an option we could not deny – especially if it is standard practice. On the other hand, there is little point in surviving if *guanxi* is harmed. Going out of business will just take a little longer and probably be more painful and expensive. Another solution needs to be found.

Finally, foreign companies can, and should, help themselves through their trade associations. If an industry is being collectively held to ransom, then it is up to the industry *collectively* to do something about it. Differing national cultures may complicate matters. Americans worry that collective action is anti-competitive. Other countries are sometimes puzzled why the Anglo-Saxons make so much fuss about ethics. Until quite recently, bribes (and we are talking bribes, not grease payments) were legitimate tax deductions in France and Germany. As a collective US/French/UK example, the drinks industry in China found itself paying escalating amounts of corkage to bartenders.[4] They all agreed to stop doing it. There is always a bit of cheating and disinformation on these occasions but, by and large, the ban held.

In this interlude, we have reviewed the philosophy of rights and ethics and taken a relativist position. In other words, they reflect society norms and not some external absolutes. At the same time, as the world shrinks, they are co-evolving to a common, or more similar, future. After touching on consumer rights and marketer responsibilities, we moved to some pragmatic advice on bribery, extortion and grease payments. We have sought to be responsible but it is offered with no warranty: do not call us, call your lawyers.

Part II

6   Creating harmony

Establishing businesses in China

The Way (*Dao*) gives birth to the one.
One gives birth to two.
Two gives birth to three.
And three gives birth to the myriad things.
The myriad things bear yin and embrace yang.
By combining these forces, harmony is created.

(Laozi)

One of the ongoing trends in business in China is the tendency for foreign companies to establish wholly owned subsidiaries in China rather than setting up joint ventures with Chinese companies or institutions. The Chinese government classes these two alternative vehicles for entry as wholly foreign-owned enterprises (WFOEs) and joint ventures (JVs), and we will use that classification here.

Over the past ten years, especially over the past five, WFOEs have become much more popular. Some Western consultants now advise entirely against JVs, believing they are too risky. Control issues lead to problems like those experienced by Pepsi China in Chapter 5. But Chinese consultants take the opposite view. They point to the risks involved in establishing a business in China, especially for the first-time entrant. Joint ventures, it is argued, provide more benefits than just profit. A good partner can help a Western company learn very quickly about the market and business environment and can provide access to resources, labour, key officials, markets, distribution channels and the like. 'Joint ventures', says Ted Plafker, 'can deliver benefits that a foreign player would need a lot of time and cash to match, including government contracts and support as well as access to land, distribution channels, bank credit, qualified workers or business licences'.[1]

This chapter compares these and other vehicles for foreigners to do business in the PRC from the point of view of strategic and operating efficiency and effectiveness. The technical details of company formation, governance and taxation are widely available from legal firms; we are concerned here with practicalities, whether the venture will succeed and whether it will deliver the required return on investment.

The chapter is structured to follow a path of increasing commitment:

- the distinction between production and distribution
- agencies and licensing
- joint ventures
- wholly foreign-owned enterprises
- identifying and negotiating with partners
- making the choice.

Although WFOEs are certainly becoming popular and do have advantages, the JV option should not be written off. JVs can still deliver significant advantages, and while they increase some risks, they can decrease others quite drastically. No one should assume that by choosing to go it alone in a WFOE, they are free of the restrictions of partnerships. All ventures, including WFOEs, rely on cooperation and collaboration with Chinese businesses and authorities. In China, foreign-owned businesses are always in partnerships, so we need to recognise that and plan accordingly.

Second, the debate over WFOE versus JV tends to obscure the other dimensions to business which the Chinese regard as being more important, and which Western managers also need to think about. The key distinction made by the Chinese authorities concerns the purpose of the venture and the destination of the goods and services it produces. Although the World Trade Organisation has theoretically introduced a level playing field, some parts of it are decidedly more level than others. Factories that produce goods for export, bring in hard currency, and provide technology and skills transfer to Chinese workers and managers, are favoured. Marketing or selling ventures that threaten local industry and have a perceived deleterious effect on Chinese culture and society will find obstacles put in their way. One of the first questions to consider, therefore, is what the purpose of the venture is and how it will impact on the market and the environment as a whole.

The JV still offers significant value, and with even big companies like Pepsi and General Motors still starting up joint ventures, we are not alone in this opinion. It is a matter of horses for courses. The Western firm needs to look first at its own capabilities and resources, and then ask the question: will our strategy best be achieved through a WFOE or a JV? The answer depends, of course, not just on those capabilities and resources, but on market conditions and government regulations – though these are much less of a factor. Wholly owned subsidiaries have become feasible in almost any business sector or any location in China. The question is, whether a WFOE is the best option, or whether a JV would be more effective.

Distribution and focus

The key distinction from the Chinese perspective is whether the proposed venture will import and distribute foreign goods in China; whether it will produce goods in China for export (outsourcing or offshoring) or whether it will both make and sell goods inside the country.

Importing ventures are very popular with Western companies, who seek the opportunity to sell their goods to China's billion-plus consumers. The Chinese authorities tend to assess each venture on its own merits, in terms of how it will benefit the economy and whether it will directly threaten local competitors. This does not mean that all such ventures are frowned upon – far from it. Western companies selling goods that are much needed, especially those with high-tech components, are likely to be welcomed. Those selling luxury goods that do not compete directly with low-cost local products should find no opposition, nor should those who will be competing only marginally with very well-established local brands. On the other hand, the Chinese do engage in some protection (unofficial now, of course) of industries that are already overstocked with firms, or where local growth needs to be encouraged. It is rare in these post-WTO days for a licence to be refused, but it can be hedged in with terms and conditions: for example, so many local jobs will need to be created, so much local sourcing will be involved, and so on. This is particularly the case for firms producing mass consumer products such as white goods. Cars are another area where the government attempts to restrict and control the number of producers, although there has been some relaxation of this in recent years.

Ventures that are set up to make goods for export are, of course, highly popular. Exporting to Western markets has long been a key element of Chinese economic policy. It has provoked some resentment in the West, as witness the infamous 'Bra Wars' of 2006, when the European Union tried to place import tariffs on Chinese-made clothing coming into Europe. This exporting has huge benefits for the Chinese, not just in terms of the dollars, pounds and euros that exports earn, but also for the skills and technology that get transferred into the country along with production. It has also had benefits for Western companies able to tap into a pool of low-cost skilled labour and significantly reduce their production costs. At the time of writing, there is a dispute as to how long this offshoring boom will last in China: will rising wages reduce the cost advantage and send Western firms further afield? The answer seems to be, not yet. While wages are rising sharply in areas like southern Guangdong and around Shanghai, there are large areas in the hinterland still to be exposed to the boom. Bolder managers looking for offshoring opportunities will leave the coast and strike out into the interior.

Combined production and selling ventures suffer somewhat from the disadvantages of the latter. It is not uncommon for the government to request that at least a portion of the new venture's production is exported, leaving the company free to sell the rest domestically. This requirement is often levied on Chinese firms as well, and is a source of occasional complaint by Chinese businesspeople. Some of the most successful joint ventures of recent years have been structured along a two-way network, with a foreign firm allowed to use the domestic partner's distribution network to sell into China, while the domestic firm gains access to the foreign networks. These kinds of ventures are increasingly common in the car industry, as China's car-makers grow in sophistication and begin to seek export markets.

China joining the WTO has promoted the delusion that, as in the West, a company once established can distribute its goods in any way it chooses. Restrictions and opt-outs remain in some sectors, and legal and regulatory advice should be sought at a very early stage. But even where the route appears to be clear, obstacles can suddenly emerge if government – national, regional or local – does not feel the venture is in the best interests of the Chinese. And as we remarked earlier in the book, government remains a very powerful, influential and active player. That is why the suggestion that Western businesses in China do not need a partner is a fallacy.

Every business in China has a partner in the form of the government, whether it wishes it or not. Government approval and support can lay down a golden path and help businesses to succeed. Government disapproval and lack of support mean that the foreign firm has to do everything the hard way, if it can at all.

To get an idea of how government will view a proposed venture, perhaps the easiest thing to do is apply the test of the 'Three Represents'. In 2002, then-President Jiang Zemin laid down his own philosophy of the 'Three Represents': the Party and the government should work to represent the interests of (i) the growing Chinese economy, (ii) the development of Chinese culture and (iii) the needs of the Chinese people. Now apply that test to the proposed business. Will it make a contribution to the Chinese economy? Will it advance Chinese culture, or at least, not actually do it harm? Will it serve the needs of the people of China? Businesspeople in the West are not used to having to think so altruistically, but in China these considerations are a useful indicator of how government will view businesses. If the proposed venture ticks at least one of the three boxes, it is more likely to be smiled upon.

The nature of the venture determines to some extent the form it can take. Generalising to a considerable extent, we can say that there are three basic ways for Western firms to enter the China market: through agencies and/or licensing, through joint ventures, or through wholly foreign-owned ventures.

Agencies and licensing

The reader will be familiar with agency (importing) and licensing (local production by the third-party licensee) arrangements which operate in China much like anywhere else. These classic ways to enter a new market minimise the demands on the exporter and use the existing resources and capabilities of the importer or agent or distributor or licensee. For this section, we will take all these terms as equivalent. The differences are more technical than real, apart from licensing which involves the transfer of much more intellectual property.

If/when the licence expires or the arrangement terminates in some other way, the firm will have acquired an on-site competitor who can make the product cheaper (certainly) and better (possibly) than it can. There have also been quite a few cases of identical factories being opened just down the road and, coincidentally of course, producing identical goods.

Franchising, a form of licensing but with less basic brand risk, is also growing in popularity. It has the additional advantage of not requiring JV retail licences. Dairy Queen, the Hong Kong clothing retailer Giordano, and 7–11 are commonly cited examples. For retailers and service industries, franchising offers less financial exposure similar to those above, but the control problems and the consequent impact on brand identity (always a problem for franchisors) need to be estimated.

China being as big as it is, the need to develop relationships and the future strategic extension of the agency or licensing arrangement into China, all suggest some form of local representation. A full-scale representative office is expensive but some sharing may be possible. For example, the British building materials sector has a joint office representing 30 companies, which was opened in Shanghai on 28 April 1999. Having no local office and changing the firm's representative who comes visiting every few months is such a bad idea that it would be better not to start. If the Chinese importer insists on buying the goods, then bank the cash by all means but do not consider market entry. Maybe you should worry about him becoming a competitor, though.

Joint ventures

A great deal of joint venture (JV) mythology has accumulated over the years. One widespread myth is that no Western joint venture in China has ever made money. This is untrue. The history of Western JVs in China is littered with casualties, but there have been some notable and very successful ventures as well.

JVs can be difficult and risky. They are always temporary and should be seen as such, even when they are part of a longer relationship. They may be transitional to success, with one party happily buying out the other. They may be renewed, sometimes several times over, but often taking different forms or having different features even when the partners remain the same. Or, like political careers, they may end in failure, and usually for the same reasons: lack of trust and understanding. However successful the politician, sooner or later he or she will fail – a few fixed-term appointments aside. In the West, surveys have suggested that most JVs fail within the first 18 months. And if this is the rate of failure among companies within the same or very similar cultures, how much more difficult must the problem be when one firm is Western and one is Chinese?

Perhaps surprisingly, it is about the same. Some companies enter the market blindfold and set up unsuitable ventures that quickly collapse, sometimes before the ink is dry on the contract. Others, aware of the cultural differences and the risks, take more care than they might in the West and negotiate ventures that last. The key success factors for JVs in China are much the same as anywhere else: a good fit between the partners; the establishment of trust and understanding between them; and commitment to the notion that the venture is there to make money for all the parties involved, not just one. Assuming good faith on both sides, equity is important: if both sides think the balance between risk, contribution and rewards is fair, it should endure. For now.

The history of business in China suggests that JVs have always been a standard format. Certainly the *huaqiao* Chinese companies of East Asia use collaboration as an important strategic principle. The JV is a business vehicle well suited to the Chinese way of doing business, which stresses networks and collaboration. Unlike the West, where all business alliances have to be seen as temporary, Chinese JVs can last for generations. In *huaqiao* firms, joint business ventures often lead to personal ties between family-run firms, such as intermarriage between families. Large *huaqiao* firms in Singapore, Malaysia and the Philippines are frequently linked in this fashion.

From the Chinese point of view, JVs can be a way of recovering sunk costs. The newcomer is told how valuable are the assets, which the Chinese side will contribute in kind, whereas the foreign partner will be bringing cash. Herein lies the crux of the early negotiations of many JVs.

Western companies also see JVs as a way of learning more about China. They become a vehicle not so much for profit-making as for exploration of the new market and its potential opportunities and risks. Earlier we mentioned Pepsi, which still likes JVs despite its 'painful marriage' in Sichuan. Other JVs, notably those in Shenzhen, have been big successes. IBM took part in JVs for ten years before finally setting up a wholly owned subsidiary, and still prefers the joint-venture model for big projects. General Motors operates through several JVs in Shanghai, and its top (Western) management in China are on record as saying that they prefer JVs to the prospect of a wholly foreign-owned venture.

Turning to practical problems, expectation is one of the most common stumbling blocks. The goal sets of the three parties – Western and Chinese businesses and the Chinese authorities – often have relatively little in common. In particular, Western firms may need to rethink their attitude to investment in JVs. Most of the research on this subject over the last ten years has concluded that unsuccessful JVs have been characterised by a lack of investment in key areas, especially in the critical area of human resources. Of course everyone wants something for nothing, but asking for a majority stake in a venture and then failing to back it fully is a recipe for failure.

Despite rapid technological advances in China, some in the West still treat the former as a developing country in which second-rate or less than state-of-the-art products and technology can be dumped. In economic terms China may be developing, but in all other respects the Chinese consider the term insulting. They are quick to spot when they are being fobbed off with something that is second rate. Demands for leading-edge technology at second-hand prices (being a poor country entitles them to that too, or so it is sometimes claimed) leads to lively negotiations.

A JV needs complementarity: the two partners both have to want something that the joint venture can give them, be it profits, knowledge, technology, access to scarce resources or some combination of all of the above. Because of the distance and time involved, to say nothing of the capital commitments, there has to be a strong bond of trust. To say that good communications between the parties are essential is an understatement. Chinese firms and institutions often take a long time to set up a JV. The venture itself may not be complicated, but they will not move forward until they thoroughly know their prospective partners and their motives and attitudes. There is no special magic to making JVs in China, but the three Cs of courtesy, communication and common sense will go a long way.

Joint ventures are often seen as risky, but a good one will reduce risk. Shared responsibility, the bringing in of more expertise, including local market knowledge, *guanxi* with other firms, government and customers, are all potential benefits.

Another common belief about JVs in China is that they will only succeed if the Western partner takes a majority stake and has control. Consultants often treat this as a necessary condition when negotiating on behalf of clients, and several studies suggest that foreign-company majority JVs are more likely to be profitable than 50-50s or minorities. The key phrase is 'more likely'. That does not mean minority JVs should be ruled out. They can, and do, work. The most important thing is to get the right fit between Chinese and Western partners, allowing both to reach all or most of their goals for establishing the venture in the first place. Slavish adherence to principles of how a joint venture ought ideally to be established can get in the way.

Wholly foreign-owned enterprises

Consultants may claim that WFOEs are much more likely to be profitable than JVs, and have produced studies to prove it. But there is contradictory evidence, too. John Child, formerly of Cambridge University, has estimated that in general, the success of wholly foreign-owned ventures is greatly overestimated, and that JVs are more likely to become profitable and to do so quickly.[2] Slightly earlier, a study by the Economist Intelligence Unit found that 47 per cent of JVs in China were profitable within two years or less; a statistic that is unsurpassed anywhere else in the world. We know of no more recent evidence, but suspect that the same figures still roughly hold good.

With the empirical evidence decidedly mixed, we go back to basics. What is the best kind of venture, not in general, but for this particular business at this particular time? Multinationals like IBM now use a mix of WFOE and JV formats depending on what their purpose is for a specific project, and also where they are operating within the country. IBM China was established as a WFOE in 1992, only after IBM had been operating in China for more than ten years and had built up an impressive portfolio of contacts including former vice-premier Zou Jiahua. IBM China functions in every respect as a Chinese company; it pays taxes to Beijing, can hire Chinese employees directly, and can trade in local currency. Even now, however, IBM China prefers to set up JVs with Chinese partners for big projects.

Most market entry is a matter of progressive commitment. As we show later, firms do not like to gamble, so the key factor is balancing and containing risk. Accordingly, going straight into a WFOE, making a large investment in a market where the firm has no developed relationships or contacts, has high levels of regulation, poor infrastructure and rapid economic change, growth and uncertainty, carries a risk level which no sane banker should consider. However, for companies with the right experience and resources, WFOEs can and do work: good examples are 3M and Procter & Gamble.

Much of the point in a WFOE is making a fresh start and not getting tangled up in existing webs. Most WFOEs are greenfield operations, but some result from buying out existing partners and there are an increasing number of buyouts of going concerns (now that there are some Chinese going concerns to buy). Anyone feeling especially brave can buy a state-owned enterprise when they come up for auction. There may be bargains to be had.

As the reader will by now have noted, we retain a bias towards JVs. This is currently rather unfashionable. We do not by any means rule out the WFOE, and there are some very good and profitable ones around; but the same can be said of JVs. The final recommendation is that, no matter what advisers may say, there is no general solution; each needs to be teased out of the circumstances identifying target markets and constituencies, the commercial, social and regulatory context, the venture's mission and goals should provide the analysis to determine the best format.

Identifying and negotiating with partners

This section covers:

*   the go-between
*   what type of partner
*   the time horizon
*   negotiating.

The go-between

One of the key aspects of relationship-building is the role of the *hongniang* (go-between, or literally, maid-servant). The *hongniang* has a long and honourable history in Chinese society. Go-betweens are used for functions as diverse as village matchmakers and mediators who help settle legal cases. A go-between is a perfectly natural way to put a business deal together; and for the go-between to be a part of that deal and take a percentage from it. For foreign companies wishing to do business in China, the Chinese government has helpfully established a number of *hongniang* agencies, the largest of which are CICECC (Chinese Industrial and Commercial Economic Consulting Corporation) and the Shanghai Industry and Commerce Development Corporation. The Chinese government has also welcomed foreign consulting firms who come in to act in a *hongniang* role; Batey Burn is a well-known example, but there are many others. Hong Kong and other East Asian traders sometimes fill this role. In addition to these specialist consultants,

Chinese banks and investment companies can act as go-betweens. CITIC, for example, will provide consultancy advice as well as investment for some projects.

A go-between is not essential; Western companies are free to set up one-to-one relationships independently and many do. However, particularly for firms with little experience of China, the practice has many advantages. Furthermore, the go-between should not just be used to make contacts but also to give strategic advice. For example, the next section deals with the type of partner needed. By the time the *hongniang* is briefed on the mission, he may as well contribute to re-defining it. Little more time is needed and, perhaps, much enlightenment.

We have not mentioned confidentiality because it is obvious that the *hongniang* must have no conflict of interest or competitive clients. One argument for the sole operator, as distinct from the large consultancy, is that he is more likely to stay free of *future* conflicts. Otherwise the learning that the *hongniang* gathers at your expense today may be available to your competitor next month.

The growth and development of China, and the increasing sophistication of its businesses and managers, may suggest that the day of the *hongniang* is drawing to a close. We suspect the reverse is true. In the old days, the foreigner was likely to be compelled to do business with just one company or agency. Now there may be thousands. Cyberneticists tell us that the most successful and flexible systems are also the most complex, because they have so many different parts to enable responses to different situations. China's economy, as it grows and becomes more competitive and flexible, is also getting more complex. The role of the go-between, who can deal simultaneously with younger brothers (potential partners) and mothers-in-law (government officials) may well be essential to maintaining harmony within the business family.

What type of partner?

When it comes to choosing a business partner, the Daoist way would be to look for complementarity rather than similarity. IBM went into business with a railway company to deliver its computers. A US East Coast flight simulator company went into business with a Chinese provincial tobacco monopoly. Both succeeded. On the other hand, Diageo's spirits company had no success from a JV with a Chinese spirits business. No doubt other factors were at play but the point remains.

The Economist Intelligence Unit (EIU) (1995) defined three types of partner, and, by and large, their classification still holds good:

- **The 'nuts and bolts partner'.** This partner's primary function from your point of view is to help solve problems of access to land, resources, labour, government, distribution or other factors. The usual quid pro quo is technology transfer or skills training. The EIU notes that these tend to be set up with a short-term focus, and problems can arise once the immediate problems have been solved. Nevertheless, this can be an ideal type of partner for a first-time entrant.
- **The 'well-endowed godfather'.** These are more powerful partners, and the EIU identifies them primarily as government authorities, such as the Ministry of Posts and Telecommunications or the China National Automotive Industrial Corporation. While somewhat slow and bureaucratic, these partners are also very powerful and have access to resources. Their primary contributions are during the start-up phase, and as powerful 'godfathers' who can help sort out problems down the road. They normally take minority stakes and have little direct involvement in day-to-day management.
- **The 'four hands on the wheel partner'.** This is a more strategic partnership in which the Chinese partner is interested not just in technology transfer but also in building its own strategic position. The EIU cited the example of the strategic partnership between Rohm & Haas and Beijing Eastern Chemical Works, which are expanding together to set up operations across China. Instead of setting up a lot of small JVs to get national coverage, the single JV is expanding and setting up subventures. Not surprisingly, this type of partnership is believed to have a higher chance of survival.

Key factors to consider when choosing a partner in China

1 **Technical expertise**. What skills does the prospective partner have? Can the Western firm provide the missing skills, and at what cost?

2 **Facilities**. What facilities (production, distribution, etc.) does the prospective partner have or have access to? Will these need to be modernised or upgraded and, if so, what will be the cost?

3   **Location**. Is the Chinese partner geographically well placed to exploit market opportunities? This is particularly important given the physical problems associated with distribution in China. Setting up an operation in Guangzhou to market in Sichuan is likely to involve a lot of extra time and expense.

4   **Relationships**. How good is the Chinese partner's *guanxi* with other firms in the supply chain, with customers, and with government? This is the big one. If the *guanxi* is right, the partner should be able to fix anything else. The main three components (durability, seniority and onward connectivity) need separate consideration. Will the Chinese partner's *guanxiwang* complement that of the Western partner?

5   **Partner goals**. What do partners want? Are they 'nuts and bolts' partners, or might there be true strategic vision in their thinking?

The time horizon

Relatively speaking, Chinese companies care for long-term relationships and interest, although they want even quicker (if that is possible) profits. Maximising the short and long terms simultaneously is good Daoist thinking. Western companies, on the other hand, usually want to keep their longer-term options open whilst they see how it goes. Most JVs in the West are for periods of six months to three years. It can be a considerable shock to realise that China expects a commitment of 15 or 30 years.

Western companies normally want quick profits too, but investment in China is usually regarded as a medium- to long-term payback. Shanghai Volkswagen, established in 1985, repatriated profits for the first time in 1993. Chinese partners, on the other hand, usually want to see profits quickly in a JV, since they perceive the comparative advantage when joining hands with their Western partners. This disparity in expectation strains communication and a consensus over the highest NPV (net present value) corporate strategy and plan.

Negotiating

Much is made of the difficulties of negotiation in China. They can be long and frustrating, and there are plenty of tales of negotiations dragging on for months or even years. Some are amazed when all is concluded within a few weeks, but the home office should be prepared for the long haul. Negotiations mostly run into trouble in China for the same reason that they run into trouble everywhere else. The days when negotiations were bedevilled by political issues and cultural misunderstanding are largely over. The Chinese now understand the Western game, although the reverse is less true. Ian Rae,[3] who managed his own company in China for many years, believes that while Western negotiators spend a large part of their time trying to figure out what their opposite numbers are thinking, Chinese negotiators seldom worry about what the Westerners are doing. They focus, and refuse to deviate from what they believe to be the best outcome, whereas Westerners are sometimes too quick to conciliate in the mistaken belief that they will give offence on cultural grounds.

Chinese negotiating techniques can take some getting used to. A typical ruse is to conceal the identity of the most senior player. Westerners, on the other hand, typically exhibit the pecking order all too clearly. When Wall's (Unilever's ice-cream business) was negotiating a fire safety certificate for their new plant in Beijing, they worked very hard to satisfy the smart man in the suit only to find that the badly dressed, tramp-like figure sitting quietly at the end was in charge. (The owner of a Yorkshire brewery used to play the same game with unsuspecting sales reps. He would stand with a broom in the yard and accept tips for looking after their cars. Then reception would call him to the meeting and he would dish out the same level of respect he had received in the yard.)

A more typical manoeuvre is to keep the boss entirely out of sight. This slows things down quite a bit, as regular reports are made, and prevents the Westerners seeing any body language. Fortunately, the Chinese increasingly see time as money, and game-playing for the sake of it is probably diminishing.

What does not change is the Daoist advice to see the problem and potential solutions from both points of view. Defending a position politely, firmly and consistently may seem boring but will impress those who are comparing their notes with those of several hours, days or months ago. Creative new arguments may free the log jam but they may also provide a whole new area for exploration and reconciliation – especially if the language is complex or subtle.

Negotiations in China are at once both formal and personal. Due recognition must be given to protocol, procedure and precedence.

Informal small talk before and after each negotiating session is expected; and rushing is rude. If talks are going along well, they may be accompanied by drinks, dinners and even banquets. Gifts may also be exchanged. Mayfair Yang's book probably remains the best guide to etiquette on these occasions, although Kevin Bucknall's more recent book has some helpful ideas as well.[4]

We mentioned above Western attitudes to Chinese negotiators. There are two extremes: (a) the bull in the China shop approach, where the Western negotiators go in hard, lay down their demands and stick to them and (b) the softly-softly approach, where the Western party gives way too quickly (motivated by too-strong cultural sensitivities, post-colonial guilt or whatever) and thus appears weak. Deference to your potential partners is one thing, giving away the store is another. Firmness and politeness need to go hand in hand.

Key points for negotiators in China

1 Joint ventures, even when all partners appear willing, can take up to two years to negotiate.

2 It may be good manners to talk around a subject rather than address it directly, though Chinese negotiators are becoming less sensitive and more direct.

3 Conventional wisdom is never to show anger but always be polite, softly spoken and gentle. This is probably right but we have seen, very occasionally, anger used to good effect both between and with Chinese negotiators.

4 Silence is considered a valuable negotiating tool.

5 Words and gestures may have hidden meanings, especially in the early stages, and many devices are used to test sincerity and commitment.

6 Use your opponents' strengths, ju-jitsu-like, rather than taking undue advantage of their weaknesses; the latter they will remember and resent. That may seem a bit gnomic but what we mean is that the negotiators' arguments should give face.

7 The time component, or pace, of negotiation is actively managed. For example, they will be conscious of when the foreigners have to leave and of the pressure from the home/ head office to reach a deal.

8   Know where the exits are. Leaving the prospective partner an exit demonstrates trust and increases the probability of goodwill. If he takes it, then all the better to find out sooner. Leaving oneself an exit is more tricky (shows lack of commitment), not least because your partner should have left one for you. That does *not* mean he wants you to use it.

Research and a tight definition of strategy and goals are an essential part of preparation for doing business in China. All the warnings about negotiating in China can add to the usual fever of speculation until the Western team get spooked by a dinner cancellation which is no more than they said it was. Holding on to a clear agenda and being unfazed by any side issues, still less the possible motivations for them, works wonders. If it is boring to say the same thing, in the same words for the umpteenth time, think how much more boring it is for them to write it down. As a general rule of thumb, distrust and paranoia are usually reciprocal unless the other side is a truly professional team. In that case, ring your *hongniang* for someone to bolster the skills of your team.

Tamarack

Tamarack is a Canadian clothing company specialising in branded outdoor wear including boots, shooting vests and mackinaw jackets. Like many other Western firms, it found the cost of production at home growing increasingly expensive and made a strategic decision to relocate production to China. John Dawson, Tamarack's managing director, began seeking advice on how and where this could best be done. The advice proved to be contradictory and confusing, with some urging him to set up a WFOE and others to establish a JV with an existing Chinese firm.

Consultations with the local authorities in Guangzhou province in 2002 convinced Dawson that his venture would be welcomed by the government. The new plant would export all its product, and would create more jobs in the garment industry which, though already huge in Guangzhou, was continuing to grow. On his first visit in late 2000, Dawson was approached by several Chinese garment makers who offered to set up a JV with him. They promised him access to supplies of skilled labour and local management, so that there would be no need to bring in expatriates. Dawson wondered, however, whether some of these potential partners might not be a little over-eager to do business with him.

The longer he spent in Shenzhen and Guangzhou, the more attractive the WFOE option seemed. It promised control, and there were none of the risks associated with partnerships and JVs. While he conceded that if he were establishing his factory in a more remote and less developed part of China he would find the JV option more tempting; here in Guangdong, distribution networks were good and labour was plentiful.

Dawson recommended to his board that a WFOE be established. In 2005, Tamarack (China) opened its plant in Shenzhen. But problems began almost at once. One of the Chinese firms Dawson had consulted in 2002 claimed that Tamarack had agreed in principle to set up a JV, and the Canadians were not honouring their word. Although untrue, the allegation was widely believed, and the local business community regarded Tamarack as partner who could not be relied upon. Suppliers tightened their terms of delivery and began demanding payment in advance. Even the workforce became disaffected, and suddenly turnover became a problem, with skilled workers especially moving on to other jobs. Tamarack (China) was losing money quickly, with no end in sight.

Several options presented themselves to Dawson and his board. Legal action against the company that had started the rumour was unlikely to be productive. Their first inclination was to close the plant altogether, lay off the workers and try again, perhaps in Shanghai or Tianjin. But at the eleventh hour another opportunity presented itself. Another Chinese firm, whose directors Dawson had met in 2002, offered to establish a JV with Tamarack. This was a well-respected firm, and its reputation would be useful to Tamarack in building up its business. For its part, the Chinese firm was producing its own branded clothing and wanted access to Tamarack's North American distribution networks. For Dawson the question was: could this potential competitor be relied upon to be a useful partner?

Making the choice

Each strategic option carries its own levels of risk and reward. The usual evolution is to use organisational learning in such a way that risk is reduced at the same time as commitment is increased. In the Chinese context, *guanxi* is part of that, because *guanxi* is

Table 6.1 An analysis of commercial investment risk in China

Type of venture	Type of risk		
	Investment	Presence	Control
Agency	Low	High	High
JV	High/Moderate	Low/Moderate	Moderate
WFOE	High	Low	Low

the traditional way to manage and reduce risk. Thus firms like IBM began with agency arrangements, then JVs, then a WFOE and now a complex mix of both to cope with their R&D, production and distribution interests.

In making the choice, it is worth analysing risk more closely into investment, presence and control risk components. Table 6.1 shows the approximate levels of risk of each type, based on the experiences of past ventures in China.

Investment risk is the likelihood of loss multiplied by the amount at stake; in other words, what is the expected downside? Agencies where the Western partner puts in little if any money, obviously have a much lower risk level than WFOEs, where the Western firm puts up all the capital and takes all the risks. JV risk levels in this category vary, depending on exposure and situation, but at least the Western firm has the (sometimes dubious) comfort of knowing that the Chinese partners are also risking their investment, although that assumes they put in cash or valuable assets. If they contributed dud assets in the first place, or have a matching plant up the road, the comfort will not last long.

Presence risk refers to the rewards that may accrue from a lack of physical presence in China, or the penalties that may be associated with absence. Being there may hurt, but *not* being there may hurt more. As noted in earlier chapters, the Chinese, especially the Chinese government, value commitment from Western firms and tend to reward it eventually. Companies that show they are prepared to 'stick with' China (IBM and Volkswagen are two prominent examples) tend to have higher levels of success when negotiating new ventures and securing permission to expand. WFOEs and high-profile JVs are a way of demonstrating commitment. Agency relationships may give brands some profile in the Chinese market, but their lack of commitment could tell against future expansion. Presence risk has to be assessed against the firm's own future plans for China and the region. It may be that a loss-making initial investment can be the key to unlocking further, highly profitable investments.

Control risk refers to the ability of the firm to control its operations and products in the Chinese market. WFOEs obviously offer far higher levels of control risk than agency relationships because so many more things can go wrong, and each from a higher base. In JVs, the risk varies, as different partners will agree to different levels of control. However, the worst-case scenario is one where the foreigner has, de facto, to pick up all the risk without having enough managerial control to spot and prevent the leakages. This, in essence, is why WFOEs have become favoured. Control will never be absolute, however, as even WFOEs always have a 'hidden partner' in the form of the Chinese government, which can and does interfere in the workings of business.

Risk management is an important exercise, but we would refer the reader back to Chapter 4 and the role of *guanxi*. In China, *guanxi* plays an important role in minimising risk because relationships are both based on trust and enable further trust. The starting point for a risk assessment in China, then, should be the level of *guanxi* that has been built up over time with potential partners. The type of venture comes second. This does not mean that the kinds of risk we describe above are unimportant: rather, the level of all three is in part dependent on the level of *guanxi* that has been cultivated.

We have focused on risk even though most feasibility studies focus on profits and cash flows. Firms should surely continue with upsides and their usual forecasting methods but China requires a good hard look at the gloom. Even for the best managed companies, the short term is probably only a 50-50 bet. Unless one is sure one can beat those odds, e.g. one has something China really wants, China is simply not a worthwhile short-term bet at all.

On a long-term view, however, the picture improves. If one has to be there one day, now is cheaper than later. The only good time to do it is when the firm can afford it; not when the accountants fantasise about an optimal net present value. *Guanxi* will gradually take care of risk if it is properly and patiently managed. So quantify the range of likely NPVs and the three risk components for all three types of entry. Have everyone take part, even though you will never silence those who will later claim prophetic powers.

Xian Janssen (Johnson & Johnson) launched their JV in October 1985, when WFOEs in that sector and region were not available. It went into production in May 1991. Those five and a half years spanned the Tiananmen incident and the amount of nay-saying in the home office can be imagined. Today it is a huge success, with market leadership and competitors trailing far behind. We can count the cost but it is still too soon to count the profits.

The overseas Chinese

Even though most overseas Chinese communities operate in considerably freer market conditions than in the PRC, the JV remains a favoured device in Taiwan, Indonesia, Malaysia and other countries in the region, especially in manufacturing and distribution. Why? Because JVs can provide local knowledge and access to key players in vital networks. *Guanxi*, as we have said before, is possibly even stronger in the rest of East Asia than in China. JVs allow a firm to tap into someone else's *guanxiwang* without having to go through the arduous process of building their own.

This chapter has shown an obvious predisposition to the JV. Yes, they can be tricky to manage; but who ever said management was supposed to be easy? Yes, they can also be risky. Yet at the same time, the right JV with the right partner is a terrific means of laying off other forms of political and economic risk. Don't believe all the statistics you read, and don't automatically discount the JV as an option, no matter what country you are working in.

7 The marketing mix

The plan of Heaven is more certain than the plans of men.
(Chinese proverb)

Marketing is not a subject that commands as much attention as some other aspects of doing business in China. Very few recent books on China discuss marketing in detail, and many mention it only in passing, preferring to focus on issues such as organisation, managing people, regulation, ethics and the like. The reasons for this are quite understandable, as the cultural issues involved in organisation behaviour and human resources management are demonstrably huge, while for marketing they are arguably less so. Some even argue that there is no real difference between marketing in the East and in the West. When we discussed marketing in China with professors of marketing in 2001, they failed to identify any area of marketing where China differs from the West. With greater contact, consultants increasingly recognise that marketing in China may be different, but generally recommend that the difference be managed by passing on responsibility for marketing to local staff or affiliates, who will be aware of cultural differences and better able to respond to them.

The weakness of Western firms in marketing to China was recently commented on by Michael Backman and Charlotte Butler, who argued that in the future – perhaps the very near future – it will not be enough for Western companies to leave marketing to the locals.[1] Backman and Butler do not go far enough. The Chinese government historically excluded Western firms from 'distribution' and thus encouraged this hands-off approach. But business in China is no different from anywhere else, in the sense that the first priority is to identify and then empathise with the end users (consumers) of your products. That is where cash flows from. Most Western firms in China have inadequate knowledge about their consumers, including buying patterns and decision-making, competing local products and prices, and how the competition operates.

That said, many Chinese companies are bad at marketing too. Another observer, Martin Roll (2006), has commented on the number of Chinese companies and managers who think that branding is no more than advertising and a logo. Branding, and marketing generally, are seen as cost centres, not value-adding exercises. Although sophisticated Chinese brands like Haier and Lenovo do exist, they are not representative. Chinese managers, like their Western counterparts in China, often have little idea of who their ultimate consumers are, or what they want, and have done little or no market research. Thus we have the paradox of a country where marketing is extremely important, and yet local managers are not very good at it.

In fairness, as we will discuss in the following chapter, doing market research in China is extremely difficult. Getting accurate statistical information of *any* kind is very hard in China, in a society where statistics are regarded with fascination – witness the streams of economic data pumped out by various ministries and state councils – but where, to paraphrase Peter Fleming (1959), in any given situation there will be at least two competing accounts and the only verifiable fact can be proved conclusively to be wrong. We are not discriminating against the Chinese by saying this, by the way; Chinese friends are equally rude about Chinese statistics, and one economist friend cheerfully admits in private that his own bureau's statistics could be out by as much as 10–15 per cent. That's not so much a margin of error as an informational black hole!

Turning marketing wholly over to local managers is unwise. Even more than marketers in the West (no slouches in this respect), you should expect Chinese marketing specialists to be making it up as they go along. In other words, lacking accurate data, marketers in China are forced to do what they have always done: fall back on intuition and on trial and error. What follows in this and the next chapter is a series of observations, our own and those of others, on what is involved in marketing in China, and on where the differences and similarities lie. Our conclusion is that marketing in China does have quite a number of similarities with the West, and that the globalisation/localisation decision in particular is not so different from that made in other markets. But there are also some key market-specific issues. The attitude of Chinese consumers to brands is one. The problems of distribution are another, especially when moving outside the relatively well-developed eastern parts of the country.

This chapter is structured as follows:

- looking back
- marketing strategy
- product and branding issues
- pricing
- promotions and advertising
- place, i.e. sales, channels and distribution.

The last is probably the most difficult and is likely to remain so. The picture in different parts of China varies largely, according to local acculturalisation with Western standards and also the strength of the local economy.

Looking back

Under the centrally planned economic system before the reforms began, the marketing mix[2] was not an issue for businesses in the PRC. Product line and design decisions were made centrally; any changes began on the production line, with little reference to trade customers or consumers. With the major economic goals focused on boosting output, production was guaranteed to be bought by government buyers. The system was known as *tong gou, tong xiao* (unified purchase, unified sale). Producers found this a 'relaxing' time: industrial businesses focused on making their quotas and on celebrating their successes. As in the old USSR, the heroes of labour were those who beat their quotas. More commercially aware managers, however, became anxious about overstocks and realised that the recorded income posted by their businesses was artificial.

Advertising and promotion were considered unnecessary during the early years of Communist rule, and were totally banned during the Cultural Revolution of 1966–76, when they were labelled a tool of 'bourgeois capitalism'. Pricing levels were determined by centrally controlled pricing bureaus, and were invariably subsidised by government. As all output was predetermined, producers generally had no input as to the distribution for their products. Distribution channels were unduly long, and in some instances moved through three levels of wholesaling on their way to the retailer.

After economic reforms began in 1979, advertising was reinstated as a legitimate business tool. Enterprises now advertise in all the classic media and a few others besides. In the first decade after reforms began, the advertising industry grew from just ten people in 1979 to 11,100 agencies with total employment of 128,000 in 1989. These agencies were controlled by the state with responsibility in advertising planning, creative execution and media planning. During this time, the media developed their own in-house services, both creative and production, directly for advertisers. Larger advertisers created their own in-house advertising departments for creative and, more rarely, for production. Private domestic agencies had gained perhaps 10 per cent of the total advertising market by 1993. That year marked something of a turning point; the number of private agencies tripled or quintupled (depending on which set of figures you use), and advertising expenditure reached $16 million.

Almost all other major multinational agencies that have set up in China have done so primarily to service multinational clients. By the end of 1993 there were more than 40 international advertising firms with offices in China, most concentrated – like their clients – in Beijing, Guangdong province and Shanghai. Chinese advertising agencies, struggling with competition both from media, advertisers' in-house departments and the multinationals, cried 'unfair'. Some order was needed and the government introduced a set of Interim Regulations on Advertising Agency System. In essence this introduced traditional Western practice, limiting print and broadcast media to display and turning the rest over to agencies. Commission rates were set at 15 per cent. There is some interpretation on issues such as who does 'production', and it is likely that some agencies will rebate some part of the commission. Formerly, Western ventures (JVs and WFOEs) were required to pay higher media prices, but the playing field has since been levelled – officially, at least.

Today, most of the ad agencies established in the 1990s have failed. The advertising market is consolidating, and at the same time becoming more professional and technically adept. There is little to choose in technical qualitative terms between television advertisements produced by multinational agencies and those produced by Chinese agencies. Loyalty, habit or linguistic barriers mean, however, that most Chinese advertisers continue to use Chinese agencies and most foreign ventures use the multinationals, though there are exceptions.

Distribution was one of the last areas in Chinese business to be heavily regulated (along with banking and finance), but here the barriers have been falling. Most importers and manufacturers are now free to choose their own distributor on the open market, and since 2000 foreign companies have been allowed to set up increasing numbers of JVs with Chinese distributors, or even wholly owned distribution subsidiaries. Being legally allowed to set up such a company is one thing; making it work in the organised chaos that is China's transport infrastructure is another. Many still prefer to use Chinese distributors on the grounds that these know how to work the system and have better *guanxi*. This may be good advice, but that does not preclude a thorough understanding.

Marketing strategy

Chinese marketers need no introduction to the writings of Sunzi. On the other hand, they may well be graduates of China's business schools and trying to write plans according to textbooks that do not mention him. As part of the transition to a market economy, China's leading universities rushed to provide MBAs. By 1999 there were 56 MBA programmes and by 2004 there were 90. Strategic thinking is even more important in China where there are, by and large, more options and fewer resources. Furthermore, we are not dealing with big, conventional warfare issues. Very few Western companies – Procter & Gamble, Unilever and maybe Johnson & Johnson being exceptions – are in that position. The Western brand, and we refer equally to industrial and services marketing here, is engaged in a long guerrilla campaign. Focus is crucial and that means sacrifice. By 'sacrifice' we mean not pursuing most of the attractive opportunities presented and especially not those suggested by senior management. Success stories from other markets are relevant, hence Unilever's success with Wall's ice-cream; however, as a general rule, the bigger the market, the narrower the marketing campaign should be.

Conventional market planning in today's China is a nightmare. To be accurate, competitor analysis needs to be done almost daily. New entrants to the markets come and go like the wind. Chinese entrepreneurs can take a business from start-up to full production with astonishing speed, and can enter the market and be in full-scale competition almost before one is aware of their presence. In part this is because the use of *guanxi* networks means it is possible to pull resources together quickly. Moreover, Chinese entrepreneurs think and make strategy on the fly, in true guerrilla-warfare style, reacting to opportunities as they come up. A Western company may well be able to identify a market opportunity, but by the time its cumbersome planning process has creaked into action, the plan has been modified and then approved by the board, resources have been found, a budget created, a partner identified, a site built, workers recruited and production begun, the market opportunity will not only be filled but the market itself will be saturated. This is precisely what happened to makers of white goods in the late 1990s and early part of this decade. There were a lot of casualties among Chinese manufacturers: those that survived, like Haier, were able to leverage both a strong brand and relationships with distributors. Today, Haier products are sold all across China.

Many people's marketing thinking about China starts with helpful phrases like 'one billion new customers'. It sounds tantalising, the pot of yuan at the end of the rainbow, but it is best forgotten. Even if a Western company could reach all those customers, could they actually serve them? It is with a shock that we realise that the largest producers in terms of volume sales in many markets – cigarettes and vodka being two – are Chinese. Those big Chinese firms have already captured the high ground and are in command of large portions of the market. So, for the Western company, it is farewell to dreams of conquest and back to guerrilla warfare.

Segmentation is essential, and can lead to real success with the right application of creative thinking. Kentucky Fried Chicken, whose appeal is universal in the US, targeted children in China. The product was not to conventional Chinese tastes, but they knew the 'little emperors' would be indulged. This strategy has worked: KFC remains (anecdotally) the number one venue in China for children's birthday parties. Much advertising in China for other products focuses on children for one-child family reasons; following the herd may or may not be a good strategy.

Guerrilla strategy (and Mao Zedong is a good guide here) dictates reining-in one's territorial ambitions and selecting the smallest, most favourable ground (market) one can hold. Never mind where the brand 'should' be, where can it win? Inner Mongolia and Xinjiang are not, we admit, the most attractive options and, as with the Long March, the brand strategists need to consider where they can win, not necessarily where they want to go next. Nevertheless, overall strategy and a feasible path to success do matter. Westerners tend to act conventionally and start in one of the big three centres (Shanghai, Beijing or Guangzhou), which are easily accessible, rather than the hinterland where competition may be weaker. Once you get on the ground, you can overlay the geographic strengths of each competitor on a map of China before choosing. The good news is that Chinese marketers have just as much trouble crossing provincial borders as do Westerners; a tough competitor in Beijing may not even be a presence in Shanghai.

Most China market entry products find themselves in an awkward gully. On one side will be the imported international brands with a higher reputation but tiny sales. On the other side will be the massive volumes of Chinese products but at prices below the foreigner's reach. So the campaign has to be fought on two fronts: international brand equity and affordable pricing. Both are fragile. Pabst Blue Ribbon was long the leading Western-style beer, albeit brewed in China. That rested on the belief that it was also a major brand in the US. When the word got around that it was small in the US, sales tumbled. On the other hand, 555 remains one of the largest cigarette brands, perhaps still bolstered by its legendary lead user (Mao), even though enough people must know by now that it has virtually disappeared elsewhere.

Leading marketing companies, having analysed the competitive environment and empathised with the end user's situation, write the brand's 'positioning' down in a short statement. By 'brand', we mean the thing being marketed, whatever the sector, including the product and its packaging. Reputation is just as important in industrial marketing as branding is for the consumer. A positioning statement is effective when it is focused and sacrifices all the easy compromises. It should identify immediate customer and end user and pick out the single reason why it is (a) different and (b) better from their point of view relevant to the most threatening key competitor. Not a woolly 'everyone' but the firm you would most like to take business from and least like to lose it to. A few other key strategies may need inclusion but a positioning statement should not exceed one page no matter how big the brand or market (China).

Products, branding and packaging

A *Harvard Business Review* article of 1994 describes *guo qing*, which means 'Chinese characteristics' (or perhaps more accurately 'Chinese circumstances') or the 'special situation in China', and advises that foreign companies need to adapt to it in order to reach Chinese consumers.[3] There is, of course, a broader debate about localisation and globalisation more generally, and each has its proponents. IKEA has the standard international approach of opening a market with their usual range of products and only adapting when they have to. In the USA, IKEA took many years before the eventual adaptions suited Americans and the stores began to make money. History is repeating itself. In 1999, Chinese visitors thronged into the new IKEA stores in Beijing and Shanghai, but few bought. The furniture seemed too expensive. IKEA has now managed to establish itself in the market, but our point is that adaption needs to be based on what is necessary in reality, not theory.

One good example of how creative adaptation can create a market in a China seemingly out of nothing comes from the diamond merchants De Beers, who already had a successful track record in adapting their product to the Japanese and other East Asian markets before going into China. On the face of it, diamonds do not willingly lend themselves to adaption. But what De Beers set out to adapt was not the product, but people's *perceptions* of it. In the West, diamonds are marketed with heavy connotations of romance, not just engagement rings but gifts on wedding anniversaries and the like. The assumption is that men buy diamonds for their wives, partners and girlfriends. But the Asian notion of romance, just like the Asian notion of law, is different from that of the West. In the Tiger economies, De Beers started marketing diamonds directly to women themselves. The attractiveness of the stone itself, not the romance surrounding it, became the key feature, and women were encouraged to buy diamonds to make themselves feel good and more desirable.

In China, a different approach still was taken. Many young Chinese are decidedly materialistic, so the East Asian approach might have worked, but De Beers decided there was another way to position diamonds: as a symbol of an enduring relationship. Harmony, rather than love, was chosen as the key connotation, and ads featured husbands giving wives rings on their wedding days and then flashing forward to show subsequent years of happy and prosperous marriage. Michael Backman and Charlotte Butler, commenting on this, note that 'the diamond ring in China has come to symbolise not so much love as a successful joint venture. That's some adaptation'.[4] And a highly successful one too, as the large De Beers store in the fashionable shopping district of Wangfujing clearly shows. In fact, Western-style weddings have become big business in parts of China, with couples getting married in formal gear and white wedding dresses in the morning – sometimes even in a Christian church – before going on to a traditional Chinese banquet in the evening. Adaptation takes place on both sides.

Some new products introduced from the West may well have perception problems in China. Marketers introducing unfamiliar products might do well to consider using methods such as personal demonstrations and sampling. Mary Kay Cosmetics and Avon used these methods when introducing their health and beauty lines in Guangzhou and Shanghai, though they have since had regulatory problems. Colgate, Rémy Martin and Orange Tang all used this method, as did Coca-Cola.

For consumer goods, therefore, a small sampling and/or demonstration promotion in a key entry market should be standard practice until it is shown to be unnecessary; that is, when more sophisticated techniques prove more productive. For products like automobiles and farm machinery, a showroom is necessary. Before 1949, major international automobile companies all had showrooms in China, employing salespeople to persuade potential buyers to have a close look and take a drive. Now, cars and farm machinery are being displayed once again in showrooms. In the early 1990s, these showrooms were usually the offices of the agents who imported the products, and they tended to lump many different products together. This has changed, certainly as far as the luxury car market is concerned, and some companies have experimented with setting up networks of dealers specialising in their own cars. (The Chinese government has an ambivalent attitude to the car. Auto production was at first encouraged and then discouraged, but popular complaint over the lack of cars to buy forced the relaxation of production restrictions. As a result, the pollution problems and traffic jams are getting worse.)

But this is by the by. The importance of branding and packaging simply cannot be overstated. Packaging is one of the ways in which economic reform has changed some aspects of Chinese culture. The universal big bag (*midai*) for carrying home the rice has been replaced by packaged rice as supermarkets take over. The brightly coloured shopping bag carrying the retailer's brand has also become commonplace. Packaging's key role is communication; it is the carrier of the brand name and symbol. This is where Chinesing has to start. Specialist consultants are available to explain how Western brand names and packaging will be seen, said and understood – in all the major Chinese languages.

Orange Tang, which is advertised as a 'fresh-squeezed-orange-taste instant drink', has the Chinese name 'Guo Zhen' (fruit treasure).

The mark and the package are both very appealing: the latter carries the wording 'Selected by NASA for U.S. Space Flights', and the advertising strap-line is, 'the drink in space time'. The Changsha Refrigerator Factory, which uses Italian technology in its manufacturing, adopted the brand name 'Zhongyi', which means both 'Sino-Italian' and 'satisfactory' or 'to one's liking'. Sometimes successful brand names can be construed from Chinese words which sound like the company's Western brand name; thus Gillette used the Chinese name 'Jili', which means 'lucky'.

Numbers are also important: for example, 8 is lucky and 9 is everlasting. Animals have symbolic significance: the tortoise stands for longevity, while fish mean wealth. Colours also have strong significance. The scarlet, imperial yellow, and gold are now a cliché; you will see them most commonly on Chinese goods that are destined primarily for sale to the West. White is the funeral colour and seen as unlucky.

Unsurprisingly, in a culture where symbols are so powerful, brands need to develop a unique iconic symbol. Research in the West indicates that non-letter logos (e.g. those for Apple or Shell) communicate more effectively than words or letters (BP or IBM). In Chinese culture, non-letter symbols can be even more powerful. Rémy Martin's centaur ('man-horse') has positive associations and has much to do with that brandy's dominant market share.

Some commentators have written off the Chinese attachment to brands as a passing phase, and have compared it to attachments to brands in other developing economies. The reasoning is that, once consumers reach a certain level of sophistication, they become more cynical about brands and less likely to remain loyal. Certainly the Chinese are less uncritical of *foreign* brands than before, and foreignness no longer has the cachet it once had. But whether this is because the Chinese are becoming less enthusiastic about brands, or whether it means that domestic Chinese brands are becoming more sophisticated and more appealing is a moot point.

The quality of consumer goods has improved markedly over the past few years; even where quality is still not as high as for Western goods, the price differential more than compensates for this. Chinese marketers have been getting better at reinforcing their brands, too, and can offer the additional appeal to Chinese cultural values. In Beijing, the modern shopping district of Wangfujing may have all the big foreign names, but go south and west of Tiananmen Square and you will find that Chinese shops selling Chinese branded goods are booming. The restoration of the centuries-old pharmaceuticals brand Tongrentang, in its elegant flagship store off the market street of Dazhalan, is a symbol of the resurgence of Chinese brands. In the nineteenth century, Tongrentang had a nationwide presence; today, as it opens or reopens stores all over China, it is about to achieve this again. Other old brands like the shoe retailer Tongmenghui are also beginning to re-emerge.

The reassurance of a famous brand, whatever the price, is still important, but that brand need not be foreign to be successful. Consider too that many consumers quite happily buy counterfeit brands. They are not fooled; but they believe that, if the counter-feiters have gone to so much trouble, the quality is probably a reasonable match for much less money. Experience with rip-offs will reinstate the importance of genuine brands, in time, but without much help from the law.

Brands will be *more* important in China than internationally in the long term. Our reasons concern overseas Chinese behaviour, *guanxi* and the associated lack of consumer rights enforcement. Overseas Chinese consumers, who have been buying in sophisti-cated free markets for some time, still exhibit high levels of loyalty to brands. In an uncertain world, consumer–brand relationships should prove enduring once they settle down. One should not read too much into the teenager-like early process of infatuation and rejection. Brands will remain more expensive than local unbranded, or private label (which are actually retailer brands), or counterfeits. But they are also reassurance and reducers of risk. Economic factors play a part and the long-term strength of brands needs a big enough middle class willing to pay this marginal extra cost for these benefits.

Earlier we mentioned the old adage about how Westerners seek the meaning of life while Chinese seek a way to live. Brands convey status and achievement; their possession signals one's place within one's social group and community. The associative aspects of Chinese culture are significant. Individuality matters, but so too does the need to belong to a certain group. As people leave villages for the cities, they need to find new ways to express that. Hong Kong is a good example. Once a brand has the reputation of being powerful and 'good', people will wish to be associated with it.

Certainly branding is not limited to foreign products, and compa-nies like Qingdao (beer), Forever (bicycles) and Lenovo (computers) have developed strong brands, along with the historic brands we mentioned above. In 1997, the state announced a programme of support to 17 domestically produced brands, including consultancy support and funding for advertising and marketing. It is probably only a matter of time, and getting the quality right, before Chinese brands start becoming major players in Western markets (see Chapter 4).

Product issues

- Start with the packaging. What does it communicate not just in meaning but in price, quality and other associations? How does the brand name sound; indeed is it sayable, in all the main Chinese languages?
- As anywhere, forget the intentions and the rest of the world. How would/does the *Chinese* consumer use this product? What problem does it solve for them? How could it do that better, e.g. a smaller pack size? What is the primary competitive advantage from their point of view?
- Consider using demonstrations and personal selling when introducing new products, not only as a good way of introducing the product, but as a crucial market research to check on the two points above.
- Then consider sampling on a wider scale. It is expensive but it does get the product into the hands of the end user.
- Finally, consider the long-term brand–consumer *guanxi*. What needs to be done to reinforce that, build confidence and reduce risk to the consumer?

Pricing

We have already referred to the need for sensitive pricing between imported and local products. Consumer readiness to pay import prices for locally manufactured goods has largely evaporated along with economic growth. The skimming route is certainly an option. McDonald's successfully entered at a premium of four to five times the costs of eating out, but that may not now be possible. Every generation of marketers believes that earlier times were easier and that 'today the pressure on domestic prices is strongly downward'. The reality is that pricing has always been critical but the premiums and discounts that customers will accept do change. Careful judgement is needed; once the brand's novelty value wears off, or once other high-profile competitors enter the market, prices need to come down to support continued brand growth.

McDonald's did just this, by gradually reducing its premium, and the brand has grown well. Kentucky Fried Chicken, however, held on to its margin for too long following entry to Hong Kong in the mid-1970s. The business dried up; at the same time there were disruptions at a higher level as the parent company in the USA was bought and sold a couple of times. Consequently, it was not until the early 1990s that KFC re-entered the market, on a small scale and well behind many of its fast-food rivals. Today KFC, problem fixed, is widely prominent.

No one should imagine that price is not an issue for Chinese consumers: the reverse is true. Studies in Hong Kong and Singapore show that they tend to be much more canny and discriminating shoppers than the average person in the West. But for most brands, price has a display as well as an economic role and that needs to be factored in.

Pricing issues

- Consider two entry strategy options: skimming and shooting straight for the target. If you enter too low, it may be tough to get back up.
- Be 'premium' by Chinese, not international, standards.
- Pricing should be determined by the brand's strategic positioning and consumer empathy.
- If sales fail to show up, or evaporate, you will be told that price is to blame. Do not panic: that is the easy rationalisation by inexperienced marketers. Look again.

Promotion and advertising

Advertising

We are fairly sure that advertising in China is more strongly correlated with sales than in, say, Britain but that does not mean that it is more effective. Perhaps Chinese businesses are just quicker to hand cash to their agencies when sales are rising and to take it away when they are falling. Most Chinese advertisers and their agencies have very little idea of what advertising does for them, which is refreshingly honest.

Partly as a result, a large cultural gap exists between Western clients and their multinational advertising agencies on the one side and their Chinese counterparts on the other. The Chinese view is that their ad agents, who may have little expertise beyond media buying, do not deserve much remuneration and that attitude rules out the multinationals. Conversely, the multinationals expect more expertise on the part of their clients. Chinese clients admire the quality of the foreign agencies' work (though the gap is rapidly closing, and in terms of television advertising may even have closed) but do not want to pay the bills.

Given the importance of brands, advertising should play an important role in terms of both brand awareness and reinforcement. Some Western advertising campaigns have proved even more effective in Asia than in the West; Michael Jordan became a household name among children in Singapore. But advertising in East Asia does have its pitfalls for the unwary, and most of them concern culture. Simple problems with translation are of course responsible for many of these – almost everyone has probably had a laugh by now at the expense of Coca-Cola, whose slogan 'Coke adds life' was translated in Taiwan as 'Coke will bring back your ancestors from the grave'. The transmission of cultural values is often more difficult. Many 'sexist' ads on television and in newspapers are simply not acceptable in the Chinese cultures of East Asia, where relatively high moral standards prevail. This is particularly true of China, but less so of the Hong Kong SAR; ads on Star TV broadcast into the PRC are noticeably more risqué than those on China Central TV. Ads that show children rebelling against their parents are also unlikely to be well received. Finally, the problem is compounded by cultural diversity in those countries with indigenous as well as Chinese and/or Indian immigrant communities. But this chapter deals with the PRC.

Attitudes to advertising can be paradoxical. Advertising, in China as elsewhere, is disliked as undermining national culture, lowering standards, increasing demand for the 'wrong' things, and intruding into the landscape and/or media. Foreign advertising can be particularly offensive when it oversteps the bounds of cultural sensibilities, awakening not-so-very-deeply buried Chinese memories of foreign domination. On the other hand, advertising makes economic sense and consumers enjoy advertising and find it useful.

Television is the main vehicle for advertising, with all the provinces, autonomous regions and municipalities and a great many large and medium-sized cities having their own television stations penetrating every corner of the country. There are now 3,000 television stations, though most have limited reach. The most powerful station is China Central Television (CCTV). CCTV has at present 17 channels devoted to news and current affairs, sport, family and games shows and has national reach; there is also an English-language channel, CCTV International (formerly CCTV 9). Accordingly, products advertised on its channels do tend to become household names. As a result in early 2008, CCTV was charging between 3,600 and 243,000 yuan (Y7.2 = $1) for a 30-second slot depending on the time.

According to the World Advertising Research Center (WARC), China is an oddball in terms of media costs. Compared with 35 other major markets, it is the most expensive place for advertising, in terms of cost per thousand (CPT) for cinema and magazines but the second and fifth cheapest for TV and radio respectively. In the case of TV in 2006, the cost per thousand (CPT) in China was only 8 and 7 per cent that of the USA and UK respectively.[5]

Within China CPT's vary considerably as they do in other countries, to some extent correlating with the buying power of their readership. For example, among China's 20 leading newspapers by circulation, *Southern Metropolitan News* (Guangzhou) has a CPT (2007) of 3.3K RMB compared with 2.5K for the next highest (*Xiandai News*) and on down to 0.3K RMB for the cheapest (*Reference News*). The great majority ranged from 1K to 2K RMB (2007).

For Chinese TV, the music channel was the most expensive, with a CPT of 0.6K RMB. Channels 9 and 11 were just over half that and the remainder were only about 0.03K RMB.[6]

The *Futures Worldwide* January 2006 review (Initiative media network) estimates that cinema's global cost per thousand is $59.43; Internet CPT is $16.38; magazines $11.14; newspapers $9.23; TV $7.06; radio $6.32; and outdoor $5.37. In 2007, advertisers queued up to pay 200,000 yuan for 7.5 seconds immediately after the main early evening news. Ten years earlier, the figure was around 20,000 yuan for 15 seconds.

This represents reasonable value, given the size of the market, but the trick is actually getting a top spot. Formerly, agencies used to send their staff to queue for the release of the most popular spots, but now air time is sold at auction to the highest bidder. As a result, advertisers with deep pockets claim virtually all the space. In a highly unscientific study conducted by one of the authors in November 2002, it was found that fully 60 per cent of CCTV ads were for one of three product groups: hair care products, alcoholic beverages and Chinese medicine. Cars came a long way fourth; white goods and computers barely showed on the register. A similarly unscientific sampling in January 2008 showed advertisements by insurance companies, home furnishing companies and car makers, but beauty products and medicines still dominated.

Newspapers also play an important role. Until the 1980s, given that the lack of newsprint limited the size of newspapers (eight pages is the norm) and newspapers were controlled by the Communist Party, advertising was almost non-existent. Now there are no limits. At the top end of the range, the official mouthpiece, the *People's Daily*, charges between 40,000 and 100,000 yuan for a whole page, while the popular *China Youth News*, with a million circulation, charges between 40,000 and 70,000 yuan. On 15 January 1993, history was made when Shanghai's most popular daily newspaper, *Wenhui Bao*, sold its entire front page for a Xileng (refrigerator) advertisement costing 1 million yuan. Most newspapers now, like their counterparts in the West, make the bulk of their revenue from advertising.

Pricing is complicated by a brokerage system in which entrepreneurs corner particular niche markets and hold out for higher prices. The marketer can hold his nerve and hope for last-minute deals. Some of these arrangements are hedged by the original media owner being prepared to buy back unsold space. Another local peculiarity is that space booked may not run when expected or even at all. As a result, advertisers have to pay for tracking systems to monitor what ads actually run.

Posters are also important, though curbs on some of the biggest users, notably tobacco, have cooled the market. Much of the disposable income lies in densely packed urban areas. As elsewhere, messages do not need to be complex for famous brands, but in frenetic major Chinese cities, stand-out is even more important and more difficult.

Guanxi brand–consumer principles apply. If one can afford it, advertising early, before the product is available, and long can pay off even though the short-term financials are unattractive. Normally, in Europe and in North America, advertising should follow distribution. In China, a number of Japanese brands, such as Sony, were advertised for some years before coming onto the market. With hindsight, this was a smart investment, especially as advertising rates were a great deal cheaper then.

Admittedly some time ago, but it is still a good story, an advertising lecturer came to Shanghai with a television commercial he had designed for Ivory Soap. In it a Chinese family – father, mother and children – all go to the paddy field to transplant rice shoots. Later they emerge covered in soil and use Ivory Soap to clean up. This commercial was completely off the mark. For one thing, this particular task is now done by machine; more importantly, no one who is experienced in this work becomes so soiled. The image of dirtiness, which may be used with some appeal abroad, is simply insulting to the Chinese working consumer. Evidently the commercial was made with a minimum of research. 'Ivory – the soap that floats', is still the best approach in China.

A good idea of the kinds of advertising currently used on Chinese television can be gained from watching CCTV or other main channels. Spot the differences between East and West. Most ads for Western brands are produced in China but against international strategies. Much of the Chinese advertising is imitative. Lager always seems to be promoted by clean-cut young Chinese men in a Western-style bar, while Chinese spirits use images of the Great Wall, people dancing in ethnic costume, and elderly men proclaiming how the product has helped them to reach a wise old age.

We do not take up space with advertising regulations which, following WTO, are being brought theoretically into line with the rest of the world. The guidelines in the box below are not intended to be taken too rigidly. In advertising, rules – but not government regulations – were made to be broken.

Some advertising dos and don'ts

- Be careful with comparative advertising and exaggeration; most of the problems with the censorship board have been in this area.
- Translate outwards and then back when approving advertising copy. Have an independent translation of the translation made, and see if the original matches.
- Where direct response is being used, understand the communication and distribution problems for the responder. Be convenient for the buyer.
- Don't assume your agency knows and applies the regulations.
- Don't say your brand is the leader (especially if it is).

- Don't use models whose appeal is based on sex. (Of course Chinese companies do, but from a foreign advertiser it is all too easy to portray this as exploitation.) One 1995 Beijing regulation stated that female models cannot expose their bodies between the shoulder and 15cm above the knee (Article 9.2) apart from swimsuits, and only then in relevant context. Check on local regulations before starting to shoot.
- Don't put ads on the backs of envelopes.

New media

It is arguable that China has leapfrogged the conventional landline telephone infrastructure and jumped straight to mobile (radio) communications. Notwithstanding the phone boxes appearing in the streets, mobile phones are everywhere. As of January 2008, there were 547 million resgistered mobile phone users in China, equivalent to the entire populations of the USA, UK, France, Germany and Italy. A fascination with gadgetry and technology, peer group competition, and the burning need to keep in touch all lead to the same outcome. You can expect your host to be waiting at the door because your driver will have made half a dozen calls as you faltered through the traffic.

After a slow start, the Internet is growing fast. Government regulations and restrictions on the Internet remain tight; usage is widespread, especially among the young. In January 2008 government statistics claimed there were more than 200 million Internet users in China; a big number, but less than 20 per cent of the total population. As Google among others has learned, usage is heavily monitored and controlled. Any advertisement on the Internet should avoid controversy of any kind.

Golden Hall sausages

The Jen Man Tang (Golden Hall) sausage company is based in Zhanjiang, about 230 miles southwest of Guangzhou. In 1994 they were the dominant brand in their own market, but had no sales at all in the much larger market of Guangzhou, which was dominated by two other brands, The Emperor and Kung Ki Leng. The company contacted an advertising agency, the Sun and Moon Spreading Co., to advise it on how to break into the Guangzhou market.

The sausage market is highly seasonal. Like many traditional foods, consumption is ruled by the calendar rather than the weather. It begins with the Zhongqiujie (Moon Festival) in late September or early October and ends with the Qingmingjie (Clear Brightness Festival) in April. Sausages are made of 100 per cent pork plus flavourings. A sausage may be a meal in its own right or may be chopped up into other dishes. As with other meat products, sausages are not cheap.

Golden Hall sausages were shorter and thinner than The Emperor sausages, which had over half the current market share, and a lower fat content. It was believed that a 'lean appeal' might be successful with consumers. However, there were also production problems; Golden Hall sausages were not always fresh when sold, and there were quality problems such as variable levels of fat.

Competing with The Emperor would be difficult, as the rival company was a big spender on advertising, and Golden Hall could not hope to spend on the same level in the early days. Clearly some other tactics were going to be needed for the launch and the promotional period immediately following. The first and foremost objective for Golden Hall was to build up some *guanhai* (Yue for *guanxi*) in the Guangzhou market.

Other promotions

We have referred to the importance of demonstrations and sampling above, under 'product'. Point of purchase (POP) displays and demonstrations are very effective in these stores, which are, or perhaps used to be, crowded at peak times. Department stores have been hardest hit by the economic downturn and many, Chinese and foreign, have closed their doors.

Customers rely on the retailer for advice when purchasing unfamiliar products, and this provides opportunities for promotions. In 1999, for example, Asahi beer (Japan) launched a major offensive in Beijing where restaurant customers were rather forcibly offered two cans for the price of one. This was advice with a heavy A. Asahi has not made much impact in China.

The beer market is an interesting illustration of some of the points in this book. In the 1990s, the fashion for foreign brewers was to buy small Chinese breweries which they could dominate and use to introduce big foreign brands. Most of those failed by 2000.

Since then, the fashion has been to buy shares in the major breweries selling Chinese brands and operate as JVs. Sometimes, as in the case of the acquisition of Harbin brewery by Anheuser-Busch in 2004, the joint venture paved the way for full acquisition.

Service centres can be effective, perhaps because the whole notion of after-sales care is so unusual. Omega appointed a watch store as its service centre in Shanghai, Sanyo established its own service centre and Citizen has service centres in Beijing, Shanghai, Guangzhou and other cities. Ricoh recorded 28 service centres and Shanghai Volkswagen (SVW) had 32 SVW authorised service stations across China. Ensuring regional coverage is important, given the large distances and infrastructure difficulties.

The Chinese calendar with its cultural associations remains (though less so for young people) an important tool for promoting seasonal products and reflects attitudes with respect to the capricious climate. For instance, a Shanghai rubber shoe factory advertised in the 19 February 1986 issue of *Xin Min Evening News* with the single headline 'Today is Rain Water'. The message was sufficient to convince great numbers of readers to buy rubber rain shoes, even though there was no sign of water. In another promotion, McDonald's gave away 'lucky' red decorations; these can still be found in many homes. Those were early days, however, and the consumer is now far more marketing-savvy; approaches will need to be more subtle.

The Pine Nut King

In 2001, made redundant from the state-owned agriculture concern in Hangzhou where he had worked for most of his life, Liu Xiandong decided to put his 50,000 yuan redundancy money into a venture harvesting and selling pine nuts. This was a risky venture, as there was stiff competition with many established players, and Liu had little business expertise or capital. He had done no market research, and was simply aware that there was a large potential market. Pine nuts are a feature of cuisine in Hangzhou and the surrounding province, and are used in many dishes, by ordinary families as well as in restaurants.

Liu found he could make some headway in the market by concentrating on quality. Hand shelling of the nuts was time-consuming and wasteful, but Liu hit on the idea of using vapour machines to steam open the shells without damaging the contents. This gave him an edge in the market, as his larger rivals used chemical processes to soften the shells. Liu's pine nuts were organic, and suddenly he had found his first marketing advantage. He then began experimenting with different varieties of nut. Hearing of some particularly large pine nuts that were grown in Iran, Liu travelled to western China and there met some of the Iranian dealers who had access to supplies. He quickly cornered the market in this large and delicious variety, and his sales grew rapidly. He also began developing other product lines such as pumpkin seeds. By 2005 his business was producing 1,500 tons of nuts and other food products which were selling in supermarkets and shops in Hangzhou and across the province.

In October 2005, Liu took a further step, withdrawing his products from supermarkets and setting up his own chain of retail outlets in Hangzhou. This was risky, but Liu argued that the supermarkets were taking too large a share of his profits. Despite retail overheads, he found he could sell his products profitably for a lower price than they had been selling in the supermarkets. A further advantage was that he could brand the entire business, not just the individual products it made and sold.

By the end of 2007 Liu was in a strong position, with more than a dozen retail outlets and an annual turnover of more than 2 million yuan. His next step was to expand beyond Hangzhou, into other cities of eastern China and ultimately across the entire country. But so far, nearly all his contacts were in Hangzhou and his business was unknown outside his home province. How to replicate a successful business format in parts of China he did not know and where he had no existing relationships was proving to be a tough problem to solve.

Place, channels and distribution

Poor infrastructure and distribution have discouraged more than one investor. Billions have been invested in infrastructure over the last ten years, but need always outstrips capacity. There are ways around the problem, but they often require some creativity. Fosters, in expanding its interests in China, has set up a whole network of joint ventures, first with producers in a number of regional centres, and second with the Hong Kong conglomerate Wheelock, which has experience in transport and distribution in China. By establishing many regional centres rather than a few large breweries, Fosters has cut down on the distance its goods need to be shipped; and where shipping is required, Wheelock's expertise and contacts help cut down the problems.

Mary Kay Cosmetics in Shanghai used party plan selling to reach its potential customers, who were mostly young working women. As most people in Shanghai have fairly limited residential space, Mary Kay established its own premises and made meeting rooms available to its sales agents, who could invite potential customers to parties on the premises (where, of course, they could be exposed to other forms of point-of-sale promotion). They, and Amway and Avon, were surprised to be included in the 1998 ban on pyramid selling.[7] After 50 per cent losses, they renegotiated themselves into a new regulation which requires, inter alia, that their salespeople pass an exam administered by the local authorities. They may be operating outside the normal retail regulations and in uncharted waters but they have done astonishingly well. By 2005, Mary Kay claimed to have around 350,000 agents and China was fast outstripping the US to become their largest market. Apparently, they had been profitable since 2001.[8]

Retailing has had a chequered history. The first retail joint venture was established in Shenzhen in 1991, and since then retail JVs have proliferated. Manufacturers are allowed their own stores or rent counters in department stores in the cities, ostensibly as 'windows' to get market information. The realisation is dawning, however, that retailing should be left to specialist retailers. As a result, retail quality is rapidly improving. A walk through Beijing or Shanghai shows the smartening up of department stores with traditional Chinese goods but, more importantly for the future, Chinese versions of international goods made to improving standards. The prices of imported goods leave plenty of space. Department stores remain a major force in retailing, with 400 in Shanghai alone. As noted above, however, their strength is waning as consumers, as in the UK, turn to chain stores. 'Sincere', part of the Hong Kong department store chain, closed after only two years.

Before the traumatic events in the early twentieth century, China, even more than England, was a nation of shopkeepers. Under Maoism, small enterprises were largely swallowed up by the state. After reform, the *huaqiao* from Singapore, Thailand, Malaysia and elsewhere moved into distribution and trade, often via family members still living in China. Wangfujing in Beijing was one of the first areas to be opened up to JV retailers and was largely developed by Hong Kong money; it could be a shopping street anywhere in East Asia. Dazhalan, on the other hand, is in a historic quarter of the city and was developed using local money, and remains more distinctively north Chinese. Shanghai has also thrown open its doors to foreign retailers, including Isetan, Sogo and Yaohan of Japan and Taiwan's Sunrise, along with a variety of Shanghai and Hong Kong-based operations.

The strategy of the Hong Kong real estate companies, in particular, has primarily been to build large-scale commercial buildings for rental to international chain store groups. However, some real estate companies have also sought to include retailing in their permitted scope of business. Where they do not, they simply set up subsidiary companies to engage in retailing directly. Kerry Everbright and Cheung Kong have both used this strategy with success.

There is also a significant European and American retailing presence. Some, such as clothing and fast food, lend themselves to franchising, as discussed in the last chapter. Metro (Germany), Makro (Netherlands) and Carrefour (France) are represented; the last is something of an East Asian success story generally. The British are represented by B&Q (Kingfisher) and Tesco which bought 50 per cent of Hymall in 2004 as a JV with Ting Hsin International of Taiwan. Hymall then had 25 stores. By the end of 2006, Hymall had grown to 44 outlets compared with Carrefour's 81 and Wal-Mart's 66, the latter then expected to grow by 100.[9]

The physical problems of distribution are caused by an inadequate infrastructure. Fast as China's road network has grown over the past two decades, the number of vehicles has grown even faster; companies shipping by road will face increased costs and uncertain delivery times and outcomes. The rail network, largely geared to the defence of China from foreign invasion, is inadequate to the task of shipping goods. Water transport is usually efficient, and accounts for about 20 per cent of all freight, but is slow and does not reach all areas. Air freight tends to be quicker but less efficient. Companies wishing to ship directly between two minor centres will often be told, in effect, 'you can't get there from here'. Manufacturers can also expect to face problems in road travel and transport of goods across borders as a result of inter-provincial rivalries. Some provinces in the past have erected barriers at their borders, preventing or charging high fees for certain goods such as rice or cotton.

Everyone has their favourite story about air travel in China; here is one example. One Western firm anxious to ship a large package on a Saturday flight from Shanghai contacted the local air cargo firm earlier in the week and gave the dimensions of the package. Would there be room for it on the plane? No problem, they were told. Come Monday, the package had not been shipped. Contacting the air cargo company again, they were told that there had in fact been no space. When reminded that they had confirmed that there *was* space, the cargo company conceded that, yes, there was indeed space on the plane that went the day the inquiry was made. There was no space on the Saturday plane, which was smaller.

Distribution issues

• Although distribution has been greatly liberalised in the last few years and state-owned firms no longer play a major part, both sales channels remain under-developed.

• Inadequate infrastructure greatly complicates distribution problems, and will probably continue to do so for some time.

• Waste no time before working out paper solutions for your particular products in the territories you intend to cover. You may need, for example, a separate business with a different governance structure as well as approvals from authorities which may take a long time to arrive.

• Try to find local or foreign companies that have already set up successful distribution networks similar to what you need. *Guanxi* may help you get close to them and perhaps set up joint ventures.

• Consider getting a nucleus of the future sales team to start calling key customers before you have products to sell. Train them in providing technical advice.

Conclusions

We have boxed some points for each of the four Ps of the marketing mix and will not repeat them here. We began by saying that marketing in China is becoming much like anywhere else but there are enough differences for the foreigner to need to take care − especially with distribution.

We have paid attention to the PRC and to consumer brands, leaving the reader to adapt the implications for other Chinese markets and sectors. The principles really are the same:

- Of the four Ps, the product really does matter most.
- To gain trial, first impressions (packaging, demonstrations, sampling) are a crucial gate (*guan*).
- Once through that gate, the goal is to build long-term consumer-brand *guanxi*. For consumer goods, that is the role of advertising; but in business to business, industrial and services, this role falls to the customer-facing employees. Industrial business may not see themselves as branded but that is what they are: their reputation makes the difference between profit and not making it through the door.
- But more important than those communications is the satisfaction from the use of the product itself.
- Pricing must be seen, within the context of the brand–consumer relationship and competition, as fair.
- Finally, the marketer has to think it all the way through, and see it through, to the end user.

The way a firm goes about marketing strategy is also the same for all sectors: segmentation and geographical concentration to gain enough focus and leverage to win. Too many marketers try to do too much with too little. Define the positioning in a crisp, half-page statement; that way, everyone should be able to understand and be motivated by it.

The overseas Chinese

The main differences between selling into PRC consumer markets and those of Chinese communities elsewhere in East Asia lie in better distribution networks (meaning easier access to the market), and in greater consumer sophistication. Thus, it may be easier to get your goods in front of the consumer, but it may be harder to persuade them to buy.

Overseas Chinese customers have, by and large, become accustomed to modern advertising and branding. More subtle approaches are needed, just as they are increasingly needed in

China too, as the consumer wises up to Western marketing methods. Nonetheless, many Chinese cultural attributes mentioned above are important when it comes to marketing in overseas Chinese markets. For example, many of the same sensitivities to advertising apply, through in some countries more than others. Marketers considering Taiwan, Thailand or Malaysia can certainly use this chapter as a starting point, before going on to research local regulations and market preferences.

8   The marketing process

> The general who wins a battle makes many calculations in his temple[1] before the battle is fought. The general who loses a battle makes but few calculations beforehand. Thus do many calculations lead to victory and few calculations to defeat: how much more no calculation at all.
>
> (Sunzi)

This chapter is in effect a continuation of the last, and many of the points made there – about the need to know more about Chinese markets rather than simply handing marketing over to local affiliates, and about the difficulty of acquiring reliable factual information – apply here too. The latter is particularly critical. As Sunzi pointed out 2,500 years ago, apart from focus, the other key to winning battles is having, and using, superior information. A plan built on poor information is as useless as perfect information which is not acted upon.

So what is new? Forty years of practising and teaching marketing has convinced one author of this book (and the others are quite prepared to believe it) that every marketing plan ever written fails one or both of Sunzi's tests. As another great strategist, the Prussian field marshal Helmuth von Moltke, remarked, 'No plan ever survives contact with the enemy'. We would amend that to simply, 'No plan ever survives'.

This chapter begins by returning to the subject of market research, discussed briefly in Chapter 1. We then move on to look at other information and discuss a practical strategy for integrating information needs. There is a tendency, in writing about business in China, to note *guanxi* as some sort of local peculiarity, and then get back to business as usual. We think it needs to be made intrinsic to the whole planning process. Here we make suggestions how.

Market research in the PRC

It is easy, albeit expensive and time consuming, to obtain PRC market research; it is somewhat more difficult to determine whether it is reliable. Published sources of quantitative data include those from the state Statistical Bureau, foreign research agencies, and collections such as *The China Business Handbook* from the media. This last group is the cheapest, and in some ways most convenient, but they are very general and recycle other sources, so consistency is no confirmation.

After reviewing those, we turn to bespoke quantitative and then qualitative research.

Published sources

Data in China are likely to be used to paint a picture rather than give precise information. An enormous system collects and analyses information for central planning purposes. This information used to be difficult to get hold of because it was scattered among various agencies (including commissions, ministries, national corporations and industry councils), and the 'right' person to approach within any particular agency might be unidentifiable. A Westerner who approaches a ministry for help is likely to be referred to the foreign affairs department within the ministry. Industry-specific market analysis can be undertaken, but the results may be crude. It may take a few hours to examine an industry yearbook.

However, the situation is now much easier so far as access is concerned. The state Statistical Bureau and some ministries have set up information service centres and much of their data is accessible, on CD-ROM and increasingly on the Internet. We still recommend that trusted local intermediaries are first commissioned to obtain data from these sources. Unreliability requires independent verification and interpretation, which is best done by people with experience. They need to know the purpose of the research and the level of accuracy required.

Generic information about consumers and their behaviour is available from these sources. For example, China's high-potential consumer markets are concentrated along its east coast in three distinct areas. Getting at each cluster of consumers is, therefore, possible through geographical focus. The key markets are usually seen as being Shanghai, Guangdong, Beijing and, to a lesser extent, Tianjin. Although only 50 miles from Beijing, Tianjin is a very different market; in particular, prices are lower there than in the capital, as is the standard of living. However, with a population of around 10 million, Tianjin should not be overlooked. Of other major centres, Chongqing in the west is often overlooked but is the largest city in China (around 30 million). Wuhan is a crossroads, very important in terms of transport links through central China. Because of its location, many people thought that it would become a key centre very quickly and a number of foreign firms went into Wuhan in the early 1990s. Initial results were disappointing and some of these firms quickly pulled out again. However, with the east coast becoming increasingly congested, foreign firms are starting to see opportunities in Wuhan once more. Other centres likely to experience major growth in future are Changsha, Xi'an and Chengdu, as well as the big Manchurian cities like Changchun, Shenyang and Dalian. It all depends on one's strategic priorities – in particular, on how long one can afford to wait. Growth statistics for all these centres are available from the sources above, and increasingly this information is being made available online.

Bespoke quantitative research

Obtaining research is easy, primarily because of the number of Western and Chinese market research agencies. In 1994, there were over 100 market research agencies in the PRC, including state, private and joint-venture agencies. Nobody knows how many there are today, but telephone directories are full of advertisements. Quite what quality of information one will get from using these agencies is an unknown; many are one-man bands working from homes or small offices, trawling the Internet and published sources for the same material one could easily look up oneself. The number of companies able to conduct original quantitative research such as surveys, questionnaires, retail audits and the like is much more limited. Consultants in Beijing and Shanghai advise their customers to ask for references before employing any market research agency – Chinese or foreign – and to ask what previous customers have thought of their work. Many consulting firms have relationships with local agencies, and the latter are probably among the most reliable.

Survey Research Group (SRG) was probably the first major external agency to establish itself, in 1984. Run from Hong Kong, it has offices in Shanghai, Beijing, Chengdu and other centres as well as their original joint venture in Guangzhou. It also has links to a worldwide market research network. Their main clients are foreign, mostly US; global clients tend to feel more comfortable with global marketing services. These big companies expect modern marketing services (using the logic of 'you get what you pay for'), and also, being big, they prefer to put their faith in statistics rather than intuition. Chinese marketers, being generally smaller, have fewer inhibitions. Chinese market research tends to be based on feedback from salesmen, test introductions and personal field experience. Incidentally, this is quite similar to Japanese experiential research preference.

SRG's Guangzhou offices told us that in-house customised (door-to-door) usage and attitude studies for consumer products were their main item, followed by focus groups, in-depth interviews, retail audits and media monitoring research. Media monitoring is also important in China, and tracks whether advertisements actually appeared when and where they should. SRG's business-to-business work consisted mainly of desk research, for reasons noted above, and professional in-depth interviews. Interesting too is these agencies' perception of their own role: SRG, like other researchers, see themselves as interpreters of consumer/customer preferences and behaviour for foreign businesses.

The methodologies these agencies use are standard and would be familiar to most Western market researchers. The results they achieve, however, can be confusing. One survey showed a substantial demand, among over 500 million smokers, for products to help them quit. This turned out to be nonsense: the respondents were being 'helpful'.

There are three main reasons for unreliability. First, there is the differing nature of Chinese consumer psychology. People's responses in China do not always fit into the neat pigeonholes that our market research methods would like; so a research programme which gives a clear and sharp segmentation when applied to a US or European market may give a much more fuzzy picture when applied in China. Providing information is treated as being valuable. Not only do respondents expect payment, as is becoming increasingly true elsewhere, but the mindset of respondents does not match those of the people setting the questions.

Second, there are regional differences. As noted earlier, China consists of, basically, as many markets as you would like it to. The good news is that this makes it easier to position market entry: one can make mistakes in market entry in one place, learn the lessons, and start with a fresh sheet somewhere else. The bad news is that every new market in another region of China needs a fresh start. Chapter 2 discussed some of the regional variations that can affect the nature of markets and consumers. Let us consider just one: language. When conducting surveys in Guangzhou or Fujian, should you do so in Mandarin on the grounds that you have already learned and used Mandarin in Beijing and Shanghai? Or should you adapt to the local language? Most people will speak Mandarin, but they may be less willing to express themselves fully and honestly than they would in their local tongue. Closer is better: we strongly suggest that the data gatherers operate in the appropriate local vernacular. Written questionnaires, of course, make this easier.

The third problem is that of the layers of processing and subcontracting that the data may pass through. Each time it does so, some subtle spin may be applied. Inspection of the literature of Chinese agencies, for example Hengtong Marketing Consultant Corporation (one of the largest Chinese marketing research firms in Shanghai), reveals that many of the Western marketers and research agencies seem to be subcontracting to them. Perhaps therein lies the explanation of how relatively small firms can offer such a wide range of services across such a large market. There is probably quite a lot of laundry exchange (firms working for each other). Given the difficulty of understanding the market in the first place, one should always check who is collecting the original data and how many hands/interpretations it then goes through. Research that gets the Chinese whispers treatment is likely to be both more expensive and less reliable.

Market researchers are rationalists and so are consumers *when they are reporting their behaviour*. Yet much of the time, consumer behaviour is *not* rational. Applying (Western) logic to Chinese consumer behaviour is especially dangerous. Yet that is exactly what a firm applying Western market research methodology in China is likely to do. If the report is not littered with contradictions, it has been oversimplified. (This is also true of books on China, including this one.)

In consequence, the marketer cannot just commission the research and then accept the glossy, or otherwise, report. The research process has to be checked all the way through to the ultimate respondents, both when commissioning and afterwards.

The option of commissioning two identical surveys and comparing the answers may be no solution for the following reasons:

- It doubles the costs.
- The second firm may find the same mismatch of questions and answers that the first encountered.
- How will the differences be explained?

These problems are less severe with retail audits and media monitoring, which are really only checking the system and are more factual, as distinct from strategic.

That said, if the budget will stand it, there is benefit in using two research agencies in China: one Western-style and one Chinese. When they come up with conflicting results, picking through the various findings may increase the chance of getting close to the real picture. If there are no differences, we would suspect collusion, or else both subcontracted the work to the same firm.

The simplest quality control system is to collect similar data through one's own distribution channel (the salesforce) and to compare the answers. This has the advantage of improving the market orientation and understanding of the salesforce itself but is of little help until they are in place. New salespeople seeking to ingratiate themselves with the 'right' answers are a particular hazard and one should at the very least insist that the salesforce obtain customer points of view, not just provide their own. Those collected views should include the name of the source, phone number and date for later verification if required. The possibility of later verification should help reliability even if it does not take place.

Statistical information on China remains, at best, unreliable. But even if we could be sure that the information were accurate, what would it tell us? Quite often, one only needs to know that the number is big enough: 1 per cent of a billion people is still a lot of people. It is easy to find a group of consumers: for most firms, getting into two or three of China's big cities or provinces gives them enough *potential* customers to last them for many years. Increasingly, the advice from consultants in China is not to worry about the numbers: a company with a good product will find plenty of customers, or the customers will find them, provided that the fundamentals of promotion and distribution are in place. Many see the big issues as getting the product and distribution strategies right, and that means knowing what it is that Chinese consumers want, where they go to buy it, and how they make their buying decisions. The focus, increasingly, is on qualitative research.

Qualitative research

In the previous chapter we talked about the need for Western companies to become less reliant on Chinese partners for marketing, and to know more about what is taking place on the ground. That is true, but there is one important exception, agreed on by almost everyone: qualitative research into what makes consumers tick in China *must* be done by Chinese people. Never mind the language barriers, some say there is no way that most Chinese will open up to foreigners in their homes or in the workplace in the same way that they would to their fellow Chinese. That is hardly surprising; how many of us would open up and speak as freely to a Chinese market researcher as we would to a fellow Briton, American, etc.? But some advice goes so far as to suggest that even the presence of a foreigner during the interview process can taint the proceedings. There are ways around this, of course; sitting behind a two-way mirror in focus group sessions, or (less satisfactory) listening to tape recordings can give that all-important whiff of gunsmoke. And there are likely to be different reactions to foreigners for different products too; interviews concerning luxury products are less likely to be tainted than those for lower-priced consumer goods.

This being China, the opposite can also be true. It depends on the product category, how self-confident and used to foreigners the respondents are, and how skilled the foreigner is in merging into the wallpaper. The early part of any focus group is unnatural and needs to be discarded anyway. Typically the respondents forget about the microphone and the two-way mirror once they get going.

Bearing in mind the purpose of qualitative research, namely to get close to end users, it may be worth risking distortion from having too few respondents, but being involved, rather than turn the problem over to the professional researcher to do more efficiently. The choice may depend on the researcher's empathy with client and respondents.

In setting up focus groups, be aware that Chinese are probably more visually and less aurally focused than Americans, and probably to Westerners in general. Given the subtleties of spoken Chinese, this second result is not intuitively obvious, even though the two-dimensional visual nature of Chinese written characters relative to the (topologically) one-dimensional Roman script makes the first suggestion predictable. The consequence is that Chinese consumers should *see* names and other marketing stimuli more than they should *hear* them. In other words, research, and focus groups in particular, should provide more visual stimuli than they might in the West.

Thus the process of converting the raw gathered data into the neat folders presented to management carries the severe risk that the insights will be lost. No psychologist hired to run a focus group has the experience of the brand that the marketer should have. There is a good chance that the psychologist will miss the significance of what was said.

In particular, research should endeavour to bring cultural values, the usage occasion and the product *together* as realistically as possible. The less hypothetical or artificial the research situation for the consumer, the more reliable it will be.

Other information

In principle, many other sources of information are available, including own staff, especially the field staff, customers, trade associations, journalists and competitors. Even if there were time to track all these down, one would have to know what one does not know and what is important. And one would need much more openness than one can expect in China. Nevertheless, the difficulties with market research prompt reconsideration of the sources of intelligence used before modern methods became available.

Essentially, we are talking about reducing all the flotsam floating around marketing decision-making to the few key issues that (a) will make a major difference and (b) are the subject of substantive uncertainty within the top marketing team. Once identified, the collective *guanxiwang* can help to piece together some answers with or without formal market research.

In China, all information needs triangulation before one can take it seriously, or so they say, i.e. three or more independent sources. On the other hand, it only needs to be near enough to make the decision; it needs to be *relatively* accurate. Too often in the West, information is disconnected from its use; in other words, the required degree of precision and the relevance of information depend on what it will be used for. The West tends to seek quality in information for its own sake.

Planning

Plans are not important: planning is. Rehearsing the future can open up more options and develop more skills than waiting to be surprised by the daily events. You can practise as many times as you like, at some cost to today, but tomorrow only comes once. Or if you prefer a different cliché, there is Gary Hamel: 'to get to the future first, a company must find the shortest path between today and tomorrow'.[2] We have no idea what that means either, but it has sold tens of thousands of books and it feels right. One can get ahead of the game by engaging the brain sooner rather than later.

Planning is also learning: learning from the past, from other business units, functions and competitors and from seniors and juniors in the hierarchy. We need to understand *why* something works, so that we can extend the principles in new situations. Otherwise we can never distinguish context, or simply luck, from good marketing. Most plans are simply adaptions of those that went before. They are evolutionary not revolutionary. What works is extended, what doesn't is cut back. Darwinism, in effect, beats economic analysis. Successful behaviour is more convincing than theoretical calculations but this is no help to those preparing their first ever plan in China. Should they bring in experts, e.g. consultants, with previous experience of preparing marketing plans in China? Probably not, but having someone on the planning team with previous Chinese experience obviously helps.

Experiential (early) plans are quite different from experienced ones. The latter, as noted above, essentially build on that experience. Where little or no experience exists, then the planning process itself has to provide the best proxy for that experience. For example, the team can debate the likelihood of alternative scenarios. Rather than forecasting exact numbers, they can forecast how big – and how small – they could be. Thus the planning process itself simulates what will happen as best it can.

A plan is also the minutes of all the meetings, possibly over many months, that went into its preparation. Most Western firms, including those in China, spend far too long working a plan around the hierarchy. They begin before they can tell how the last plan worked out and then finish after the new year has already started.

They would be better off working twice as hard over one-quarter of the time.

While the whole state apparatus, including SOEs, is built around formal planning, few Chinese family businesses, not even the big ones, have any formal marketing plans. What they actually do evolves along Darwinian principles, part reacting to external stimuli (threats and opportunities in the market) and part based on the firm's own abilities and the nature of its business. This leads to some decisions that appear to make no sense – food retailers diversifying into bicycle repair being one recent example – and yet in terms of cash flow and profitability, they seem to work. So long as the current approach is bringing in satisfactory amounts of cash, it continues. When a new strategy is required, either because cash flow is drying up or because the leader has greater ambitions, the top team will analyse and test alternatives.

Experimentation, trial and error are endemic to market development (one Chinese maker of embroidery machines tried over 100 different products before hitting on one that worked. It was so successful that they were bought out by a Scandinavian firm two years later, each of the original partners making several tens of millions of dollars as a result). Procter & Gamble are no different in this respect. Where modern methods do help is in what Sunzi called the 'calculation'. From a range of possibilities, one can calculate which ideas can be tested on the smallest possible scale. One can calculate whether a full-scale model is feasible, e.g. the resources needed and the competitive response. And then when the experimental results are in, one can calculate which is, preferably singular (focus, sacrifice), the best to pursue. In short, well-managed businesses frequently fail small in order to win big. China has the great advantage of providing plenty of opportunities for failure. The question is whether one can learn enough, and survive long enough, to win big.

Reasons why Western companies think it important to write marketing plans down, and traditional Chinese businesses do not, include the following:

- managers change (average 16 months) in the West five times faster than in family businesses
- approvals are needed from different sites, perhaps cross-border
- the financial (budgetary) system is far more formalised and a main plan function is to gain financial approval

- lack of trust
- intolerance for ambiguity.

Linear Western logic has many advantages but it also drives out the opportunity for unusual solutions gradually to evolve. Explicit information-sharing is given greater weight than implicit. Nonaka and Takeuchi show how the Japanese are better than the US in developing strategically new businesses because they are more patient with implicit information and codify it (make it explicit) more carefully.[3] Professor Max Boisot, who started China's first MBA school in the 1980s, independently came to much the same conclusion.[4]

So where does this leave us in practical terms? We suggest a small cross-functional team is assembled both to plan and to implement the plan. Planning for other people is a waste of time. Notwithstanding our reservations about formality, bridging the East–West cultural gap is helped by the written word, so long as the Western side does not give the plan itself too much authority. It is not a legal contract but merely an *aide-memoire*, indicating where the market learning has reached. Flexibility and the door to new learning must be left open.

A plan should be developed over three phases and then, if the calculations reveal that the objectives have not been met, it needs to recycle through all three until it does:

- strategy
- *guanxi*
- calculation.

A bad but frequent practice is to do it the other way about. This starts with the required bottom line, deduces what marketing expenditure will be authorised, and then forecasts the sales needed to balance the books. Since the end result looks much like the previous plan with the date changed, this tends to work quite well, which in turn reinforces the behaviour until something goes wrong.

Good marketing practice, however, begins with the customers and what they want, or might want in the context of the competitive environment and the company's own capabilities. We call this the E+3Cs analysis (Environment, Customer, Competitors, own Company). From this, as we have noted above, emerges the brand's positioning statement (one page or less). A plan without this crisp positioning statement can be consigned to the rubbish bin. The positioning will include customer segmentation and geographic focus.

Having established who the friends and foes are, why the friends will love the brand and how it will kill the competition, we can move on to develop the specifics of building the brand–customer relationship that is the essence of marketing. Who exactly make up the brand's *guanxiwang*? Draw the network and prioritise those who matter most. Draw the network of the key players and their relationships. Players form nodes and relationship lines. No relationship means no line.

Every brand has many relationships and it is just as important to prioritise time as money. What activities will most enhance those relationships? Why should they want to buy more, more often, and at higher prices?

Guanxi is at the heart of creating demand, which is what marketing is all about. Supply, even in China, *should* be easier.

Finally, and only finally, we need to quantify everything thus far. If financial numbers can be assigned, well and good. Quite often, brand equity (the brand–customer *guanxi*) can only be estimated non-financially and even then the numbers are fuzzy. Concepts like awareness, salience, perceived quality relative to the competition, satisfaction, trust and commitment are important but vague – especially in China where, as we have seen above, market research data are less reliable. Nevertheless these calculations are worth making, using estimates where hard research is not justified. The process of measurement brings focus.

Planning should be fun but it rarely is. It should be fun because it is the annual opportunity to learn, to be creative and to play with wild ideas. We only live once (although that is just a majority opinion) but we certainly have the opportunity to rehearse next year's life as often as we like.

Smirnoff in Shanghai

Smirnoff vodka, owned by Diageo, is (2007) the world's largest premium spirit brand. In 1995, Diageo's predecessor company's Chinese arm, IDVC, began to consider the launch of Smirnoff on the China market, and chose Shanghai as its point of entry.

The Chinese imported spirits market was dominated by brandy (mainly cognac). Since 1980, the market had grown in volume by about 40 times. Local products are mostly white spirits, of which Mao Tai is most famous. Most are highly aromatic and heavily flavoured. They are also relatively cheap, considerably less than imported cognac. The local makers are highly fragmented, however, with the top 17 names accounting for just 2 per cent of volume. There are around 40,000 distilleries in China; the largest name, Fen Jiu, was selling, at that time, some 17 million cases annually.

The Group's usual policy was to spend on advertising *behind* distribution, partly on the grounds that there is no point in inviting consumers to buy the brand if they cannot find it, but also to fund advertising out of sales revenue. However, such is the potential value of brand equity in this case, that establishing a strong position was perceived as necessary to support distribution of a high-price product. The key task, then, was to develop a promotional strategy to support this goal.

Given IDVC's limited resources, the alternatives were seen as twofold:

- Spend whatever could be afforded on a focused TV campaign and measure the results. This would mean spending ahead of profitability.
- Build word of mouth through targeted, on-premise promotions (one example might be JJs, then the most trendy and popular nightclub in Shanghai) and later build advertising behind distribution.

Juxinghe

In 2004, Guo Yongsheng opted for voluntary redundancy from Capital Steel, the Beijing-based state-owned enterprise where he had worked for the past 16 years. 'I wanted to see what I could do without the iron rice bowl [the cradle-to-grave social security system enjoyed by workers in SOEs]', he said. Unemployed, he at first faced a bleak future, but then his local social security department arranged for him and other unemployed men to visit a small business entrepreneurship fair in a Beijing suburb. One of the displays at the fair featured waterless car-wash products. According to Guo, he knew at once that this was the future. Car ownership was rising rapidly, at a rate of about a thousand a day in Beijing, and so was environmental consciousness. A 'green' car-care product was sure to be a success, and importantly, government approval of the concept got him permits to operate and access to funding without delay.

By 2008 Guo's company had established four car-wash outlets in the city and was planning to open more, using a franchising model rather than directly owning them himself. The business name, Juxinghe, means 'cooperation leads to prosperity and friendship leads to wealth'. Guo chose his franchising partners carefully, often from among his own employees; he said he would never choose a partner who was not willing to wash cars himself. By establishing himself in suburban residential areas, Guo has managed to get a 'neighbourhood feel' to his business, employing people from near each outlet who often know their customers personally.

His method of market research is simple; he walks around different districts, counts numbers of cars on the street to determine the market potential, and engages passers-by in conversation to determine their attitude to waterless car washing. He does not employ an agency or researchers, nor even his own staff, feeling that this task is too vital to be delegated. Only by coming face to face with his potential customers does Guo feel certain that he can understand their attitudes and wishes.

Conclusions

Victory in war requires intensive research of the rival. Entering an unfamiliar market and making big money needs good intelligence too. Market research contributes crucially to the foundation of corporate strategy and the detailed corporate plans. But because in China it is expensive and unreliable, it needs to be used more selectively and with quality controls. And given the highly dynamic environment and regional variety, it may soon be outdated. However, we need plans, since planning is vitally important to learning about this particular world – China. The next challenge, to convert planning into action, is the reason why plans must be constructed by those who will have to execute them – which is why we can save money on consultants.

China has masses of statistics and available research, far more than any company can handle. Many of these data are inconsistent and unreliable. This bothers Westerners more than it does Chinese, who usually look for pictures rather than precision. A fuzzy focus is quite good enough.

To navigate through all this, a Western firm will need to be tough-minded in distinguishing between what they must know and what may be nice to know but perhaps should be abandoned. Integrating research needs and the planning process, be it the one outlined above or some other, is critical to distinguishing between essential and inessential information. The process needs to be seen as a whole, whereby planning supports information and information supports planing.

The overseas Chinese

As far as this chapter is concerned, differences between marketing to the overseas Chinese and to markets in the PRC are differences of degree, not of kind. As mentioned at the end of Chapter 7, overseas Chinese markets are more discriminating and less naïve; but the mainland Chinese are catching up very fast. The approaches to marketing planning and thinking outlined here should work as well in Taipei or Singapore as in Shanghai, always providing that the detailed planning and thinking have been adapted to local market conditions. But that adaptation has to be made inside China too; see Chapter 2 on China's geographical and cultural diversity.

9 Rightness and correct form

The *yi* and *li* of organisation
in China

> People say that we [the younger Chinese generation] are only interested in money, but that's not true. We want to succeed at our lives, to make the most of the opportunities our parents never had. Westerners think all they have to do is pay us and we will eat out of their hands. But we want opportunity, not charity.
>
> (Anonymous young manager, Beijing)

> I want to do something different besides working the earth all the time. If I cannot succeed with my own efforts, then I deserve my failure. But please first give me a chance.
>
> (Bian Chengyu, Sichuanese entrepreneur)

At the beginning of Chapter 8, we remarked that there were few formal studies of how Chinese firms do marketing. The same cannot be said of organisations and human resource management (HRM). The nature and culture of Chinese business organisations continue to be intensely interesting to both Chinese and Western scholars. The big question is whether Chinese businesses will turn to Western models of organisation and HRM, or whether they will continue to use essentially Chinese models with a few borrowings from Western best practice.

Views range from the notion that Chinese management is rapidly adapting Western methods of organisation and people management, to the exact opposite, namely that China is distinct and will remain so. A third alternative suggests that both are true, and that what is emerging is a synthesis that will incorporate key features of Western- and Chinese-style management and create a new model or paradigm. But that reconciliation of paradox is not Daoist. The fourth, and probably most likely, alternative has the two philosophies existing side by side and without reconciliation, in much the same way that Western and Chinese medicine co-exist in China.

As ever, the theories help us to understand what might be happening behind the scenes but, ultimately, the approach to managing organisations and people (organisations being, after all, collections of people) in China must be based on pragmatism. If we follow Alfred Chandler's dictum that 'structure follows strategy', then we need to work out what that strategy is and then design an organisation that will 'work', without getting too worried about following any one theory too closely. Experience suggests that strategy and structure are actually much more interdependent – that is, the kind of organisational structure we adopt influences the strategic choices we make. But this merely reinforces the point that there are no hard and fast rules. The best strategy and the best organisation are the ones suited to the time and place.

That suggests that when working in China, we need to consider Chinese models of organisation, similarly to Chinese models of strategy back in Chapter 3. Obviously, Chinese notions of hierarchy, role and function are different from those in the West. But should Western firms in China adapt to the national model? Or is the Chinese model outdated and should Chinese firms adapt to what is taught in Western (and also Chinese) business schools? Some consultants follow a recipe-book approach, trying to reorganise and restructure every Chinese firm until it looks like a Harvard case study. Sometimes this works, but more often it does not. There has been an unfortunate tendency for consultants to expect Chinese businesses to adopt a Western model of organisation and hierarchy, and then to blame the local managers when things don't work out. Many Chinese managers freely admit that there are things they can learn from the West, but they also believe their own style of organisation works. So, just as with marketing, some adaptation is necessary.

Come to that, it *is* marketing. Consumers are the ultimate people the firm has to satisfy but it has to satisfy its own employees first. The last 25 years have seen increasing recognition that internal marketing (to employees) uses many of the same disciplines and tools as external marketing. It follows that top management need to think about, empathise with, and market the firm to Chinese employees with as much adaptation as they need to market to Chinese customers.[1]

There is also disagreement about what motivates Chinese employees and managers. There have been a number of large-scale motivational surveys conducted, and each seems to paint a different picture. Some say that salaries are by far and away the most important factor, others that salaries are relatively unimportant and that chances for personal development and growth such as training and travel are often critical factors. There is little to be learned from this, save to underscore the perils of conducting statistical research in China. When we come to look at actual cases, some companies have been able to attract and retain key staff by paying higher wages than their rivals. Others, like General Motors in Shanghai, pay less than their competitors but offer more chances for development, training and promotion.

Therefore, let us follow the rule of thumb adopted early in this book, that any position may be true, but so simultaneously may its opposite. Depending on where, when and how the company is operating, salaries might be the only real factor; or they might not. Adaptation to Western models of organisation might work; or it might not. As a reader, you are probably saying at this point that this is somewhat less than helpful advice. But in this chapter we are going to look at some of the reasons *why* things differ. And our conclusion is that adaptation is, on the whole, preferable to an imposed Western model; furthermore that while salary is a strong motivator, there are many other factors at work as well. In the end, structure doesn't just follow strategy; it also follows the needs of the people who go to make up the organisation. Successful management in China may depend on the ability to manage in 'Chinese style' and provide Chinese employees with the kind of organisation that suits their needs. As more than one recent book has suggested, building *guanxi* between employers and employees can be a critical factor (though by no means the only critical factor; salaries and working conditions matter too).[2]

The first section of this chapter deals with hierarchy. Almost all organisations are hierarchic: the differences lie in the shape of those hierarchies (flat or vertiginous), and interfunctional and senior/junior relationships, i.e. how they work. Western companies are more likely to make decisions up and down the hierarchy, whereas Chinese managers are more likely to wait to be told.

An even larger adjustment needs to be made when working with Chinese employees, who have different sets of work values and often quite different goals. Many Western companies are currently experiencing severe difficulties in recruiting and retaining staff in China. Some of their difficulties may stem from trying to manage in

'Western style'. Nothing is more fatal than assuming, when human relations are involved, that Western management techniques are more advanced; the hardware technology may be but the people are not.

After hierarchy, we look at the question of specialisation – or the lack of it – and then decision-making and leadership. People management has much to do with coping with risk. The West uses controls, especially financial controls, to do that while China uses *guanxi*. No wonder Western accountants struggle in China. Both systems work in their own context but severe losses can, and do, occur when they collide. Finally, we will briefly review some basic HRM bread and rations issues, such as unions and the Party, pay, bonuses and training. Today, enough experience has built up for HR managers from both cultures to be thoroughly trained in the PRC context, e.g. using video materials.

Chinese organisations are strongly permeated by Confucian values which do not always match short-term business interests. Some years ago, Oled Shenkar summed up the key distinctive features that characterise Chinese organisations as follows,[3] noting that all have parallels in the *Analects* of Confucius:

- Formalised, detailed rules are destructive to human relationships.
- Flexibility and versatility are essential qualities for a leader.
- The leader must set and enforce standards of commitment and morality through personal example.
- Economic incentives alone will not motivate subordinates.
- A leader must be courteous, friendly, helpful and sincere when dealing with subordinates (*ren*).

This being China, the opposites are sometimes also true. The Chinese have plenty of formal rules in business, success comes from determination (inflexibility), and Mao was not famous for his morality, at least in his later years. Money sometimes is the key and some Chinese bosses are downright rude. There are differences within China too: southern Chinese complain that northerners are too formal and too rigid; northerners respond that their southern counterparts are too informal and do not pay attention to detail. Stereotyping any culture is dangerous, but Shenkar was more right than wrong. There will always be variations in some of the dimensions he describes, but most will hold good most of the time.

Hierarchies

Most Chinese organisations are strongly hierarchical when compared with their Western counterparts, in the sense that the channels of reporting and authority are more formal, if not authoritarian. On the other hand, the distance between the bosses and the workers would be shorter, with a few strong leaders at the top, a few managers running around in the middle, and the majority of employees at or near the bottom. The majority of Chinese small and medium-sized businesses are led by a single dominant owner/manager/director. The same is true of most large businesses as well, though in some cases there will be a dominant group, perhaps 3–4 directors are most, who are clearly *primus inter pares*. Very often, these dominant directors were also the founders of the business, or joined early in its history.

But some of the difference is temporal rather than cultural. British businesses used to be like that before middle management expanded. In Chinese SOEs and British nationalised industries, aimless bureaucracies took over the asylums. There is not much evidence that China is ready for the leaner, flatter organisations now thought to be best practice in the West. Eventually, yes, but now, possibly not.

The majority of overseas Chinese businesses are family affairs. Hong Kong businesses are most often very family-oriented; Li Ka-shing's son Victor is prominent in Cheung Kong and Hutchison Whampoa, while Peter Wu 'inherited' the managing of Wheelock from his father-in-law, Sir Y.K. Pao. A dominant family member, usually the father, is head of the business; other family members occupy key posts; and employees lower down the organisational pyramid look to the father and the other members of the family for leadership.

In mainland China the situation is somewhat different. We have already noted that the Communist Party tried to re-make society along Confucian lines by casting itself as the 'father' or 'head of the family' for all Chinese. In business terms, that became a little confused as the Party cadre member, who held the ultimate power, was not usually the general manager. Power gradually switched in most businesses away from the cadre but the Party should not be forgotten when considering organisational matters.

This history can be glibly recounted but it has had devastating effects on individual people. For example, Wu Zinan inherited a silk factory in Suzhou from his father in the late 1940s and ran the factory until 1956 when it was nationalised. The Party asked him to stay on as manager, which he did, believing genuinely in the Party and wanting to help improve the Chinese economy. During the Cultural Revolution he was sacked from his job and forced to clean the factory floors wearing a dunce's cap; his erstwhile employees were encouraged to mock and abuse him. In 1976 he was reinstated; in the 1990s, well past retirement age, he was working to take his factory into the new age of the enterprise economy.

Today in the private sector, there has not (yet) been time for long-standing family-owned businesses to have emerged. Single dominant owner-managers are common, or else there will be a group drawn together, either by ties of kinship or by bonds of community or education. It is not uncommon for classmates at university to hit on the idea for a business and, upon graduation, to jointly set it up. Other small entrepreneurial groups emerge from SOEs, neighbourhoods or villages. One such example is the little group of rice farmers who founded what later became one of China's largest bottled-water companies. It is entirely possible, even likely, that classic family-owned Chinese businesses will emerge as the founding generation hands on to their children. And even where family ties do not exist, the concept of *guanxi* still dominates. University alumni and the village community are merely substitutes for the family.

The Confucian ideal of the family is thus translated easily and naturally to business. One of the consequences is that decision-making and power are highly concentrated and the 'power distance' (the barrier sensed by those lower in the hierarchy between them and those who run the business) is significantly increased. Cross-cultural studies have shown that power distance is greater in China even than in Japan.[4]

Why these cross-cultural studies are misleading

The problem with much of the cross-cultural analysis is worth a short detour. The most famous of these studies is that by Geert Hofstede, a Dutchman, who processed responses from about 100,000 employees of IBM, which removed any confounding of his results due to varying corporate cultures. Multivariate analysis originally yielded four dimensions of culture, of which power–distance was one. When the analysis was subsequently recalculated in Hong Kong, they discovered a fifth: individuality–collectivism. Japan was seen as being highly collective whereas the USA is individualistic.

China, however, is highly individualistic and highly collective at the same time. Tony Fang, originally at MIT and then an academic in Sweden, was a pioneer debunker of the Hofstede approach which is as much a reflection of his own Dutch culture as a description of the cultures being observed.[5] As Fang was attacking what was by then the conventional wisdom, he had a problem getting published.

The issue turns on the different mindsets (linear v. circular thinking) being applied to the research. The West typically uses the equivalent of Euclidean space and describes things like culture with the smallest number of orthogonal (independent) dimensions. Chinese thinking employs relativist, curved space.

This is most easily explained by considering two people walking off in opposite directions. The further they walk in Euclidean space, the further they are from each other. The more individualist one is, and the more collectivist the other, the further apart the two are. But suppose the path they are taking is not a straight line but a circle. Although they set off in opposite directions, they will ultimately meet up. In this visualisation, one can be either collectivist or individualistic, or both/neither.

A simpler explanation would be that the two are independent dimensions; but that would not accord with Hofstede's mathematics.

One consequence of this family-styled system is that Chinese businesses have can have short lifespans. The Chinese tend to be at least as bad at succession planning as foreigners. Wheelock is an exception to the rule that the business tends to die with the leader. In Hong Kong, nearly as many businesses disappear as appear each year. The majority of closures are due not to insolvency, but simply because the owner dies, or wishes to retire and does not have a successor. The retirement of a strong man often causes a large decrease in profitability. Not all these businesses simply close their doors, of course; many are sold or merged with those of their neighbours, but for all practical purposes they no longer exist.

The three conclusions we draw are, first, that the organisation should be seen as a family. In China, where business and private lives are not so clearly demarcated, this makes sense. Second, the formal structure is developing along the same lines as elsewhere but, for historical reasons, empowerment is some way behind.

Third, respect for authority and power is much greater. Chinese managers have a greater need for approval both in the sense of getting permission or instruction and in the sense of positive reinforcement.

Lack of specialisation

It may seem odd in the light of the foregoing, but Chinese businesses tend not to employ specialists. The hierarchies that exist focus on power, responsibility and salary; they are less likely to be task-related. This was particularly true of old-style SOEs. In a Chinese steel mill, for example, individual employees are likely to be notionally capable (though not necessarily trained) to carry out a variety of tasks ranging from stoking a blast furnace, to skimming slag, to sweeping the floor. Traditionally, a work unit is given a production quota to fill; it is up to the members of the unit itself to decide who carries out which tasks.

Before deriding this notion of management, we should remember that it was long employed in the West. Many heavily industrial enterprises in China, and this includes many of the early private sector ones as well as SOEs, are run on the lines of purest Taylorism. Taylor's theories on scientific management met with a mixed reception in his own country (and even more mixed in Britain), but they were adopted enthusiastically in Russia by one of Taylor's greatest fans, Vladimir Ilich Lenin. Stalinism has even been called 'a weird blend of Communism and Taylorism' by one American observer. The Plekhanov Institute in Moscow trained many young Marxists from around the world, including from China. When the People's Republic of China was established in 1949, this approach to enterprise management was one of the Western ideas that Mao was keen to see adapted to meet Chinese needs. The point to this story is that some Chinese, at least, are aware of their production system's history and origins. A manager in Shanghai, when told that his company should adopt Western management methods, responded, 'Why, when they worked so well the last time?'

This style of management is proving hard to break; the old systems are still in place. People have a hierarchy within their work unit based on salary and position, not on task. The work unit in turn has a hierarchy within the business, based on the nature of its work and, very often, on its past success in filling production quotas. In the past this has led to serious problems of overproduction. Early in this decade, white-goods makers around China were cheerfully pumping out a huge volume of goods, pleased with the efficiency of their production lines and only dimly aware that the market for their products was saturated. Many of these companies disappeared as a result.

Only gradually are functional distinctions beginning to emerge, and with them a focus on markets and customers rather than the internal workings of the business. Although many Chinese students study marketing, few companies have formal marketing departments. HR departments are beginning to emerge, but are criticised as not being very effective. *Plus ça change*; the first grumble when Western managers meet for a Friday night drink is likely to be the incompetence of their HR department. Finance is one area where progress is being made, as firms learn the advantages of staff specialists who can understand and work in the newly emerging equity and debt markets. Even so, surveys that have looked at specialisation have found that Chinese businesses have a much higher proportion of the total staff directly concerned with the production of the company's main product or service – probably 90 per cent of the total. Exceptions can be made for companies such as Lenovo which have borrowed more ideas about organisation and function from the West and have larger backroom and support departments, but these exceptions are still very rare.

Decision-making and leadership

The typical (good) Chinese manager operates in a very hands-on style and is familiar with all aspects of the business. He or she delegates far less than his or her Western counterpart, spends less time in meetings and formal consultations, and more time actually making decisions and implementing policy. Some surveys have suggested that Chinese managers believe that travelling and meetings are the least important aspects of their jobs; they would rather spend more time doing desk work, assessing and evaluating information and making decisions. It is interesting that in one survey, only 31 per cent of the sample believed that scheduled meetings were an important activity and only 4 per cent believed that unscheduled meetings were important.

Decision-making in Chinese organisations tends to be autocratic and takes place at a high level. Decisions are usually made by one individual, the owner/manager/director, and in private. The results of the decision are then announced, usually without explanation. It is assumed that the decision has had sufficient consideration before it is made and will be understandable to those people under the influence of this decision.

However, there may well have been extensive informal consultation first. The good Chinese manager listens to the workers and takes their opinions into account, up to a point. There may also have been lateral discussions with ministries, local officials and the *guanxiwang*. Decision-making in China can be remarkably quick or remarkably slow. The quick ones are where experience provides the (apparent) solution. Nevertheless, there is not much democracy about all this; the leader makes the decisions and the employees are expected to carry them out exactly.

Challenging a decision once it has been made is often considered a serious offence; it causes the superior to lose face. At this stage, workers are expected to keep their views to themselves. There is a saying: 'Honour the hierarchy first, your vision of truth second.'

One consequence is that people lower down the hierarchy tend to be bad at taking responsibility. There is a great deal of buck-passing and procrastination in Chinese organisations: more even than in the West.

Management by relationships

Western companies use systems to control relationships. Chinese organisations use relationships to control systems. Western companies use a legalistic framework of procedures and controls to police relations. One must not exaggerate: both cultures operate both arrangements, but the balance differs. This legalistic and financial control framework is confusing for Chinese managers who feel mistrusted and do not know how they stand in relationship to the boss. It also tells them something very dangerous: if this is the Western game, let us find out how it works and beat the system. Of course, this confusion is also a function of novelty. Once these systems become commonplace and accepted, the problems should decrease.

Chinese managers believe that one of their key tasks is to maintain harmony within the organisation, both between people and between work units. This is particularly the case where Confucian values are strong. When the workers create discord or challenge leaders' decisions, their actions create bad feeling and cause loss of face.

Leadership anywhere in the world operates on the basis of respect. One may not like, or even admire, the leader but if he or she has established a good track record and observes the main principles laid down by Sunzi, the troops will follow. On the other hand, leaders are certainly expected to develop a relationship with their employees. This is formalised as *wu lun*, the relationship of unequal pairs; each employee should feel a personal connection with the employer or manager, and should feel to some degree dependent on that leader. This relationship gives the employee a claim on the leader as the surrogate father-figure who owes the former protection and help. There are all sorts of stories of Chinese business owners and senior managers being approached while walking in the park or playing golf by employees with problems to solve. For example, a few years ago a Shanghai manager was visited at his home by an employee at 11 pm in order to help patch up the breakdown of the latter's marriage.

At the same time, management is not just about leadership. One can argue which matters more, but persuading people to follow is just part of the story. A tactical plan needs to be drawn up, practical decisions need to be made, and resources need to be in place – and not diverted. Business schools do not teach much about leadership for the simple reason that they teach management. It will be interesting to watch the principles taught in China's MBA schools (from Western textbooks) collide with the practices in their workplaces. They are taught mechanical controls, but operate in a *guanxi* environment for handling risk. The vast majority of MBA places are part-time; the students are also holding down middle management jobs. In our limited observation, the students do not so much attempt to synthesise the cultures, as learn to operate in both. Conversations with Western managers and consultants in China confirm this. What is interesting is that some of the Western managers are growing more comfortable with this and even learning how to do it themselves.

The relationship approach to risk management clearly works better in small family businesses than in multinationals, though it has to be said that the mafia, with similar if criminal and fear-laden characteristics, seems to span continents without difficulty. But note the need, as with *guanxi*, for close family-like ties. Maintaining these relationships requires constant communication – hence the significance of the mobile phone.

Western firms do not need, even if they could, to abandon the control systems that have served them well elsewhere. On the other hand, in China they need to understand why their Chinese colleagues find them awkward, to say the least. They should develop *guanxi* and Western control systems in parallel.

The 'personnel problem' for Western companies in China

Polls of Western businesses asking respondents about the problems of doing business in China usually show that recruiting and training managers and staff come at the top of the list. This is a little odd; after all, Western companies have been honing and refining their personnel management techniques for decades. Most have a senior HR person at director level, influencing policy and making certain that the company remains focused on its staff. Chinese companies, on the other hand, have no concept of personnel management; instead they have *ren shi quan* or personnel authority. The company personnel manager, if there is one at all, has responsibility for hiring and firing, promotion (or punishment) and salaries. The situation become odder still when one reflects that most Chinese managers approve of Western management styles and believe they are more suited to the needs of business than traditional Chinese authoritarian management.

Why then are Western companies failing to cope with the Chinese labour market? Some companies continue to report annual labour turnover of as much as 80 per cent, and over 20 per cent is common. A survey in late 2007 found that China has the highest labour turnover rates of any country in Asia. Various explanations have been proposed:

- By providing higher salaries, Western companies are encouraging Chinese managers to become more mobile.
- Traditional Chinese values are breaking down and China is becoming a much more fluid society.
- Chinese employees may feel loyalty to Chinese organisations, but not to Western organisations.

There may be some truth in all these explanations, but none is complete in itself. Certainly there is no excuse for the hands-in-the-air attitude adopted by some Western companies, which simply believe that high rates of turnover are a given factor in China. The ability to recruit and manage a stable, loyal, committed workforce is a key success factor, in China as elsewhere. There are of course two separate and related problems: (a) where does a company find managers and skilled people more generally, and (b) having found them, how does it keep them?

In the 1990s, finding Chinese with managerial experience and talent was not easy. Western companies brought in expatriates, at vast expense and not always with great success. Some expats and their families adapted easily to the adventure of life and work in China, while others could not cope. But the ideal for both Western and Chinese companies was the Chinese expatriate, the overseas Chinese with business experience in Southeast Asia or North America or Europe, who was willing to come back and work in the homeland. Such managers were able to command considerable salary premiums over and above their mainland Chinese counterparts. This caused resentment in some cases among the mainland Chinese, who felt they were being undervalued. The demand for these overseas Chinese managers was also very high, and they were prone to job-hopping, easily lured away by salaries and benefits superior to those they were already receiving.

Today, the salary gap has narrowed as more and more skilled and well-educated mainland Chinese managers are emerging. The gold standard now is the mainland Chinese manager with a degree from a good Chinese university and then an MBA from an American or European business school, especially one with a recognised brand such as Harvard, Stanford, MIT or the London Business School. Once again, there are not enough of these to go around, demand is high, and they are paid accordingly. There is a significant salary differential between Chinese managers with an overseas MBA and those with an MBA from a university in China. A smaller salary gap exists between graduates from mainland schools and those from institutions elsewhere in Southeast Asia, especially from established universities in Hong Kong and Singapore.

The nature of the problem has changed but the problem remains. The rapid growth of the Chinese economy means that the demand for managerial talent, and for skilled workers more generally, continues to outstrip supply. The best and the brightest are going to the biggest companies, the Lenovos and other large Chinese companies, to the domestic and foreign banks and finance houses. Ask the senior managers of these institutions if they are worried about the war for talent in China, and they will tell you no; they work hard and invest heavily in identifying the best talent, have deep pockets and can offer good career prospects to any ambitious young Chinese manager. They concede, however, that they are still willing to hire expatriate Western managers too, especially if they are young, have few ties, and have taken the trouble to learn Mandarin and to read Chinese. But all this leaves the smaller and less attractive companies, Western or Chinese, with a problem. Until the supply side catches up, they will have to do their recruiting from among those the big companies have left to one side. This calls for a creative approach to recruitment, and to people management more generally.

Training and development

There are marked differences in education among Chinese employees, depending on the region and also on the age group. Those who should have been at school during the Cultural Revolution received no education at all for several years. The generation that entered school after 1976, however, has been educated to a fairly high standard. Many more people in China speak English than in England, although certificates of proficiency should not be taken at face value. In some JVs, English may seem to have been adopted by the seniors as the working language, but that is just being polite to the expatriate(s).

Technical training is usually of a very high standard, given the variable technology levels with many hundreds of technical training institutes around the country. In areas such as electronics, training is rapidly catching up with that available in the West. However, especially in the last two or three years, demand for workers with technical skills has increased rapidly. Local authorities are scrambling to establish more training facilities, but some of these are hasty affairs and the products (graduates) they turn out are of lower standard. It is advised that, where possible, graduates of the older and more prestigious technical schools should be sought.

There has been an explosion in management training in recent years. By 2002, 56 universities were authorised to offer MBA programmes; by 2007 the number had increased to 230. The number of MBA graduates (including those from EMBA, Executive MBA programmes) from Chinese institutions doubled from 2004 to 2007, from 10,000 to 20,000. Several notes of caution need to be sounded here. First, 20,000 is a big number, but according to recent estimates, nearly double that number of graduates is required annually to keep up with demand. Second, evidence suggests that most people signing up for MBAs are doing so, rather like many of their counterparts in the West, because they hope that the letters 'MBA' in their résumés will advance their careers and give them better salaries; there are real doubts about how much they actually learn. Academics teaching on these programmes and companies recruiting their graduates have complained that MBA students at Chinese universities appear to be interested only in rote learning and are poor at decision-making and problem-solving, which are key managerial skills that the MBA is supposed to provide.

The MBA is a useful tool for helping young managers to learn some of their tradecraft, but is not a magic bullet guaranteeing managerial success. Having taught on MBA programmes at a number of universities in different countries, the authors of this book have observed how the quality of MBA programmes can vary widely. And the quality of most Chinese MBA programmes leaves a lot to be desired. Lecturers with little work experience or education use out-of-date and often badly translated Western business textbooks with scant relevance to China. Little attempt is made to teach marketing or other soft skills; only mathematics, economics and accounting attempt to keep up with modern best practice.

The most trenchant criticisms of Chinese MBA programmes come from Chinese managers. Possibly this is because, having had access to Western-trained MBAs for some years, their expectations are higher. Western managers tend to be more tolerant, but they acknowledge that the Chinese MBAs they hire require much support and mentoring before they are ready to take on managerial roles. This involves costs in terms of money and time.

Many young Chinese realise this, of course, and opt to go overseas for management training, with the costs sometimes picked up by families. They cite the need for better training in areas such as corporate finance, marketing and international business, which are the areas where Chinese business schools are especially weak. Again, the quality of some of this training varies; some Western universities push these young people quickly through sub-standard courses while collecting large fees and handing over a diploma of sorts.

That is the gloomy side. The bright side is that in some Chinese institutions, quality is improving rapidly. Investment has been made in top-quality staff, Chinese and foreign, and standards are high. Jiao Tong University in Shanghai was ranked 41 in the world by the *Financial Times* in 2007; in the Chinese-speaking world, only Hong Kong UST Business School was higher, and the prestigious Nanyang University in Singapore was several places lower. Also in Shanghai there is the China–Europe International Business School, which trains Chinese managers to European MBA standards. Other rising stars include the School of Economics and Management at Tsinghua University, the business school at Zhejiang University, the Guanghua School of Management at Peking University and the privately funded Cheung Kong Business School, also in Beijing. The hope in China is that the high standards being set by these business schools will force other Chinese business schools to raise their game. However, recent experience in the West, especially the UK, says we should not count on this. A two-tier system is more likely, with a few high-quality schools and a number of also-rans.

Many of China's new companies are led by men and women with no formal management education at all. They have grown their businesses through hard work and common sense, but with the environment growing more complex, they are finding that these are not quite enough. So top-level executives, directors and even chairmen and CEOs are signing up for MBAs. With all the caveats on quality above, this trend is helping to create a generation of business leaders who are essentially Chinese in outlook but can speak the Western business language and understand the concepts by which Westerners manage. We noted above that successful Chinese managers are those who can work in both systems.

Of course, not all good managers or potential managers have MBAs. In the past, Western companies recruited heavily from the graduates of the best Chinese universities, especially but not exclusively from the faculties of science and economics. The rising popularity of law as a field of study also offers opportunities. These universities train people in the techniques of analysis and rigorous thinking, which are foundation stones for good management in every case. For companies wishing to avoid the rat race of competing for MBA graduates of unknown and sometimes dubious quality, the universities still offer an interesting alternative.

In sum, the quality of management education in China is uneven, to put it kindly. But there are strong indications that quality is improving at a number of institutions, and that some like Jiao Tong and CEIBS can claim with some justification to be world class. Just as in the West, it is not enough to know that a potential hire has an MBA, or technical qualification or whatever. Where the qualification came from and how it was obtained must be checked.

Recruitment and rewards

Dismissal of an employee in China may be difficult but it is not the main problem: keeping people is. Western managers in assigning roles may well cause loss of face, and where that happens the individual is likely to resign. In both recruiting and terminating employees, face is of prime importance.

Although, as mentioned above, Chinese employees at all levels are eager to improve their own skills and make themselves more marketable, Chinese managers are not currently seeing personal career development in the same way that foreigners do. Westerners job-hop too. Firm comparisons are not available and the diminished loyalty by firms to employees has been matched, not surprisingly, reciprocally. Younger managers look to the market rather than their pensions as security. Critics of young Chinese managers, however, suggest that they are doing themselves no favours by accepting the next higher pay-cheque that comes along, rather than building a strong career (or CV/résumé, if you wish to be cynical). It is alleged that they move from one job to another with no personal goal beyond that of making money. The chance of a trip overseas is an important incentive for managers who have never been out of China, though one survey shows that managers who have been out of China once often do not want to go again. Been there, got the T-shirt.

The old SOE culture provided housing, education and health benefits to make up for low wages. However big the salary from the JV, these benefits are hard to make up, especially in areas such as Shanghai where housing is particularly expensive. A favoured solution was to leave one partner on the state payroll, with the benefits, whilst the other works for a JV or WFOE. Today, with SOE employment declining, both partners are taking the plunge.

Company benefits are, therefore, important. Where housing is particularly expensive, companies can either provide employee housing directly or a cash housing allowance on top of the pay-cheque. More important and more widely provided are benefits such as health care. Pensions are becoming increasingly important too, as the state pension system is being de-emphasised (possibly a code word for 'cut back', though it is too soon to tell). Benefits sometimes amount to a 50 per cent supplement to the base salary.

Benefits can have a direct impact on retention. IBM and Procter & Gamble both offer comprehensive benefits packages, and both have very low staff turnover rates. Ciba, Bell and Shanghai Volkswagen also pay well, offer internal chances for promotion and good benefits packages, and have low turnover rates. Those with high turnover rates are usually smaller operations or representative offices, with limited offerings to employees.

Promotion equals status. Before economic liberalisation, workers were often restricted in their choice of employment. They therefore worked hard to work their way up the promotion ladder in their own organisation.

One of the consequences of a planned economy is that, in many organisations, the drive to meet production quotas took precedence over health and safety issues. Certainly health and safety standards have suffered in China, and there have been a number of serious accidents in recent years.

There are virtually no restrictions on recruitment, and the end of many internal travel regulations means most Chinese are free to take jobs anywhere they can. For all practical purposes, China is now a free labour market. (But beware the existence of 'surprise' local regulations; consult before you place your 'help wanted' ads.)

Some commonly used channels for recruitment are as follows:

- **local human resources exchange centres** (*rencai shichang*) hold databases and manage job fairs for management staff
- **local labour bureaux** (*laowu shichang*) provide a similar service for workers
- **campus recruiting** is favoured particularly by top multinational companies, especially for graduates with scientific or technical knowledge and/or formal business training
- **media advertising**, usually in newspapers (broadcast media and posters appear to have little effect)
- *guanxi*: knowing someone who knows someone who is qualified for the job.

Experience suggests that the vast majority of jobs are filled using the last method. Employing friends and relatives is now considered nepotism, or at least unprofessional, in the West but that was not always so. Families joined in groups and introduced new generations as they left school. There is much to be said for engaging families, especially when trying to get as close as possible to the style of a Chinese family business. Warmth is good. One of the authors surprised a very successful young brand manager by asking if she had a sibling with similar talents and then engaging the sister without even meeting her.

Of course, a bad family in key positions can wreak devastation, so we are not suggesting this is a panacea. At the same time, we are suggesting that the *guanxiwang* culture exists and should be made the most of. Is job-hopping new and, if so, why did Chinese managers not do it before? Chinese managers and workers stayed put because they had to, by government order and because of social pressures. But the traditional Chinese organisation offers something else. As a community, with strong leadership and values, it can offer the worker or manager a home and a sense of belonging. A set of concentric relational circles could be drawn around the organisation and the employee's place in it. JVs and WFOEs, however much they develop their staff, have a real problem here. At the end of the day, they are still foreign.

Obviously there have been changes over time. The values of young Chinese today are as different from those of the Cultural Revolution as those of the Cultural Revolution were from the 1930s. There can be no doubt that the Chinese, especially the young and educated members of society, are influenced by the West and see Western managers as role models. But the job seeking and holding patterns currently in evidence do not so much suggest Western influence as no influence at all. With the communal organisations and their Confucian influences disappearing, Chinese managers are finding that the new-style organisations offer them no sense of values. Chinese managers go on to new jobs simply because there is nothing to hold them in place.

What can hold them in place? One solution recommended by bigger Western companies working in China is *training*. Paradoxically, given that recent research suggests that young Chinese do not have planned career paths and their definition of what 'career' means is much more fluid and hazy than in the West, there is also plenty of evidence that these same young Chinese value training and professional development. This is true of many workers, not just managers. Companies that invest in training and development report higher levels of retention than those that do not. There is of course the phenomenon of 'train and run', as workers and managers take their new qualifications and go elsewhere to seek better jobs. This is used by some companies in China as an excuse not to invest in training. In response we would make the following observations:

- 'Train and run' is a two-way street. If compensation packages are good enough, well-trained workers and managers from other companies will want to join too. Also, some departing employees may well want to return to the original business at some date in the future. Training in this sense becomes a case of casting bread on the waters.

- Training is not a unique event. Rather than putting employees into one training programme and expecting them to stay, you should consider developing staged programmes that will last for some years, encouraging them to stay and complete the programme (at least) before departing.
- Nor does training have to mean formal programmes like MBAs, technical programmes and so forth. Mentoring and on-the-job training can be ongoing, and there is evidence that Chinese employees value both highly.

One recent book for Western managers in China, Fernandez and Underwood's *China CEO*,[6] offers four tips for Western companies wanting to retain employees:

1   Offer the right compensation package. Money is obviously important but not all-important; fringe benefits matter too. With property prices going up quickly, loans and assistance to help employees buy their own homes might be attractive; but depending on local conditions, there may be other factors too. It is not always necessary to pay top dollar, or top yuan, to get the best people, but managers are advised to track comparable salaries in their area to ensure they do not fall too far behind. Chinese employees are generally resistant to the idea of performance-related pay; some Western firms have managed to introduce it, but doing so takes time and careful management. This is not for the uninitiated.

2   Think carefully about recruiting. Develop a profile of the people you need and invest time and money in recruiting them; then take steps to integrate them into the firm. The orientation process is particularly important and has to consist of more than showing new managers where their desks are, how to use the phones and where to make tea. Make sure new managers understand the company's procedures and operating systems fully, particularly if these are likely to be new concepts. Remember too that younger Chinese-educated staff will know how Western businesses work only in theory, and that imperfectly. Gordon Orr, long-serving director with McKinsey & Company in China, recommends treating orientation as a training programme, helping new managers to understand the new company's culture and history; this being China, the history does matter.[7]

3   Use training and professional development as a retention strategy, as described above.

4   Offer chances for promotion and new responsibility, especially to those employees who are most needed. Be aware that those who wish to be promoted and are not may suffer from loss of face and will depart accordingly. (Of course, on the flipside this can be a useful way of shedding employees who are not fitting in or not pulling their weight; letting them know quietly that their promotion prospects are nil could encourage an early exit.)

All this seems like good advice, but as many Western managers interviewed for the book acknowledge, all this is no more than best-practice HR management in the West. One lesson seems to be that companies that have sophisticated HR policies will have less difficulty in adapting to China than those that do not. Planning and investing in recruitment and retention are becoming ever-more important in the West too.

What it comes down to is the need to develop *guanxi* with employees, from senior management to shopfloor workers. Cultivate and build strong relationships with employees, just as with customers. Of course, even with *guanxi*, turnover rates will remain high, key staff will disappear at intervals, and wages will continue to go up. Building relationships will not eliminate the problem, but, if skilfully done, it should be possible to keep turnover to a manageable level.

Shatou Sports

Shatou Sports Company is a new venture, a partnership between David Chan, a Chinese-Canadian entrepreneur and Professor Wen Jun, an academic with one of China's leading faculties of medicine. The company has developed a sports drink, for which Professor Wen holds the patents, which it hopes to launch first in the Chinese market and later worldwide, with the ultimate aim of competing with long-established brands such as Gatorade. The brand name chosen for the new drink is Xuebao (Snow Leopard), which the partners believe has connotations of strength and speed but also is associated with Chinese culture. They have come up with a sophisticated marketing plan, timing the launch of the drink with the opening of the Beijing

Olympic Games in 2008. They think they have a winning formula, in terms of both the drink and the marketing plan. The Construction Bank thinks so too, and has lent them half of their start-up capital, with the rest being raised privately.

Unfortunately, the early high hopes have begun to turn sour. The company is based in eastern Guangdong province where labour mobility, especially among skilled workers, is very high. Skilled workers follow rising wages, job-hopping two or three times a year, sometimes even more often. Shatou Sports is finding it very hard to keep technical staff, and even harder to keep managers. Even though the company is paying very competitive salaries, working for a sports drink company is not seen as sexy enough by young people who see themselves as potential high-flyers and want to go to work for international high-tech or finance firms. In its first nine months, Shatou Sports lost two finance directors, a key production manager and several senior marketing staff.

This constant turnover means high costs and, worse, no continuity in terms of key programmes. The production system is full of bugs, and the first trial batch of the drink was spoiled and had to be poured down the drain when some ingredients became contaminated. The marketing programme is months behind schedule; for example, designs for logo and packaging are still on the drawing board. The opening date for the Olympics is drawing ever closer, and Mr Chan and Professor Wen are beginning to wonder if their fine product will ever reach the marketplace.

Conclusions

Western companies in China can and should market themselves as employers using the techniques of the last two chapters. The concept of the 'Employer Brand' is gaining ground in the West and it makes just as much sense here. Status can be attached to working for a particular company.

As part of that process, companies can actively manage employee expectations. Disappointment with salary increases, unrealistic expectations and general job dissatisfaction are all responsible for job departures. Non-financial incentives also have an important role to play in employee retention. Although the present move is away from the iron rice bowl and full security, many employees value these things highly, particularly in the inflationary areas of Shanghai and the southeast. Benefits can be a powerful inducement to employee retention.

Perhaps what is developing in China now is a subtle mix of the best of both worlds. Most Chinese recognise that Western management systems have a lot to offer in terms of efficiency, use of technology, and development of creativity. Thus it is a mistake to see Chinese business culture as 'anti' any of these things. As noted above, there is no either/or in Chinese management; it is both structured and unstructured. Our own stereotypical view of the entrepreneur as a free-wheeling loner does not make much sense in China (one can question whether it makes sense in the West either). China has entrepreneurs, but they work within concentric circles and networks of *guanxi*, not as lone wolves.

The overseas Chinese

As Chapter 11 points out, many overseas Chinese firms are actually a synthesis of value systems as they typically (especially the larger ones) employ a variety of different nationalities. That said, the prevalence of (especially) Confucian and Buddhist values elsewhere in East Asia means that employees and managers in these countries often share similar workplace values to their counterparts in China. In fact, countries like Thailand exhibit even more strongly an attachment to hierarchy and to personal relations in the workplace. Taiwan, too, is noted for strong bonds between employers and workers.

We should also bear in mind the difficulties already encountered by many firms when employing overseas Chinese managers in mainland firms. There is no doubt that these managers offer a firm many advantages. However, the pay differential and the more general problem of clashing cultures can lead to tensions. (The same problems can be encountered when moving managers between regions inside China.) Instead of looking to hire managers from Hong Kong or Singapore, if possible look for mainland Chinese who have worked or had part of their education in one of these two places, and so have learned more about Western methods.

---

10 Doing business with the sojourners

The overseas Chinese communities

This chapter looks to the Chinese community living 'overseas', i.e. beyond the mainland PRC. Taiwan has a business culture distinct from that of the PRC. So too do the Hong Kong and Macao Special Administrative Regions (SARs), which is why comments up to this point about differences between PRC and overseas Chinese managers included Hong Kong and Macao. But with Hong Kong and Macao formally back in the PRC, we will skip over them here, and concentrate on Taiwan and Southeast Asia. A number of these comments apply also to Chinese communities in other parts of the world.

Understanding the overseas Chinese communities is important for two reasons. First, the overseas Chinese communities can be useful routes of entry into the Chinese market. Overseas Chinese intermediaries are often used by Western companies as *hongniang*, and overseas Chinese capitalists in Malaysia, Singapore, Thailand, Indonesia and the Philippines are major investors in China on their own account.

Second, the countries of East Asia where the Chinese community is a major business presence represent major markets in their own right. Singapore and Taiwan are Chinese societies, by any reckoning. Overseas Chinese dominate the economies of Malaysia, Indonesia, Thailand and the Philippines. There are strong links between ways of doing business in these countries and ways of doing business in the PRC, and the concepts in this book are applicable to a greater or lesser degree all over East Asia. There are also many differences, however, and we shall be looking at variants in business practice and behaviour between China and the rest of East Asia.

The overseas Chinese

There are an estimated 60 million Chinese living outside the PRC (this is entirely an estimate, as no cross-national census of this community has ever been done and national censuses in the regions where they live are often little more than guesswork). Eighty per cent of these live in East Asia, and about 6.5 million live in North America. The remainder, about 4.4 million, are scattered across South America, Europe, Africa and West Asia, with sizeable communities in Jamaica, East Africa and the Seychelles. The largest single overseas Chinese community is in Taiwan, 98 per cent of whose 20 million people are Chinese.

These figures are obviously quite small when compared to the population of the PRC. However, these communities exercise an economic power all out of proportion to their size. These 60 million people had in 2005 a gross domestic product in excess of $740 billion and current assets of $3.1 trillion. The East Asian Chinese have been powerful forces in the regional economic revolution, and are increasingly important players in the world economy.

Who are the overseas Chinese?

In China, expatriate Chinese are referred to as *huaqiao*. The name means 'overseas Chinese', but there is a connotation that the *huaqiao* are only overseas temporarily, and will one day come back to China. They are also sometimes known as 'sojourners'.

Huaqiao refers to both Chinese nationals and ethnic Chinese who are citizens of other countries. There are also a number of sub-categories:

- *huaren*: ethnic Chinese who live abroad
- *huayi*: 'persons of Chinese origin'
- *Taiwan tongbao*: Taiwan Chinese.

The Chinese do make considerable distinctions between these and other categories, and are acutely conscious of where the *huaqiao* come from and their backgrounds. The three subgroups above can experience vastly different treatment, depending on where they are in the country. Taiwan Chinese are sometimes treated with reserve or even suspicion, while *huayi* from Canada and the United States are often warmly received as prodigals returning to the fold.

There are other divisions within the community which are not necessarily recognised in China. Political divisions were important throughout the post-1949 period, with some overseas Chinese supporting the Communists and others vehemently opposing them. Geographic divisions of origin, between north and south Chinese, occasionally appear but are less important as the majority of overseas Chinese families come from south Chinese backgrounds, with the second largest group coming from Shanghai. The most important distinction concerns the degree of acculturation and integration. In this respect, some overseas Chinese regard themselves as being citizens of their host country and have adopted much of that country's culture, while others emphatically regard themselves as Chinese.

Taiwan: on-again, off-again relationship

In 2008, Taiwan's love–hate relationship with the PRC continues and no solution has yet appeared. Beijing's hope that a peaceful transition in Hong Kong might inspire more Taiwanese to look favourably on the idea of reunification has not worked – at least, not yet. There have been moments of tension in the past few years (which often happen to coincide with elections in Taiwan), but relations remain comparatively peaceful. Restrictions on trade have relaxed, Taiwanese airliners have landing rights in China, and Taiwanese tourists play a small but substantial role in the economy of eastern China.

Taiwan was damaged by the Asia Crisis and many of its cherished business and economic traditions went by the board. Commitments to lifelong employment lapsed as companies were forced to shed jobs or die. Many small firms did go to the wall, but enough survived to keep the economy in a reasonably healthy state. One consequence of the crisis was that Taiwanese learned that, like it or not, the shape and nature of the mainland economy is a major influence on their own. Many of the more pragmatic Taiwanese now favour closer ties with the PRC, even if they stop short of endorsing full reunification.

Another impact of the crisis was the partial dismantling of Taiwan's heavily protectionist economy. Although the Taipei government claims to have made great progress in this sphere, it is widely assumed that much protectionist regulation remains in 'hidden' forms, or that new regulations are interpreted by officials in a protectionist light. One of the many things the Taiwanese have in common with their mainland cousins is the presence of a powerful bureaucracy which can and does shape economic and business policy at every level. Far from being swept away by reforms, the bureaucrats have simply adapted to and co-opted the reform process so as to bolster their own power.

Taiwan has a strongly entrepreneurial culture. Both government and big business encourage the growth of small business, and people wanting to start their own companies are encouraged. Ninety-eight per cent of businesses in Taiwan have fewer than 50 employees: the Taiwanese themselves have a saying, 'Throw a stone out of a window and you will probably hit a company president.' There are big and prosperous firms in Taiwan: Acer Computers and Taishin Bank have international reputations, but this remains predominantly a land of small and medium-sized enterprises.

Origins of the overseas communities

If one excludes the debatable case of native Americans, the earliest Chinese emigrants were possibly the groups who moved to Japan in the period before the Japanese Warring States and the closing of Japan's borders in the eleventh century AD. During this period, the Chinese had a powerful influence on emerging Japanese culture, bringing Buddhism and pictograms (among other things) to Japan. Japan served as a useful outlet for Chinese emigration for about a thousand years.

The modern period of Chinese emigration began in the seventeenth century, when the economic dislocations caused by the Manchu conquest and Tibetan invasions led to a wave of refugees. Many from the southern provinces fled into Southeast Asia, while the Sinification of Taiwan begins from about this time, with refugees from Fukien absorbing the native Taiwanese. Many Chinese were also encouraged by the Spanish authorities in the Philippines to emigrate there, as there was a great need for labour.

Through the next two centuries, economic migrants and refugees from political strife continued to swell the numbers of the Chinese communities overseas, especially in Taiwan and Southeast Asia. From the early nineteenth century, the British authorities began encouraging Chinese emigration to other parts of the British Empire; Singapore became a major transshipment point for Chinese labour going to the Malay tin mines or on to Burma and India. The Dutch also recruited Chinese labour in Indonesia.

The discovery of gold in North America coincided with a period of great civil unrest in South China. The first wave of immigrants arrived in San Francisco shortly after the start of the gold rush of 1849; a second wave began around 1858, spurred by the devastation of the Taiping Rebellion on the one hand and the discovery of further gold in British Columbia on the other. More Chinese labourers were hired to help build the western links of the transcontinental railways in the 1870s and 1880s. Tens of thousands of Chinese emigrated to these two centres, most of whom came from a small strip of Guangdong province between Hong Kong and Guangzhou.

In the twentieth century, the foreign invasions and civil strife that had damaged China so badly produced new waves of refugees. The era of the warlords produced new emigration to Southeast Asia (the United States and Canada were by this time restricting Chinese immigration). After 1949 there were large immigration movements from mainland China to Hong Kong and Taiwan, many of them middle-class refugees. The Chinese populations of Southeast Asia were further increased when a number of Guomindang army units that had fought in Burma refused to go back to China and dispersed through Burma, Thailand and Laos.

However, not all the migrants of this period were fleeing Communism. The Indonesian and Malayan communities had substantial groups supporting Mao and espousing Communism. This led to considerable tensions in Indonesia, while in Malaya the Communist insurgents active until about 1957 were mostly Chinese.

Controlled movements out of China began again in the late 1960s, when the Chinese government began supporting the Non-Aligned Movement after the split with Russia. Chinese workers and technicians were exported for a variety of civil engineering projects in the Third World. The most famous of these was the TanZam railway project in East Africa, which was largely built by Chinese labour. After the conclusion of the project, some of the Chinese workers applied for and received permission to stay on in Africa. The movement of overseas labourers continues nowadays, especially in the Middle East. To these workers should be added the growing numbers of Chinese who go overseas to undertake graduate or postgraduate university studies, not all of whom return home immediately their programme of study is completed.

Canada has long been popular due to a relatively looser immigration policy. The run-up to Hong Kong's reunification with the PRC led to a mass movement of people and capital to Canada and a corresponding boom in the economy of western Canada especially. When reunification went ahead peacefully, many of the people and much of the capital returned home (and the western Canadian economy promptly collapsed). But some did stay, joining their compatriots who had moved there a century and a half earlier. More generally, young Chinese with limited prospects at home continue to take advantage of opportunities to go abroad to work. The tales of overseas self-made billionaires motivate quite a number of native Chinese to move abroad, sometimes even illegally. More recently, the people-smuggling gangs have begun enticing people abroad with false promises. In mid-2002 one such gang was luring young Chinese cooks overseas with promises of jobs paying up to $60,000 a year. Most of these emigrants, without papers or employment rights in their destination countries, were lucky to find jobs paying a tenth of that amount. Some did not survive the journey. The gang was broken up by the Chinese government later in the year and its leaders jailed, but the problem remains.

By 2008, and this looks to be part of a long-term trend, China was investing significant money and manpower in Africa in a bid to secure raw materials. Whether this will lead to the establishment of permanent overseas Chinese communities of any size in Africa is not clear, but it is certainly a possibility.

Singapore: the crossroads

'Thailand is a Buddhist country, Indonesia is a Muslim country, Singapore is a capitalist country,' commented one investment banker in the city. If capitalism were a religion, it is easy to imagine shrines to it being erected on Orchard Road. As in China, the patriarchal figure who dominates government and society, Lee Kuan Yew, exerts much influence on Singapore with his dream of a developed Western-style economy under Neo-Confucianist values. His successor is successfully following Lee's belief and holding Lee's edifice together, while Lee himself remains a venerable and venerated figure.

Seventy-eight per cent of the population of Singapore is Chinese, with the remainder being of Malay or Indian extraction. Ethnic Chinese dominate the economy and the government. In contrast to nearby Malaysia and Indonesia, where Chinese business activity is restricted, Singapore is one of the great achievements of Chinese capitalism.

Singapore is possibly the most modern city in Asia. Its high-tech achievements are formidable; cyberpunk author William Gibson recently called it 'the first city of the computer age'. Singaporean Chinese, however, for all their modern lifestyles, tend on the whole to be socially conservative. The drive against corruption, the strictly regulated society and the intense and complicated hierarchies might almost be a deliberate model of rule according to Confucian principles. Look closely, however, and you will find them driving over the causeway to scatter their wilder seeds in Johore. Strangely, Singapore has quite a low level of education spending as a proportion of GDP, much lower than Taiwan and lower even than many Western countries. But that may be due to the high level of GDP rather than any criticism of educational spending.

More recently, Singapore has been diversifying away from banking and finance into other areas, notably the creative arts. Everything from film studios to fashion houses are being encouraged to come to Singapore and to set up shop, with the result that *Time* magazine in 2005 described Singapore as a 'funky town'. This might be overstating the case, but certainly Singapore is working hard to become more than just the financial capital of Southeast Asia – it has aspirations to be the region's intellectual capital as well.

What sets the overseas Chinese apart?

The nature of their origins should give some clues about the nature of overseas Chinese communities today. Wherever they are, overseas Chinese communities have a number of distinguishing features, as outlined below.

Commonality of background

Except for students and experts, the vast majority of Chinese emigrants over the last several centuries have been refugees, fleeing either economic disaster or political persecution and war. Even those Chinese who were recruited as labourers, in Malaya, the Dutch East Indies (Indonesia), the Philippines or North America, suffered discrimination from locals who saw them as a threat to the local economy and jobs. There is a common heritage of hardship and alienation in the overseas Chinese communities, which is responsible for a number of further features such as community and identity.

Low profile

In Taiwan and Singapore the *huaqiao* form the majority of the population and control government and society as well as the economy. In other countries of East Asia, fear of persecution has in the past – sometimes the very recent past – led them to maintain a low profile. The first massacre of overseas Chinese took place in the Philippines in the late sixteenth century, when hundreds were killed; 10,000 died in ethnic riots in Batavia (now Jakarta) in 1740. Hundreds of Chinese Communists died in Malaya during the 1950s. There were more deaths, perhaps several hundred in Indonesia around the time of the fall of Sukarno, and dozens more when Suharto's government collapsed. Even today a number of countries, principally Malaysia and Indonesia, have laws restricting Chinese participation in business; as a result Chinese businessmen tend to work behind the scenes, using local businesses as fronts. A low profile means a quiet life.

In North America, discrimination mainly took the form of legal restrictions on work. In Canada, for example, local legislation in the early twentieth century prohibited farmers from hiring Chinese labour. However, most of these restrictions were repealed by the middle of the century and Chinese communities have gradually become more visible, moving out of their Chinatown ghettos in cities such as San Francisco, Los Angeles, Seattle, Vancouver and Victoria.

Curiously, lack of discrimination does not necessarily mean that Chinese communities become more visible. Instead, it seems to lead them to become more deeply integrated into the local community. In North America and in Thailand and the Philippines, the boundaries between the Chinese and local communities are becoming porous. For example, in Thailand, local Chinese commonly ask to be called by the Thai versions of their names (although this is also a legal requirement). This is low profile of a different sort, achieved by blending into the local community. This blending does not, however, mean that Chinese identity is in any way lessened.

Malaysia: uncertain future

Malaya was created in the nineteenth century by the British colonial authorities from a collection of colonies and theoretically independent principalities on the Malay peninsula and in north Borneo. Independence was granted in 1957 but there was an uneasy relationship between the Malay-dominated mainland and Chinese-dominated Singapore. In 1963 they agreed to go their separate ways and Malaysia was born. The cracks still sometimes show in the patchwork.

Malaysia took a beating in the Asian Crisis of the late 1990s but still came through better than others. More damage was done by the government of Dr Mahathir, which turned increasingly authoritarian with the passage of time and became more concerned with protecting its own position and fighting a series of post-colonial battles with the Western powers. This has hampered economic cooperation and investment alike. Dr Mahathir has gone, but his successors have found it hard to rebuild trust on the part of Western investors. That said, Malaysia remains a key player in Southeast Asia, and its Chinese community have close links with China and provide much investment there. Rising commodity prices are giving the economy a boost, and Malaysia's sovereign wealth fund, Khazanah, has aspirations to be a global player alongside the likes of CIC and Temasek.

The Malaysian government is dominated by *bumiputras*, or ethnic Malays, who like to preserve a fiction that they actually run the economy. In 1971 the government introduced laws restricting participation in business by Chinese, but in the last 30 years the share of the economy controlled by Malaysian Chinese has increased. Many companies are fronted by *bumiputras* but are actually controlled behind the scenes by Chinese entrepreneurs.

Malay and Chinese employees and managers do work together, however, which can cause problems, even more so when Malay Muslims, Indian Hindus and Chinese of various beliefs are mixed together in the same workplace. For example, while pork and beef are staples of the Malaysian Chinese diet, Hindus may not eat beef and Muslims may not use utensils that have touched pork, meaning they cannot be served in factory canteens, for example. These and a host of other small issues greatly complicate HR management.

Thailand: three steps forward and two steps back

Thailand is a Southeast Asian anomaly. Never formally occupied by any colonial power, Thailand is also the only major state in Southeast

Asia apart from Burma to have been a unified nation for more than one thousand years. Like the Chinese, the Thais have a long cultural tradition of which they are very proud.

Thailand is a monarchy but is virtually ruled by the army, which is almost a state within a state. Despite very high levels of corruption, the Thai economy has generally prospered and Thai companies such as CP (Charoen Pokphand) have reached multinational status. But the Thai economy remains plagued by instability and corruption. Until very recently the country was governed by a military junta, which had replaced an allegedly corrupt prime minister who seemed to spend more time planning how to buy an English football club than actually running the country. At the time of writing, elections have been held and democracy restored, but no one knows for how long. A low-level insurgency in the Muslim districts in the far south of the country is also causing headaches. Despite many assets and a potentially strong economy, Thailand never quite seems to achieve the prosperity it should.

The Chinese population of Thailand is believed to be about 3.5 million, but it is difficult to tell because the Chinese have assimilated into the Thai population. Many Thais, including the royal family, are proud of their Chinese ancestry. Many Chinese are equally happy to be taken for Thais, and some have adopted Thai versions of their names.

Sino-Thai businessmen probably control about 45–50 per cent of the capital in Thailand, with ethnic Thais and Indians controlling the rest. Most large companies, including CP, have strong Chinese backing and also invest heavily in China.

Chinese identity

Where the overseas Chinese have been discriminated against, they have tended to fall back on themselves, reinforcing their identity as Chinese. Fourth- and fifth-generation Chinese in Southeast Asia and North America have grown up in their own isolated communities, speaking their own languages, celebrating their own festivals, and having only marginal contact with the host country.

Chinese identity can even transcend internal political divisions within the *huaqiao* community. In Indonesia, a Chinese-owned printing business did work for both the pro-Nationalist, pro-Taiwan section of the Chinese community and for the Indonesian Communist Party (PKI). The Indonesian government put pressure on the pro-Nationalists to transfer their printing business to an

Indonesian firm. The indignant Nationalists promptly telephoned their enemies in the pro-Communist Chinese community, who in turn informed the government that if harassment of the Nationalists did not cease, the entire Chinese community in Indonesia would take sanctions against the government.

These sanctions can be very effective, given the massive Chinese control of capital and business noted at the beginning of these notes. In South Vietnam in 1967, a Chinese businessman was arrested and executed for profiteering. The entire Chinese community in Saigon, from bankers to porters and rickshaw drivers, went on strike; within days the South Vietnamese economy was paralysed. Consequently, the government released several Chinese who were due to stand trial and made no more arrests.

Indonesia: hoping for stability

Like Malaysia, Indonesia became independent after the Second World War, after a struggle led mainly by radicals from Java against the Dutch colonial authorities and other ethnic groups such as the Moluccans. A strong government backed by the military took control in the 1960s and governed the country until 1998, when a combination of the Asia Crisis and domestic unrest toppled President Suharto. Elections have since been held, but the political system remains highly unstable with demands for independence from the fringes. Some foreign analysts believe it is only a matter of time until there is another violent attempt to change the government.

Until the Asia Crisis of 1997, Indonesia was the fastest-growing nation in East Asia, and when the crisis hit it crashed further and with more devastating effects. There were anti-Chinese riots and deaths in the capital and elsewhere. Following the fall of the late President Suharto, elections were held, but the first democratic governments were chronically unstable. The Bali bombing of 2002, when Islamic militants targeted a nightclub full of foreign tourists, was another shock. Indonesia also bore the brunt of the tsunami of 26 December 2005, which killed 160,000 people in the province of Aceh alone.

That said, the current president, Susilo Bambang Yudhoyono, known as SBY, has made some headway. The reconstruction of Aceh has on the whole been handled well. There have been some economic reforms with plans for more, along with a drive against corruption. The president's 'Unleash Indonesia' campaign is meant to stimulate economic growth once more. Potentially, with its rich resources and large population, Indonesia could become an economic powerhouse. Certainly, if SBY remains in power and reforms go ahead, it is a country to watch.

There are 3.25 million ethnic Chinese in Indonesia, most of whom live on Java. They make up about 3 per cent of the total population. However, they exercise an influence over the economy all out of proportion to their numbers; it is estimated that they control 75–80 per cent of Indonesia's capital.

The Indonesian economy is usually divided into four main sectors: the state sector (the largest), the military sector, the private sector backed by Chinese capital, and the private sector backed by ethnic Indonesian capital. In fact, as in Malaysia, Indonesian businessmen are often fronts for Chinese capital, and the Chinese have heavily penetrated the state and military sectors as well.

The Indonesian Chinese community was heavily penetrated by Communist agents in the 1960s, and provided much backing for the Indonesian Communist Party in its abortive revolt against Sukarno. Since then the entire Chinese community has been harassed and there have been pogroms and expulsions. However, their economic clout provides the Chinese community with protection against any serious threats to their existence. Under a system known as *cukong*, Chinese businessmen finance the Indonesian military to a considerable extent, in exchange for which the military (almost a state within a state in Indonesia) provide licences, credit monopolies and physical protection for Chinese businesses.

Family identity

The same isolation and need for self-sufficiency have led to an even greater emphasis on the family. Surveys of overseas Chinese communities have found that Confucian family values are far stronger than in mainland China. This is partly because in mainland China from the late 1950s to 1976, the Communist Party launched a sustained assault on the family, attempting to replace loyalty to the father with loyalty to the Party. Even without this, however, it seems logical for family values to be stronger in the overseas community.

The Confucian family model is well suited to withstanding an adverse environment. Advocating strong leadership at the top and intense loyalty at the lower levels, the family model has served very well as a model for business; and it is largely through its business activities that the Chinese community has been able to survive.

No accurate figures are available, but it is believed that around 85 per cent of overseas Chinese around the world work for firms that are Chinese-owned.

Entrepreneurial qualities

All the pressures described above have served to increase the development of entrepreneurship in the overseas community. To the overseas Chinese, wealth means security; there is anecdotal evidence that their economic leverage over their host communities was gained with the idea of creating security. As far back as the 1860s the Singapore-Chinese tycoon Whampoa said: 'When we are poor, they despise us to our faces. When we are rich, they despise us behind our backs: but to our faces, they bow.'

Sociological and psychological studies of the overseas Chinese communities in comparison with China show these communities to be more flexible and with a higher tolerance of ambiguity than in China. This means in effect that there are likely to be more people within the population interested in going into business for themselves. The hardships of migration have cultivated the values necessary for business success, such as thrift and pragmatism. The story of the Chinese in Canada shows a kind of Darwinian selection at work. Those Chinese who went off to work as labourers in the goldfields and on the railways ended up impoverished and many died. Those who stayed in Victoria or Vancouver and went into the business of supplying the workers up-country (fresh vegetables were particularly needed) ended up prosperous, and their sons and daughters who took over the businesses often became wealthy.

Feelings about the mother country

Mainland China expects that eventually the *huaqiao* will return home. Some *huaqiao* expect this as well. Yet, many of the overseas Chinese do not wish to return to China and have no intention of doing so. Moreover, there is some doubt as to whether Beijing really wants responsibility for another 55 million citizens (though perhaps if they brought their wealth with them, it might be another matter).

The overseas Chinese have complex feelings about China. Even those strongly loyal to the PRC government experience some reluctance at the prospect of going home, and even a short absence can cause confusion and disorientation. Ting Gong, a Chinese academic who spent four years overseas in the late 1980s, recorded his confusion at returning home to find everyone complaining about the corruption the new reforms had brought while trading enthusiastically on the grey market at the same time.

These ambivalent feelings are by no means restricted to the Chinese. Expatriates of every culture, including British and Americans, dream about an idealised version of their own culture while at the same time criticising the present state of affairs in their homelands. The Chinese are no different in this.

Australian correspondent Richard Hughes (1972), who spent 40 years in the Far East, provides a summary:

> For generations the *huaqiao* have clung to their Chinese characteristics and traditions, united – whether impoverished or wealthy – in their blood loyalty to the great motherland and the Yellow Emperor and assured, in the face of persecution and segregation, of the transcendental superiority and inevitable resurgence of the Chinese race. Their way of life invites the discrimination of which they complain. Most of them in the past preferred stubbornly to retain the status of colonists, and this is one reason why many who now prudently wish to become absorbed as legal citizens still find the doors of assimilation and naturalisation closed to them.
>
> The giant Chinese umbilical cord links them strongly to the motherland – young and old, industrialists and coolies, bankers and smugglers, Communist terrorists and Rotarian merchants, millionaires and beggars. They may often be isolated among themselves by their native dialects, but they are united by their common written language. The elderly, amid alien temples, remember and celebrate Chinese festivals. At the local Chinese-language schools the young proclaim their Chinese uniqueness: '*Wo shih Kuo jen! Wo chu tsai Nanyang! Wo ai Chung Kuo!*' ('I am Chinese! I live in the Southern Ocean! I love China!') Yet the 'sojourners' do not want to go back home, except sometimes to die or be buried there. Nor does Peking want them to come home ...
>
> It is curious to note that the *hua-chiao* brought with them, nurtured and still preserve traditional aspects of Chinese life and philosophy which, ironically, no longer exist in their motherland.

In fact, under a new Chinese regime, whose unifying energy impresses most of them and whose pragmatic success impresses all, these anachronistic survivals have become downright offences against the mores of the new China ... To a large extent the *hua-chiao* are devoted to an artificial and outdated image of China which has been facelifted, transformed and disfigured since the forefathers of the present generation of overseas Chinese left the motherland.[1]

Hughes was writing over 35 years ago, but more recent reminiscences by overseas Chinese, especially those travelling back to China for the first time, suggest the picture is still accurate. Many overseas Chinese are living with an image of a China that no longer exists, and when they return home they sometimes feel alienated, even frightened. They are often looked on as foreigners, both in the mother country and in the lands where they live today.

Vietnam: pragmatism and *doi moi*

Vietnam is another nation fashioned by the colonial authorities, with the old kingdoms of Annam, Cochin and Tonking being welded into one by the French. There is still considerable ethnic diversity in Vietnam, and economic and cultural differences between north and south are strong.

Vietnam in the 1980s climbed out of the doldrums of the Communist era with a speed which makes one suspect that Communism never had very deep roots in the country in the first place. The Vietnamese, pragmatic as ever, are opening the doors to the West. *Doi moi*, or reconstruction, backed by foreign capital, proceeded quickly in the 1990s, and for a time Vietnam was the hot new market. The Asia Crisis dampened prospects for a time but with less to lose, Vietnam was less badly damaged and new investment was soon coming in. At the time of writing, Vietnam is becoming increasingly popular as a location for offshoring, as wages are very low and the skills base is relatively high.

About 3 per cent of the population of Vietnam are of Chinese origin. Most are concentrated around Saigon/Ho Chi Minh City in the south. The Chinese were not welcome in the north for a number of years, when Vietnam was allied with Moscow and the Chinese were backing the Khmer Rouge who killed hundreds of thousands of Vietnamese nationals in Cambodia. In the south, however, they filled their usual role as middlemen and traders.

The Chinese community in Saigon is very closely knit, dominated by a few important families who employ most of the rest in a variety of businesses. The amount of capital they held is unknown, but certainly before the unification of Vietnam, the Chinese banks played a major role in financing the South Vietnamese state. It seems likely that *doi moi* will give them a chance to flourish once more.

Doing business with the overseas Chinese

The same rules of conduct for doing business in China apply when doing business with the overseas Chinese. *Guanxi* is every bit as important as in China, and the *guanxiwang* or networks of contacts are often even more extensive. Negotiating styles are similar in most cultures. Businesses are organised in much the same way, with a strong hierarchy headed by a father-figure (often the actual head of the family).

From this position, however, it is important to recognise a number of differences. First, Chinese-owned businesses overseas frequently operate behind fronts. In Malaysia and Indonesia especially, it is not unusual for an ethnic local businessman to nominally be in charge of an organisation, but for the real ownership, hidden behind several layers, to be in Chinese hands. In China, the leadership of a large organisation should be clear. Overseas, the real decision-makers may be found behind the scenes.

Second, most *huaqiao* Chinese-run businesses are family concerns. They are small and tightly controlled by a small group who are related by blood or by marriage. There is no equivalent to the state-run or privatised ex-state-run industry, for obvious reasons.

Third, overseas Chinese businesses often come from a more entrepreneurial background. Singapore businesses are as sophisticated as any in the world, and even in emerging economies such as Malaysia and Indonesia, Chinese businesspeople tend to have more knowledge and more developed skills. They combined high degrees of spatial awareness with a strongly developed drive to succeed – a powerful combination. When compared with their mainland China counterparts, overseas Chinese business leaders tend to be highly motivated and ruthless about dealing with competitors, particularly those outside their own *guanxiwang*; but even then, relationships are often stronger than competition. When cut-throat competition between two Chinese-owned wholesale businesses in Malaysia led to the ruin of one, the winner bought the defunct company, gave his rival a position of trust, and arranged a marriage between the two families.

Fourth, and related to the above, overseas Chinese businesses are more likely to pay attention to short-term factors. Because many of them operate in more uncertain environments (either because of political pressure and discrimination, or because the markets in which they work are more developed and move faster), they tend to think more about the short term than do their mainland China counterparts. However, they still have long time horizons compared to their Western and indigenous counterparts.

Fifth, overseas Chinese are probably more likely to be concerned with Confucian values, especially respect for tradition. As noted above, the overseas Chinese are far more concerned with traditions and respecting the past than are their mainland counterparts, hence earning the description 'more Chinese than the Chinese'. Often there is also a much stronger emphasis on face, even in the North American Chinese communities, which may be surprising (unless you accept that Westerners have their own concepts of face). In a way this is no surprise: British overseas expatriate communities also hold on to old ways longer than those in Britain. As stated earlier, there is a limit to the value of the Confucian model, but the power of the family and the close links between the family and the business should be recognised.

Last, varying degrees of acculturation mean that when dealing with overseas Chinese, it is not enough to know about Chinese culture; one also needs to learn about the local cultures. Appearances are unreliable: an individual who appears to be strongly acculturated may still hold strong Chinese values, and vice versa. In American and Canadian Chinese communities, it is not uncommon to run across 50-year-old heads of families and companies who are fond of the Rolling Stones. Conversely, young men and women who wear fashionable clothes and drive sports cars, may nonetheless be devout Buddhists and observe all the festivals. It is difficult to learn about both cultures and try to understand where your partner/rival fits in, but it needs to be attempted nonetheless.

The Philippines: hope for the future?

Occupied for nearly 300 years by the Spanish and then by the Americans and the Japanese, the Philippines became independent after the Second World War. Endemic corruption and mismanagement under President Marcos nearly drove the islands to bankruptcy, and armed rebel movements threatened to tear the country apart. Guerrilla activity continues in the ethnically different, southern islands. However, the democratic experiment under Corazon Aquino and her successors has worked better than expected and the government now seems to enjoy the confidence of the army, the people and the Western banks. Special enterprise zones, modelled on those in China, have been set up on the island of Luzon, and foreign investment was rising until the Asia Crisis struck.

The future is uncertain; a ceasefire with Muslim separatists in the south brought optimism for a couple of years. However, when the ceasefire broke down in 2001, some of that optimism dissipated. Today, the Philippines still lags behind the rest of the region in terms of foreign direct investment.

Only about 1 per cent of the population of the Philippines is identifiably Chinese, although Chinese immigration under Spanish rule means that many Filipino families can claim part Chinese ancestry. Corazon Aquino's family, for example, were originally immigrants from Fukien. Nevertheless, the ethnic Chinese are a powerful economic force, controlling 33 per cent of manufacturing and 40 per cent of trading firms in the country. It seems that the Filipino Chinese community may represent the country's best hope for the future.

Cambodia/Laos: lost lands

French Indochina split after the end of the colonial period into four states: the two Vietnams, Cambodia and Laos. The latter two were ancient kingdoms which had been economic backwaters before the French arrived and continued to be so after. Both might have carried on quietly had it not been for the war in Vietnam, which quickly spilled over into both Cambodia and Laos. Both Vietnamese Communist propaganda and American carpet-bombing had their effect. Revolutionary movements began in both countries.

The Pathet Lao overthrew the Laotian monarchy without a major struggle, but the bloody war between the Khmer Rouge and the Sihanouk government and the massacres of the Year Zero killed nearly one-third of Cambodia's population.

Laos today is slowly coming out of its economic isolation. Most of the capital funding Laos's recovery comes from Thailand, primarily from Chinese firms; moreover, the 200,000 Chinese in Laos, who are concentrated around Vientiane, are also playing their part. Sino-Thai entrepreneurs dominate the tiny Laotian economy. The only other significant Chinese population in Laos is in the north, around Luang Prabang. As descendants of Guomindang soldiers who did not return to China after the Second World War, they are involved in local trade, including drugs.

In Cambodia, despite PRC support for the Khmer Rouge, the Chinese population suffered badly during the Year Zero and tens of thousands were killed. There are believed to be about 100,000 ethnic Chinese in Cambodia today, and they make up a significant proportion of the business community in Phnom Penh. However, although the conflict has ended and the warring parties seem reconciled, it seems unlikely that Cambodia will achieve a real economic revival in the near future, with or without Chinese help. The best hope would seem to lie in the discovery of offshore oil deposits, which if exploited could lead to more investment. Cambodians must be hoping that the price of oil remains high.

The overseas Chinese and China

We have discussed already the possibility of using overseas Chinese businesses as conduits into China itself, though this is not as easy as it sounds. True, most overseas businesses, especially in major centres such as Singapore, are more in tune with the needs of Western businesses; but at the same time relations between the overseas Chinese and their mainland counterparts are full of pitfalls. The much-trumpeted experiment of creating a transplanted Singapore in Suzhou is less talked about today.

Most overseas Chinese are ambivalent about the PRC. They respect Chinese culture and they are impressed by the achievements of the Chinese government, especially during the past two decades, but many of them have no wish to return to China. They are, for the most part, more comfortable in their present surroundings – even when those surroundings include a potentially hostile environment full of prejudice and restriction. At the same time, the mainland Chinese have equally ambivalent feelings about the *huaqiao*. Many Chinese feel, even if subconsciously, that the overseas Chinese have let the country down by leaving, and have in some way lost face. As noted in the last chapter, many Chinese openly resent the returned 'sojourners' from Taiwan and Singapore, who are taking senior positions with joint ventures and WFOEs and being paid far more than their domestic counterparts.

At the same time, the overseas Chinese have equally complex and ambivalent relations with their host countries. Relations can range from very good (Thailand and the Philippines where the *huaqiao* are mostly welcome and integrated with the local population) to ambivalent (the United States and Canada, where there is now little overt prejudice but where strong cultural differences remain) to poor (Malaysia, where Chinese ethnics, who are Malaysian nationals, are legally restricted from entering business). Whenever things go wrong in Indonesia, attacking small Chinese businesses appears to be the favourite diversion. Dealing with *huaqiao* businesses in these countries will not always win a Western company the favour of local governments. On the other hand, given the economic predominance of these businesses, how do you avoid them?

The Americas: survival and identity in the melting pot

The last significant overseas Chinese community is that in North America. There are about 5 million ethnic Chinese in the United States and 1 million in Canada. Most are concentrated in the major cities of the west coast. Another 500,000 Chinese are scattered around the Caribbean, with the largest concentration in Jamaica.

Ghettoised for several decades, the North American Chinese have been coming out into the wider community in the last 40 years. In California, Hawai'i and British Columbia, Chinese entrepreneurs own considerable capital and have invested in a wide variety of sectors, with wholesale, transport and light manufacturing being the most common. In the early 1990s there was a major flight of capital, and in some instances also of people, from Hong Kong to the west coast of North America/Canada. The primary destination was Vancouver, where several billion dollars of Hong Kong money has been invested in the local economy. The result was to give Vancouver and the Canadian west coast an economic shot in the arm, with this area remaining buoyant even through the recession of the early 1990s. That boost proved short-lived when much of the capital went back to Hong Kong followed the peaceful transition in 1998.

Many Chinese in North America show signs of being strongly acculturated. However, many others retain strong ties with China and some have gone back; Canadian-Chinese entrepreneurs were prominent in Shenzhen and Shanghai during the early days of economic reform, and others continue to return in small numbers.

Conclusions

The overseas Chinese are a powerful economic force and can make good partners for Western businesses. Economically sophisticated and strongly motivated, they have attained commanding positions in the economies of many countries, especially in East and Southeast Asia.

The *huaqiao* hold many of the same values as do Chinese in the PRC. However, there are also differences in outlook and attitude and it is important to recognise them. Overseas Chinese tend on the whole to be more strongly traditional and more family-oriented, while at the same time paradoxically they see themselves as more modern and more susceptible to outside cultural influences. It is particularly important, if planning to use a *huaqiao* company as a *hongniang* or go-between with China, to recognise that the relations between the mainland and overseas Chinese are complex and ambivalent. Finally, local discords may be at work, and negotiations should be handled accordingly. After all, why should a *hongniang* act merely as a short-term contact person when, with a bit of guile, he could end up as the owner of the business?

Trung Nguyen coffee houses

One of the legacies of French colonialism in Vietnam was the drinking of coffee, and as *doi moi* began to show results and a new Vietnamese middle class began to emerge, the demand for coffee started to rise. The Trung Nguyen chain of coffee houses started as a small venture in Hanoi, which proved quickly profitable. The owners chose to franchise rather than expanding directly. Since its establishment in 1996, the chain has now expanded to more than

400 outlets, and has spread across Southeast Asia, to Taiwan, China, Japan, Russia, Canada and the United States. The company has now expanded into the tea business; unlike coffee, which is not native to the country, tea is one of Vietnam's major exports. The new Trung Nguyen 'fairy tea houses' give customers a chance to drink Vietnamese coffee and tea and experience something of Vietnamese culture.

Despite having spread around the world, Trung Nguyen has remained true to its own origins. It began as a neighbourhood coffee house, something part way between a Vietnamese cooking shop and a French café, and has worked hard to keep its local feel. It cultivates custom in the neighbourhoods where it trades, and has become a popular gathering point for locals. Unsurprisingly, it has become known as the Vietnamese Starbucks. There is a long way to go before it becomes a serious rival to the original Starbucks, but its growth so far has been both steady and well-managed. Trung Nguyen shows how local cultures can be leveraged for advantage in an increasingly globalised economy.

11 China and the world

Many the strains sprung from one common stock,
Boundless the shore of the sea;
And vain are men's myriad fancies,
For every sort and kind blend into one.

(Wu Cheng'en, *Journey to the West*)

As this tour of doing business in China draws to a close, it is perhaps time to speculate on some basic trends. Readers visiting China are free, as ever, to test these ideas against their own experiences and conversations. It is our view that the expansion of the Chinese economy is not a phenomenon that affects China alone, or even East Asia alone. All of us are touched by this growth, and will be even more affected by it in the future.

In January 2008, headlines were made when the China Development Bank bought $5 billion in shares in Morgan Stanley after the giant American bank found itself badly out of pocket thanks to the sub-prime mortgage fiasco. China Investment Corporation and Temasek, the Singapore-based sovereign wealth fund, took a substantial stake in Barclays around the same time. Western journalists and politicians saw the symbolism at once; Asia's sleeping giants were starting to wake. But in truth, overseas Chinese companies had been venturing out into the West, trading and investing, for a long time, and over the past five or six years Chinese companies have been joining them in increasing numbers.

China is now the world's fourth-largest economy, and is slowly but surely overtaking Germany and will slip into third place some time during the next decade. China is becoming a world economic power. True, this process is not complete, and huge challenges still confront Chinese business leaders and policy-makers. But we need to take cognisance of this trend now. It is time to start thinking about the presence and impact of Chinese-based international and multinational businesses, even if the practical outcome may be long deferred. If we wait until the process of 'Chinese globalisation' – China's full integration into world markets – is complete, then it will be too late.

Over the last few years the Chinese economy has grown at a rapid pace, to the point where Chinese policy-makers have begun to worry about overheating. The worldwide credit crisis of 2007–8 is expected to put the brakes on for a couple of years. This is regarded by many in China as a good thing, giving everyone a chance to draw breath, and allowing time for wages to catch up with prices. Over the longer term, we expect that the Chinese economy will continue to grow at a relatively even pace, and that no sudden crises will derail it. That is, of course, a huge assumption, and there are plenty of analysts around who would contest it. The threats to China are many: social and political unrest, natural disasters such as earthquakes (look at the damage the Kobe earthquake caused to the Japanese economy) and floods on the Yellow River, or indeed the blizzards of January 2008 which caused widespread chaos, blocking roads and airports, bringing down power lines and causing misery for many. Then there are other factors, such as power outages, already an issue in some areas of the country, or political and economic mismanagement that could cause growth to falter. Many things could go wrong. But is very hard now to see China turning back the clock to the bad old days of the early 1970s.

Nor is there any sign that the Chinese people on the whole are dissatisfied with their government, notwithstanding the presence of dissidents on issues such as human rights, religion and the environment. Slowly, the ordinary Chinese are growing bolder and standing up for themselves against the government, and they appear to be enjoying the process. In Shanghai in 2007–8, residents of one district took to the streets to protest about the construction of a new railway line through their area of the city, claiming the line would damage the environment and was a health hazard. By early 2008 the mayor of Shanghai had backed down and announced a full public inquiry, promising to engage in more public consultation before such projects were planned in the future. The story was widely reported in newspapers and on television both inside and outside China. The point is that the people of Shanghai were not challenging the right of the Communist Party or the government to exist, they were simply having a good old-fashioned grumble about a policy they did not like. (That they got results is probably a result of the fact that this was quite a well-to-do district of the city. The poor in China continue to have difficulty in making their voices heard, just as they do everywhere else in the world.)

Assuming, then, that China will continue to grow and remain economically and politically stable, this chapter looks at several issues that are associated with this outward growth of the Chinese economy. First, we consider that the growth of Chinese exports is creating a linkage between Western and Chinese firms that is not necessarily geographically specific to China; doing business *with* China is no longer necessarily the same as doing business *in* China. Second, as Chinese companies continue to spread their wings and move beyond their own borders, what opportunities are there for Western firms to participate in and profit from this expansion? It is now possible for a British firm to set up a joint venture (JV) with a Chinese firm in Britain, not just in China. Managers merely need to be bold enough to take the step. This does not mean that the opportunities for business in China are in any way lessened; on the contrary, much still remains to be done. Indeed, the breadth of opportunities for business in China and with the Chinese is probably greater now than it ever was.

Skilled hands, skilled brains

The impression persists in the West that the Chinese economy is primarily dedicated to manufacturing. We have images of old-fashioned smokestack industries in sectors like steel and heavy machinery, or else vast assembly-lines turning out plastic goods, toys, lamps and the like for sale in Western department stores. For many years now, China has been a favourite destination for Western companies looking for low-cost production facilities; moreover, outsourcing or 'offshoring' as it is sometimes known, has played a role in the continued growth of China. But there is more to the Chinese economy and to Chinese business than just 'making stuff'. As time passes, the role of China in the world economy is changing. We have already seen China become an exporter of capital. We are beginning to see China as an exporter of its own intellectual property.

We have gone through several attitudinal sea-changes to business in China over the past two decades or so. In the 1980s and early 1990s, the dominant view of China was that of a vast and largely untapped potential market for Western goods, the '1 billion new customers' approach. By the middle 1990s, however, the advantages of sourcing products in China were becoming widely known. Beginning with low-tech products of the kind that China has always done well, like shoes and textiles, and gradually moving further up the technology scale, hundreds of Western companies began sourcing goods and components from China, either from Chinese partners and suppliers or through their own production facilities established on Chinese soil.

China, according to a series of reports in the *Financial Times* in early 2003, was becoming the 'workshop of the world'. China had changed from being a vast market (and occasional dumping ground) for Western goods to being a supplier of cheap retail goods and, increasingly, a supplier of labour and materials for the manufacturers of the West. Car makers are always a good bell-wether for economic trends, and when in 2003 Honda announced plans to set up a complete assembly plant in northeastern China, the writing was on the wall. By 2004, Honda was selling cars all around the world, under its own brand, but entirely made in China. And where foreign companies based in China have led, Chinese companies have begun to follow. Companies like SAIC and Nanjing Auto began investing in Western car makers; the latter's controversial acquisition of MG-Rover made headlines, but other quieter deals have been done. We are still waiting for the first Chinese-branded car to be launched on the world market, but possibly not for much longer.

In the computer business, this step has already been taken; Chinese brands have been on the market for several years. And of course, Lenovo's acquisition of IBM's PC business in 2005 catapulted it into the world league, making it the world's third-largest PC maker almost overnight. Some observers commented that this did not mean much in itself; IBM was simply shedding a division it no longer wanted, and Lenovo happened to be the buyer. From IBM's perspective, perhaps this was true. From Lenovo's standpoint, however, this is the deal that put them on the map of global companies, outranking even the other big East Asian PC maker, the Taiwanese company Acer.

The implications of this for businesses everywhere are con-siderable. First, there is the problem of competition. At the moment, Chinese costs, especially labour costs, are low while the level of technical sophistication and knowledge is increasing rapidly. In many industries, the quality of Chinese goods is not much below that produced in state-of-the-art factories in the West; sometimes it is even superior. And the cost differentials are so vast as to make up for any perceived quality differences. In most businesses in most parts of the world, management should assume that if they do not already have a Chinese competitor making the same product, that they will have one very soon. Amid the fuss over intellectual property rights in China, few have noticed that the Chinese government and Chinese companies between them are spending many billions on research and development, one of the highest total spends of any country in the world (although still less per capita than in Britain or Germany). It is not true that the Chinese are no good at innovation and rely on copying Western ideas, any more than it was true of the Japanese 40 years ago. The Chinese are a clever, well-educated and industrious people, and it stands to reason that they will be good at innovation.

Second, there is the issue of integration. In 1998, following a diplomatic incident with an American spy plane was forced down inside China, hawks in the US administration wanted to impose trade sanctions on China. American business, led by retailers such as Wal-Mart, immediately raised an outcry. The cost of any sanctions, they argued, would ultimately be borne by themselves. So great was the dependence of these retailers on goods made in China that sanctions could wipe out a large chunk of their profit margin. The same point has been reinforced several times since, and in recent years both the EU and the USA have considered trade sanctions against China over alleged unfair exporting practices. In every case, the loudest cries have emanated from Western retailers and others, many of whom depend on China utterly. China is now part of the world value chain. Of course it goes the other way too, and China would undoubtedly suffer if Western companies and consumers stopped buying its products. The point is that China is now very strongly integrated into the world economy, and short of some truly cataclysmic change, it seems unlikely that there is any way back.

This is all part of globalisation, of course, but a part that few give enough thought to. We are accustomed to the triad – America, Europe and Japan (though the latter is steadily losing power and influence as its economic crisis shows no sign of ending) – running the show. The idea that China could be a new entrant into this power game is not always taken very seriously. But we need to get over our old preconceptions of China as the 'wild East', the world's biggest market, or of China as the workshop of the world, the place we go to get our goods made cheaply. China is moving into a new stage.

The time is not far off when we will not have to go to China to do business with the Chinese; they will be coming to us. The question is: are we ready?

Beyond the Great Wall

We must now apply the yardstick that we have applied all along: the statement that China is fully integrated into the world economy is, simultaneously, both true and not true. Some parts of China, especially on the eastern and southern coasts, are pretty much integrated, although that is integration on China's own terms. Some parts, notably in the centre and west of the country, still have a long way to go.

All you need to know about China and the modern world can be summed up in a scene witnessed by one of the authors when travelling in the countryside near Beijing a few years ago, not far from the Great Wall. On the edge of the quiet high street of a small village, two women were working. One was skinning a dead sheep. The other, only a few yards away, was mending a broken video recorder. Both looked equally competent, as though these were everyday tasks that they were fully used to.

China is both timeless and modern. The ancient agrarian peasant economy and the high-tech world of the twenty-first century exist side by side. And in part, this is one of the things that gives China its strength. This is a country which faces simultaneously backwards and forwards, and draws on its cultural heritage while looking to the future. The government of China knows this very well, and spends much time promoting China's history, culture and heritage to its own people. Television programmes about history and archaeology are becoming more popular on state television. So are soap operas, masquerading as historical dramas, set in the imperial past; the Ming and Qing dynasties are favourite periods. Films depicting the mythical past, such as *Crouching Tiger, Hidden Dragon* and *House of the Flying Daggers* gained popularity in the West as well as in China. Television advertisers are following the trend; while some ads feature trendy young people in sophisticated urban settings, others use classical Chinese settings and costumes.

In 2007, according to government statistics, more than 200 online gaming companies were launched in China. Most of these failed, but of the 30 or so that survived, it was notable that many featured themes from Chinese history and mythology. So said the report; looking at screen shots from some of these games, it was rather hard to tell which bit of history or myth was being referred to. But the basic point stands. The past, sometimes imperfectly understood, sometimes crudely manipulated, is big business in China. The steady growth of the domestic tourism industry is another sign.

We must not be misled by the examples of CITIC and China Development Bank and the Construction Bank. These are now heavy-hitters in the world of international finance, just as Air China and Lenovo and SAIC are rising to prominence in their respective sectors and Jiao Tong University has an internationally recognised business school. But they are not the whole of China. In a nation of 1.3 billion people, with the second largest land area of any nation on Earth, it is possible to find extremes of poverty and wealth. China may have more billionaires than any other country but it also has 200 million people living below the poverty line. As we have remarked throughout this book, there are enormous regional disparities within the country, in terms of wealth, education, technological development and infrastructure. All of these disparities the Chinese are trying to address. And all of these disparities offer opportunities for businesses, Western and Chinese alike.

In some ways, nothing has changed. China *is* a land of opportunity; whatever product or service one is making or selling, there is almost certainly someone in China who needs it. That can be taken for granted; the real difficulty lies in locating them and explaining the proposition, and in differentiating oneself from the existing competition. That was true in the 1990s and is still true today. Makers of luxury goods will find a large market; purveyors of services will find a growing middle class with cash in its pockets and an appetite to spend; social entrepreneurs will find plenty of institutional gaps that will allow them to tackle the problems of poverty and lack of education, and if they so choose, make money while so doing. We do not exaggerate the opportunities open to this last group. The Indian sub-continent has seen a number of very successful ventures of this kind, such as Aurolab in India and Grameen Bank in Bangladesh. Their time may have come in China, too.

As for outsourcing, there is no immediate sign that the boom will end. Rising wages and overstretched infrastructure are making life more difficult for outsourcers in some areas, notably Guangzhou province. But there are plenty of untapped labour pools elsewhere.

Some have predicted that wage inflation in China will drive Western outsourcers to other countries – to Vietnam or the Philippines or even out of Asia altogether. Some may well leave, but others will see opportunities elsewhere in China. The next outsourcing boom is likely to be in central China, around Wuhan; the one after that, in Sichuan around cities such as Chongqing and Chengdu. This phase of China's development is by no means over.

But Western businesses now have other options for dealing with China. As we said earlier, it is no longer strictly necessary to go to China in order to deal with the Chinese; increasingly, Chinese businesses are coming to the West. They are doing so for several reasons. First, the banks, financial institutions and larger companies are looking to diversify their investment portfolios. It was this, rather than any desire for corporate control, which many believe was the motive behind the acquisitions of substantial chunks of Merrill Lynch, Citibank, Morgan Stanley, Barclays and others by Asian institutions early in 2008. These big Asian businesses have plenty of liquidity and are looking for bargains.

Second, Chinese and other Asian manufacturers are looking for outlets. In the old system, these manufacturers functioned as relatively passive members of the value chain, receiving and fulfilling orders from Western customers. Now, bolder and more entrepreneurial Chinese companies are looking to move down the value chain to get closer to their Western customers. They are looking for partners who can help them with marketing and distribution and general industry know-how. Cars, electronics and textiles are the sectors where the trend is most noticeable at the moment, but others will follow.

And finally, Chinese companies are seeking Western partners in order to learn: about the markets of America and Europe, about consumer demand, about ways of doing business, about culture – in effect, travelling the reverse of the path we have described in this book. Rather than waiting for the foreigners to come to China and pick them out of the herd, Chinese firms are going out into the world beyond. And they are prepared to pay for the learning they receive, not by supplying low-cost labour or materials, but with cash. 'Learning joint ventures' offer real opportunities for Western companies prepared to play teacher. But working with Chinese companies in this way may require that we change our own thinking. There is an argument, for example, that we in the West should not be giving away our 'trade secrets' to the Chinese in this way: today they are our partners, but tomorrow they will be our competitors. Exactly the same argument was advanced concerning American business in Japan in the 1950s and 1960s. The counter-argument was that the Japanese were going to learn these 'secrets' anyway, and it was likely to be more profitable in both the short and long term to work with the Japanese rather than against them.

Much the same argument can be made about China today. The Chinese economy, if not the unstoppable juggernaut that Japan was in the 1960s and 1970s, is nonetheless growing and becoming more powerful. Refusing to work with the Chinese now because they will be kicking us out of our own markets in 20 years' time sounds a bit like cutting off one's nose to spite one's face. The future will happen regardless of what most businesspeople think they can do about it – and a lot can happen in 20 years.

More cogently, there is a tendency to think of China as a developing country, and Chinese businesses as under-managed and inefficient. Once upon a time this may have been true, but the picture is rapidly changing. 'Developing country' is a label which many Chinese are beginning to question. The typical Chinese business is no longer the SOE, grossly over-manned and insolvent, its tens of thousand workers housed and fed from the iron rice bowl, churning out its quota of goods regardless of market demand. The typical Chinese business today is a small to medium enterprise run by a close group of family or friends, perhaps graduates from the same university class. They tend to be young, conscious of the fact that they still have a lot to learn, but acutely focused on a particular business opportunity and prepared to work until they drop to make it happen. These young Chinese managers are tough, flexible and determined. They know they have before them an opportunity which might not come around again. They are, in terms of intellect and commitment, our equals if not our superiors, and they deserve our respect.

One of the biggest changes in China in the last few years has been the emergence of this new generation of entrepreneurs. Born at the tail end of the Cultural Revolution or early in the reform era, they were still at school at the time of Tiananmen Square. They are well-educated and used to living with Western influences. They are prepared to take on the world. In other words, they see the rest of the world as a potential market – very much as the rest of the world sees them. That is the twenty-first-century economic battleground but perhaps a battle that both can win. China will surely get richer, but will her competitors be impoverished by that?

Implications

The most important implication of all this is, to repeat the position we set out earlier in this chapter, that all of us are affected by China's growth, and that doing business with the Chinese is no longer just a matter of doing business *in* China. Chinese customers, partners and competitors are beginning to come to the West to do business on their own account, and are doing so with increasing confidence, competence and financial backing. More and more Western managers will end up doing business with, or in competition with, Chinese firms as the years go by, and this without the Western side ever setting foot in China.

We said at the outset that this book is aimed at Western businesspeople going to China for the first time. But we think its lessons are valuable too for those working with Chinese companies in the wider world, or who can reasonably expect to do so in the near future. Just as Westerners take their values and ideas about business with them when they go to China, so Chinese managers take their own culturally based predispositions with them when they come to the West. We can argue over which side will adapt best or learn quickest, but there will be a clash of cultures nonetheless. One thing is certain though: working *with* Chinese companies offers more opportunities for fun and profit than working against them.

This is the time when some reverse strategic thinking might be in order. In other words, rather than casting around for strategic opportunities in China, managers might consider what opportunities exist in their own sectors for Chinese companies reaching towards the West. What advantages might these Chinese companies have? What might they be seeking to gain, in terms of profit or knowledge? And how can the manager's own company turn this to its own advantage, by helping the Chinese partner to find its way? This kind of strategic opportunity will become more common over the next dozen years. We believe it is time to start looking at China not as the country behind the Great Wall, but as an increasingly active player in the world economy with many advantages and many benefits to offer.

12 Western and Chinese commercial thinking

A distinguished colleague once told us, 'There's no need for books on doing business in particular regions such as China. After all, doing business in China is just the same as doing business anywhere else'. This being China, that observation is both true and not true.

Doing Business in China was written because there *are* differences between China and the West, differences in history, philosophy, politics and society. And because business is essentially a social process, there are differences in *ways* of doing business as well. This has two consequences for Westerners: when in China they have to adjust their ways to fit the environment, and in the rest of the world they can apply what they have learned from China. The Chinese are, naturally, learning reciprocally and we then have to factor in what we both have to learn from Japan and other parts of the world. Furthermore, as we argued earlier, China is likely to dominate world trade in the new century, so those of us who plan to be around for long should listen and learn.

If we took what our colleague said at face value, we would only have to understand how to do business in London, Chicago or wherever we happen to be, since the rest of the world is, or perhaps should be, the same. We were struck by the comment of the manager of the Chicago Futures Market following the Barings disaster in Singapore. Prevention was simple, we were told: the rest of the world should just adopt Chicago's rule book. The very same arrogance ('we set the standards') caused the stagnation of China through the Ming and Qing dynasties.

Our aims were twofold: to understand consumers, customers, partners, governments and other players in China and, in the process, to learn about their business methods and ways of thinking. One of the keys to success in global business lies in learning global lessons and then in applying them locally. The more we can identify with Chinese thinking, the more widely we can benefit from it. And vice versa.

Because events in China are happening so rapidly, we know that any current facts are ephemeral, although we have tried to provide up-to-the-minute information where possible. Instead, we have attempted to give you a framework for knowledge. We hope we have given readers enough understanding of the basic issues for you to go out and do research on your own, and have a context into which to fit the information you acquire.

After briefly summarising the book, we will draw out the underlying structure.

Summary of the book

The first visit

Acquiring detailed, up-to-date information about China is difficult. The pace of change in China means that books with immediate detail are quickly obsolete. There are, however, many directories and sources that specialise in helping businesses make preliminary contacts in China.

The most important requirement is to set up meetings for that visit. Conventional wisdom is that no amount of reading and preparation for the first visit is too much. We doubt that: the real aim of pre-reading is to equip oneself *socially* to impress the people you will meet. After your first visit, research will make more sense, as you build up macro-level knowledge to complement your personal knowledge. Beforehand, and apart from background reading (e.g. history), you only really need this book and a good tourist guide.

There are a number of options for organising the first visit. Solo visits or 'tours for one' are becoming increasingly easy and common, but you may find it difficult to make contacts or see people unless you have some introductions in your pocket (and maybe not even then). For others, escorted tours, organised visits and trade missions offer good introductions to the country and, depending on how efficient the organisers are, at least some of the key players in the markets you are considering.

Finding business partners is essentially a networking exercise. Do not rely on one point of entry to the network, no matter how trustworthy and well connected the person may be. Develop multiple sources of information and contacts. There probably is no one best way to find the right partner (would you advise your children on ways to find the best spouse?). A lot of it is about being in the right place and networking as much as possible. Try to find ways of identifying real people and separating them from the 'ghosts'.

Go-betweens are a good option, but then you have to find the right go-between. At least the list of potential candidates is more manageable, however, and selection should be easier. Using go-betweens saves time, uses existing networks, gives you any necessary language capability and usually some business consultancy advice is thrown in as well. Disadvantages may include longer lines of communication, with the potential for misunderstanding.

The decision to enter is not to be taken lightly. Making the decision should require several visits, a non-trivial expense for a small company.

Culture and environment

China is not a unitary whole but is a number of vastly different regions, each with its own subculture and its own language or dialect. China has a long and eventful history and a rich culture, of which its citizens are justly proud. History and culture are very important to the Chinese. History in particular exercises a powerful influence over thinking and behaviour. Bitter past experience has taught the Chinese that not all foreigners can be trusted, and that even with the best of intentions, contact with foreigners can have negative consequences. One of the most important themes here is the need for stability and the dread of chaos, which underpins not only government policy but much everyday social intercourse. Reformers who want China to become more like the West are unlikely to make much headway while this attitude prevails.

Strategy and philosophy

China is also rich in terms of philosophical traditions and modes of thinking. Many of these share common features. Respect for age and authority is commonly ascribed to Confucianism, but probably has its origins in the ancestor cult. Time in Chinese thinking is not linear but circular; the past is also the future. Daoism recognises the thirst for harmony, balance and paradox, which is both a perpetual delight and a frustration to Western minds. It is not possible to overstate the importance of 'and' versus 'or' thinking. It recurs in various forms throughout business in China, and the Orient as a whole.

Good marketing process is very often the avoidance of decisions. If you have to choose A or B, both are probably wrong. The search for consensus, for meeting all objectives, as distinct from choosing between them, gives oriental mental furniture a head start over Western logic.

Cultural values play a major role in business relationships. The most important of these are: (a) age, hierarchy and authority, which are strongly linked; (b) face and the importance of self-esteem and dignity; and (c) the balance between individual and group orientation. Past researchers have tried to determine whether the Chinese are individualist *or* group-oriented. In fact, they are both simultaneously.

Strategy is the second most important marketing, or business, paradigm in China just as it is in the West. Sunzi directly inspired some of the greatest guerrilla generals of all time, notably Mao Zedong and Ho Chi Minh. Guerrilla warfare is central to most marketers: conventional warfare is merely the final stage relevant to the surviving few. Nowhere is this more relevant than in China.

The essential lessons of guerrilla warfare are:

- Avoid the competition as long as you can.
- Concentrate your resources geographically and in time. Then concentrate again. Ruthless focus.
- Never do the obvious/expected.
- Achieve local knockout and then expand incrementally.
- Cultivate allies (relationships), steal the competitor's resources, be generous to losers: this is for the long term.
- When you are sure to win, kill the competition.

Relationships

Guanxi, relationships or connections, is the key to business in China. *Business may flow out of friendship, whereas in the West friendship may flow out of business.* To the Chinese and others in the Pacific region, relationship building is second nature, a natural part of the environment and doing business. Westerners, however, need to plan and track such networks consciously and with great care.

Corruption is seen by some as an inevitable outgrowth of *guanxi*. Indeed, some use *guanxi* as a synonym for grease. That is wrong and complicates an already complex subject. True *guanxi* cannot be bought. Pseudo-*guanxi* may be essential for survival but it can also erode future prospects.

Most advice is to avoid all forms of questionable payment. In the words of Ian Rae, 'once you start, they'll never let you go'.[1] We have no doubt that bribery (paying officials to do what they should not) should be avoided, albeit avoided with dignity on both sides. Grease payments and other borderline activities are more difficult, especially if it makes the difference between survival or not. Those brands with high brand equity are more able to set standards.

We commend the 'sunlight test' to distinguish the legitimate from the illegitimate, i.e. if it becomes public knowledge, will you be damaged? There is much to be said for cooperative policing with one's competitors – assuming, of course, that they can be trusted!

The law

Among the many myths about doing business in China one is that there is no such thing as law, or that businesspeople do not respect the law. The first is no longer true and attitudes to the second may be changing. China has an established and growing body of commercial law, and its court system and the legal profession are developing and expanding. These are early days still, by comparison to our long-established Western legal system, but certainly no Western company can afford to ignore this development.

A good Chinese lawyer can be of great value to a business – not just in interpreting the law but in managing relationships with local legal and administrative bureaucracies. The trick, as in any country or culture, is finding that good lawyer in the first place. There are, however, more resources for doing so than once there were. However, there are differences between the Western and Chinese legal systems, and probably always will be. Understanding those differences and how the Chinese system works is crucial.

Intellectual property remains a hot topic despite the progress that the PRC government has made. International law is being applied, but enforcement remains very difficult and piracy is still a cause for concern. General advice is to use a multiple strategy when confronted with piracy; legal suits are necessary to persuade government officials that it is serious. Then, via *guanxiwang*, to seek official backing.

Government, the law and *guanxi* all interweave and are hard to separate. No one 'connection', however good, is adequate.

In cultivating multiple connections, remember that they are reciprocal: favours received are credits against future favours expected. It is not a bank account but expectations for the future are created. It is easy to get overloaded, in which case doubts and distrust will creep in.

Establishing ventures

There are various options for entering the China market, including agencies, joint ventures (JVs) and wholly foreign-owned enterprises (WFOEs). The most popular has long been the JV, partly because WFOEs were not permitted in that sector/region.

Establishing and managing a JV is always difficult; one or more partners may lack a clear agenda and/or trust. A *hongniang*, or go-between, can help partners come together. The importance of this role is misunderstood by Westerners, just as the need for management consultants is misunderstood by Chinese. In practice, such misunderstandings may cancel out: some intermediaries may be seen as *hongniang* by Chinese and as consultants by their Western clients.

JVs in China are not for those who only think short-term; negotiations can take years, and the Chinese expect commitment to be long-term. WFOEs are becoming easier to establish, and many believe they should be the first preference for market entry. At the same time, many large and established Western corporations continue to use JVs. We recommend assessing both options and picking the one that works best for the situation.

Marketing mix

Brands are very important in China, and early leader advantage has more going for it in other markets. Early sampling and 'name' recognition are important. 'Name' means branding: symbols, colours and numbers all mean more than Roman letters.

Price skimming is a general strategy worth considering, though it is possible to overdo it; several recent skimmers have had trouble as consumers considered the product overvalued. Chinese consumers are now better informed and less infatuated by the 'foreignness' of brands. Today one should aim to overshoot the right price by only a small margin.

Representative offices are a must for all but the smallest traders with China. Medium-sized firms should consider sharing with

Western non-competitors. Expect to give distribution issues more priority relative to developed countries.

The full range of marketing tools is available. The less conventional may be better value, depending on the situation. E-commerce is faltering at present due to distribution and payment difficulties, but as a medium for communication it is moving fast despite government monitoring and interference.

Marketing process

Marketing process includes at least analysis, planning, implementation, measurement, both market research and internal. Some see it as including the development and motivation of managers and the host of other operational matters that bring satisfaction to customers and consumers. For this book we limited ourselves to information and planning.

China has more statistics than any company can handle. Unfortunately, they are unreliable. This bothers Westerners more than the Chinese who are looking for pictures, not precision. Fuzzy focus is quite good enough for then. To pilot through, a Western firm will need to be tough-minded about what they must know and what may be nice to know but perhaps should be abandoned. Integrating research needs and the planning process is critical to selecting, and then acting on, crucial competitive information.

Plans are not important: planning is. It is rehearsing the future. One can practise as many times as one likes, but tomorrow comes only once. The classic four Ps marketing plan format should be replaced by the Strategy/*guanxi*/Calculation sequence for China. It is not that one should adopt the Chinese format – such a thing never existed. The point is that planning, being a rehearsal or modelling of the future, should represent the Chinese market in a Chinese way. The essence of marketing is that it is outside-in learning. Absorb the context.

Management issues

Chinese businesses should be seen as families rather than as representing modern organisation theory on earth. They are more formal and traditional than their Western counterparts, with decision-making concentrated at the top. In consequence, if you want anything done by a Chinese business, you usually have to go to the top.

One consequence, as most Western companies have already learned to their cost, is high staff turnover. Smaller, leaner, flatter organisations are less likely to engender staff and managerial loyalty, and staff tend to move on as soon as they get a better offer. We looked at how Western companies, by managing in a more 'Chinese way', can improve retention and keep costs down. We also looked at training, especially for managers, where there has been a proliferation of management training programmes but many are of doubtful quality. Hiring and keeping the best people requires time and investment.

Chinese businesses overseas

The 60 million Chinese living in the overseas communities represent a powerful economic force, and literally dominate the economies of many countries outside China. Overseas Chinese can be good partners for Western businesses. However, there are perceptible differences between the overseas Chinese and their mainland counterparts, and we stressed that adjustments needed to be made when dealing with overseas Chinese in different countries.

Many overseas Chinese have ambivalent attitudes to China, and vice versa. Thus, there can be problems in using overseas Chinese as intermediaries to do business in mainland China. This does not mean it cannot be done, but Westerners need to be aware of these possibly complex relationships before setting out to build a partnership involving both overseas and mainland Chinese.

We also considered the future for Chinese businesses as they move into the global economy. That they will do so is hardly in doubt; the first steps are already being taken. This will bring threats for Western businesses but it will also bring opportunities. And there is the possibility too for some deeper learning about how we manage. Some characteristics of Chinese management may be transferable, others may not.

Doing business in China: the 'five pillars'

There is no one 'model' for doing business in China. Conditions vary too much; any model would have to be so hedged about with conditions as to be uninformative or useless. Better to summarise the course in a Confucian fashion by presenting 'five pillars', or recommendations, as a framework for anyone doing business in the area. They are presented from a variety of angles, and their relative importance will depend upon the situation.

We see the structure arranged as four pillars surrounding the first and most important: *guanxi*.

The first pillar: guanxi

Guanxi is the single most important concept when dealing with China and the Chinese in any social context, not just in business. The Chinese measure their own social position in part by the extent of their *guanxiwang*, or network of contacts. They use these contacts, sometimes almost exclusively, to do business.

It may be possible to do business in China without developing a network of relationships. However, we do not know of any examples where companies or individuals have ultimately been successful, and the recent history of Western businesses in China is full of examples of companies who have neglected *guanxi* to their cost.

Westerners often do business with people they do not know; sometimes with people they never see. This is much harder in China, and much less likely to bring success. We believe that in order to do business with a Chinese, you must first get to know him or her. You should ideally have been recommended by a reliable third party. Contacts breed contacts. It is the first stage, getting the first contacts and getting inside the magic circle, that is hardest; once in, it is possible to exploit contacts, and the contacts of contacts, and thus widen one's own *guanxiwang*.

At a more fundamental level, *guanxi* is a relationship way of seeing marketing. It puts the customer first. There is no need to recap this here but if the logical consequences are followed through, notably in planning, some of the predictable hazards, especially with joint ventures and distribution, may be safely negotiated.

The other four pillars all reflect the central importance of *guanxi*.

The second pillar: continuity

W.F. Jenner has written that China is influenced by two things: the 'history of tyranny' and the 'tyranny of history'.[2] Taoist and Confucian influences are still prominent. *Guanxi* itself is a concept rooted deep in China's past.

Any reasonably well-educated Chinese knows his or her own country's history well, and most can quote incidents from it. All are strongly aware of the events of the recent past, and of the odds that such events could be repeated in the near future. Thus while most of China's people are strongly aware of and proud of their cultural traditions, they are also trying hard to escape the cycle of boom and bust that has torn the country to pieces three times and left 200 million dead in the last 150 years.

Businesses and managers going into China need to know something about China's ancient and recent past. They need this knowledge for the obvious reasons of finding a context for the present and attempting to understand the future. They also need to know what is driving their Chinese partners and competitors. No other people on earth are so strongly influenced by their past as the Chinese.

Similarly, ways of thinking change very slowly. Tolerance for ambiguity – 'and' thinking – flow from Taoism. The Chinese do not feel the need to rush to solve problems that Westerners exhibit. This is likely to lead to Chinese advantage in the twenty-first-century race for competitive business knowledge or organisational learning.

The visiting business person should not flaunt any historical expertise. It would seem odd; all we propose is awareness and sensitivity. The 'pillar' reflects an unconscious sense of continuity: what is done now must be in harmony with what has gone before. Many things in China change rather slowly: identity, culture, etiquette and business practices all reflect the lessons of history. If you find yourself in business with someone who does *not* have those roots, beware. Continuity may slow things down; it may be frustrating but it also gives confidence in a relationship that the past is a reliable guide to the future.

The third pillar: the market

Whilst some things change slowly, it took China about one nanosecond to revert to the market concept, though the reality is taking a little longer. Trading and bargaining are as natural to China as complaining about the weather is in England: both are national pastimes. We concluded earlier that the cost of market research in China was more or less whatever you were prepared to pay. To Coca-Cola it was expensive, to others it is quite cheap. You do not necessarily get what you pay for. Those on a cheap holiday are quite likely to end up in the same hotel as those on an expensive holiday. Both paid what they could be persuaded to part with and both got what was available. The West does much the same with airline seats.

The fourth pillar: ren *and organisations*

Guanxi does not always imply equal relationships. In China, the family relationship system is consciously replicated in businesses, organisations and governments.

Ren, the obligation of a leader's responsibility to all of his or her subordinates, is a strong force in Chinese organisations which are often dominated by strong leaders, with obedience expected of the workers below. In return for obedience, the leader is expected to listen to the opinions of subordinates and to care for the lives of their employees, but is also expected to make decisions and exercise leadership alone. Workers and juniors are not expected to use their initiative or entrepreneurial skills. The leader is expected to be flexible, responsible and entrepreneurial, but always in a way that keeps his or her actions within the overall framework of the Chinese economy and society.

Obviously there are many variations of this model which, in any case, does not always work. Some Chinese are critical of their own way of doing things and would like to see the wider adoption of Western models. But equally, there is evidence that Western organisational models applied literally to China are unsuccessful as well. The flat hierarchies and devolving responsibility which are popular in the West seem to lead to lower levels of employee loyalty, and the higher salaries paid by Western companies are not always a substitute for the social and other benefits paid by Chinese enterprises. A compromise system, with the organisational freedom of Western businesses but with strong leadership and strong loyalty inducements in the Chinese fashion, may be the best model for China. It may also be a model we could usefully look at in the West.

When setting up a JV or WFOE organisation, these differences may become incompatibilities. How equal the relationships between partners (each of whom may *privately* consider themselves the senior), management styles and staff loyalties are all potentially destructive.

The fifth pillar: obstacles

China has long been seen as an impenetrable mass, protected by real and chauvinistic barriers, including the Great Wall and the Bamboo Curtain. American writers, in particular during the Cold War, were fond of seeing China as gigantic and amorphous. They noted the uniformity of fashion during the Cultural Revolution and coined empty phrases such as 'Mao's blue hordes'. Nothing could be further from the truth.

From Heilongjiang to Yunnan, from Shanghai to Xinjiang, there are vast variations in geography, climate, economy, language, food, dress, occupation, mental and social outlook – and in business conditions. The Chinese government is trying hard, paradoxically, to create more equal conditions throughout the country and spread economic development. Until it does so, China will continue to be a land of variety.

The physical barriers are gone; now tourists are the only invaders on the Great Wall, and there is unrestricted travel throughout most of the country. However, there are still some intangible barriers for a Western businessman. Chinese language, culture and regulations may scare away many faint hearts. However, Laozi tells us that there is always a trade-off between advantages and disadvantages.

Conclusions

We have met quite a few expatriates during our sojourns in China and they fall broadly into two groups: those who love China and the Chinese, and those who will soon be going home. There are dangers in both points of view, not to mention being so crass as to offend Daoist thinking with the dichotomy.

On the one hand, the world economy is not a zero-sum game. China's growth will help the rest of the world too, just as Japan has provided immense benefit to us all since about 1960. On the other hand, we are in competition. Relative wealth depends on our relative skills and endeavours. Working hard is being replaced by working smart. This is no longer a matter of how many white-overall-clad ladies are turning out how many microchips or plastic toys. That was then. Tomorrow is about the depth of understanding from which creativity and innovation can gain competitive advantage. If this book has helped, in however small a way, to improve the understanding of business in China, then we have done our part.

Notes

Introduction

1 Percy Timberlake (1994) *The Story of the Icebreakers in China*, London: The 48 Group Club, p. 13.

1 The road to Cathay

1 See Chapter 7 for more on market research in China.

2 For a longer list of UK organisations that can offer advice and assistance, see Robin Porter and Mandi Robinson (eds) (1994) *The China Business Guide*, Keele: Ryburn Publishing and Keele University Press. A. J. de Keijzer (1994) *China: Business Strategies for the 90's*, Berkeley, CA: Pacific View Press, does the same for the USA. Be warned that both these are getting a little dated; confirm contact details before trying the suggested organisations.

3 It is warned that prices can vary from organisation to organisation; some of these can be quite expensive.

4 Everyone has a right to their own opinion on contentious issues such as human rights. We simply urge caution when it comes to when and where you express these views. It is perfectly possible that an injudicious opinion will offend your hosts even if they are broadly in agreement with you. Remember the American saying, 'My country right or wrong'; it applies in China as well.

5 For example, T. Shabad (1972) *China's Changing Map*, London: Methuen.

6 See C.O. Hucker (1978) *China to 1850. A Short History*, Stanford, CA: Stanford University Press, and Edwin E. Moise (1994) *Modern China: A History*, London: Longman.

7 Their website is www.baedeker.com, but at time of writing seems only to exist in German.

8 This is an important concept, developed in more detail in Chapter 4 but referred to throughout the book.

9 This advice is more didactic than realistic: China is never so determinist. Luck may strike first time. A Chinese importer may approach the exporter's home office in the first place, saving the immediate need

to travel and search. We are not suggesting you won't get lucky; we are suggesting that you be prepared for a long haul.

2 Through a glass darkly: China from a Western perspective

1 Jianguang Wang (ed.) (1990) *Westerners through Chinese Eyes*, Beijing: Foreign Languages Press.
2 P. Fleming (1959) *The Siege at Peking*, London: Rupert Hart-Davis.
3 This chapter deals primarily with 'mainland China', that is to say, the territory of the People's Republic of China. The Chinese communities of East and Southeast Asia will be dealt with in a similar fashion in Chapter 10.
4 W.F. Jenner (1989) *The Tyranny of History*, Cambridge: Cambridge University Press; Edwin E. Moise (1994) *Modern China: A History*, London: Longman.
5 The Penguin translation of this work carries the title *The Story of the Stone*, but the title given above is more common.

3 The furniture of the mind

1 Douglas Mair (1990) *The Scottish Contribution to Modern Economic Thought*, Aberdeen: Aberdeen University Press, p. 160.
2 Ibid.
3 Huang Quanyu, Joseph Leonard and Chen Tong (1997) *Business Decision Making in China*, London: Haworth Press.
4 Ibid, p. 91.
5 M.H. Bond (ed.) (1986) *The Psychology of the Chinese People*, Oxford: Oxford University Press.
6 F.S.T. Hsiao, F.C. Jen and C.F. Lee (1990) 'Impacts of culture and communist orthodoxy on Chinese management', in J. Child and M. Lockett (eds) *Advances in Chinese Industrial Studies*, Greenwich, CT: JAI Press, pp. 301–14.
7 See Bond (1986).
8 A.S. Cua (1998) 'Confucian Philosophy, Chinese', in E. Craig (ed.) *Routledge Encyclopedia of Philosophy*, vol. 2, pp. 536–49.
9 Clive Dimmock (2000) *Designing the Learning-Centred School*, London: Falmer.
10 See Edwin Moise (1994) *Modern China: A History*, London: Longman, for a history of the Party's rise; also see Edgar O'Ballance (1962) *The Red Army of China*, London: Faber & Faber.
11 See L.W. Pye (1992) *Chinese Negotiating Style: Commercial Approaches and Cultural Principles*, London: Quorum Books.
12 G. Hofstede (1991) *Cultures and Organizations: Software of the Mind*, Beverly Hills, CA: Sage.
13 The translations come from R.L. Wing (1988) *The Art of Strategy: A New Translation of Sun Tzu's Classic, The Art of War*, New York: Doubleday.
14 Y.N. Chang (1976) 'Early Chinese management thought', *California Management Review*, Winter, p. 74.
15 Norman Dixon (1976) *On the Psychology of Military Incompetence*, London: Pimlico.

16 Taken from Ashok Som (2007), 'Volkswagen in China: running the Olympic marathon', *European Business Forum*, vol. 30, Autumn, pp. 46–9.

4 Relationships and regulations

1 Yi Zhang and Zhigang Zhang (2006) 'Guanxi and organizational dynamics in China', *Journal of Business Ethics*, vol. 67, p. 375.
2 Julia Tao (1996) 'The moral foundation of welfare in Chinese society: between virtues and rights', in G.S. Becker (ed.), *Ethics in Business and Society*, Berlin: Springer, p. 16.
3 Mayfair Mei-hui Yang (1994) *Gifts, Favors and Banquets*, Ithaca, NY: Cornell University Press.
4 Kevin Bucknall (2002) *Chinese Business Etiquette and Culture*, Raleigh, NC: Boson Books, p. 16.
5 Sally Stewart (1990) 'Where the power lies: a look at China's bureaucracy', *Advances in Chinese Industrial Studies*, vol. 1, New York: JAI Press.
6 Ian Rae (1997) 'Westerners need patience to crack Chinese puzzle', *Sunday Times*, 9 November.
7 This could be important, depending on where and in what sector the foreign firm wishes to do business. See the bibliography for books on this subject.
8 Rae (1997).
9 *Business China*, 3 May 1993.
10 Geoffrey Murray (1994) *Doing Business in China: The Last Great Market*, Sandgate, Kent: China Library.
11 Ibid.

5 Business and the law

1 The major cities include (a) the capital city of provinces and autonomous regions, (b) the city where a special economic zone is located, and (c) a city approved by the State Council to be a 'comparatively large city'.
2 Chanyeon Hwang (2005) 'A study of EU regulations', MBA dissertation, Manchester Business School.
3 *Guanyu Jinyibu Fahui Susong Tiaojie zai Goujian Shehui Zhuyi Hexie Shehui zhong Jiji Zuoyong de Ruogan Yijian*, promulgated on 1 March 2007.
4 International Intellectual Property Alliance, 2004 Special 301 Report: People's Republic of China.
5 Liu Shengjun (2006) 'Pepsi's "painful marriage" in Sichuan', *Asian Case Research Journal*, vol. 10, no. 2, pp. 281–30, media reports.

An ethical interlude

1 Julia Tao (1996) 'The moral foundation of welfare in Chinese society: between virtues and rights', in Gerhold S. Becker (ed.) *Ethics in Business and Society*, Berlin: Springer, pp. 9–24.
2 Chad Hansen (1996) 'Chinese philosophy and human rights: an application of comparative ethics', in Gerhold S. Becker (ed.) *Ethics in Business and Society*, Berlin: Springer, pp. 99–127.

3 These are traditionally given out by more senior people at Chinese New Year, by uncles to nephews, by bosses to subordinates and so on.

4 'Corkage' is a cash amount paid for every branded cork or bottle top returned by the retailer to the brand's local distributor.

6   Creating harmony: establishing businesses in China

1 Ted Plafker (2007) *Doing Business in China*, London: Business Plus.

2 John Child (1999) in *Financial Times Mastering Management Review*, London: FT.

3 Ian Rae (1997) 'Westerners need patience to crack Chinese puzzle', *Sunday Times*, 9 November.

4 Mayfair Mei-hui Yang (1994) *Gifts, Favors and Banquets*, Ithaca, NY: Cornell University Press; Kevin Bucknall (2002) *Chinese Business Etiquette and Culture*, Raleigh, NC: Boson Books.

7   The marketing mix

1 Michael Backman and Charlotte Butler (2002) *Big in Asia: 25 Strategies for Business Success*, Basingstoke: Palgrave Macmillan.

2 As noted above, the marketing mix can be represented by the classic four Ps of product (including branding and packaging), price, promotion and place (including sales, channels and distribution).

3 R. Yan (1994) 'To reach China's consumers, adapt to *Guo Qing*', *Harvard Business Review*, September–October.

4 Backman and Butler (2002: 222).

5 Summary findings of WARC's *Global Media Cost Comparison 2006 Report*, January 2008.

6 Figures courtesy of CTR Market Research Co. Ltd. Our thanks to them for generously providing this material.

7 'Pyramid selling', which depends on piling inventory on lower levels of sales representative rather than selling to real customers, is illegal in many countries and should not be confused, but often is, with 'network marketing' where the product is sold by, but not to, part-time commission agents exploiting their personal contacts. Network marketing seems well suited to China and other companies should learn from the Mary Kay experience.

8 *Asian Pacific Post* (2005) 'Mary Kay's pink gospel converts China's women', 22 December.

9 Forbes.com (2006) 'Tesco steps up in China', *Shu-Ching Jean Chen*, 12 December.

8   The marketing process

1 In Chinese ancient times, it was customary for a temple to be set apart for the use of a general for his research and planning of a battle. Further, according to Sunzi, a successful general must have the knowledge of his adversary and their behaviour.

2 Gary Hamel and C.K. Prahalad (1994) *Competing for the Future*, Boston, MA: Harvard Business School Press, p. 181.
3 Ikujiro Nonaka and Hirotaka Takeuchi (1995) *The Knowledge-Creating Company*, Oxford: Oxford University Press.
4 Max Boisot (1995) *Information Space*, London: Routledge.

9   Rightness and correct form

1 Tim Ambler (2003) *Marketing and the Bottom Line*, 2nd edn, London: FT Prentice Hall, Chapter 7.
2 Juan Antonio Fernandez and Laurie Underwood (2006) *China CEO*, Singapore: John Wiley & Sons.
3 Oled Shenkar (ed.) (1991) *Organization and Management in China 1979–1990*, Armonk, NY: M.E. Sharpe.
4 The most cited is probably Geert Hofstede (1991) *Cultures and Organizations*, Beverly Hills, CA: Sage.
5 Tony Fang (1998) *Chinese Business Negotiating Style*, Thousand Oaks, CA: Sage.
6 Fernandez and Underwood (2006), Chapter 2.
7 Ibid., p. 47.

10   Doing business with the sojourners

1 Richard Hughes (1972) *Foreign Devil*, London: Century, pp. 190–1.

12   Western and Chinese commercial thinking

1 Ian Rae (1997) 'Westerners need patience to crack Chinese puzzle', *Sunday Times*, 9 November.
2 W.F. Jenner (1989) *The Tyranny of History*, Cambridge: Cambridge University Press.

Bibliography

Ambler, Tim (1994) 'Marketing's third paradigm: *guanxi*', *Business Strategy Review* 5(4): 69–80. Describes a marketing strategy approach using *guanxi* rather than traditional Western modes.

—— (1999) 'Marketing rights and consumer responsibilities', paper presented at the Second Sino-British Conference on Business Ethics, Gresham College, London. Interesting and possibly controversial look at Western and Chinese approaches to ethics in marketing.

Ambler, Tim, Chris Styles and Wang Xiucun (1999) 'The effect of channel relationships and *guanxi* on the performance of inter-province export ventures in the People's Republic of China', *International Journal of Research in Marketing*, February: 75–87. Academic study of *guanxi* and channel management in China.

A.T. Kearney Inc. (1994) 'Capturing the Southeast Asian potential', Chicago: A.T. Kearney Inc. Useful research report, concentrating mostly on China despite the title.

Backman, Michael and Charlotte Butler (2002) *Big in Asia: 25 Strategies for Business Success*, Basingstoke: Palgrave Macmillan. Despite the 'cookbook' title, this is a really useful book, with helpful ideas and plenty of examples and cases.

Becker, Gerhold K. (ed.) (1996) *Ethics in Business and Society: Chinese and Western Perspectives*, Berlin: Springer. Mostly academic views from Hong Kong but a refreshing miscellany of topics.

Berger, Mark and Douglas Borer (1997) *The Rise of East Asia*, London: Routledge. Mostly readable collection of accounts of the rise of East Asia over the past 30 years; written just before the Asia Crisis, so a bit behind the times now.

Boisot, M. (ed.) (1994) *East–West Business Collaboration*, London: Routledge. Academic but readable study.

Bond, Michael Harris (ed.) (1986) *The Psychology of the Chinese People*, Oxford: Oxford University Press. Good academic overview of what is really known. Usefully separates ethnic from environment components of culture.

—— (1991) *Beyond the Chinese Face: Insights from Psychology*, Oxford: Oxford University Press. Abbreviated version of Bond 1986; the former is better.

Bosrock, Mary Murray (2007) *Asian Business Customs and Manners*, New York: Simon & Schuster. Up-to-date guide on manners and customs, expanded to take in all of eastern and southern Asia as well as China.

Brown, David H. and Robin Porter (eds) (1996) *Management Issues in China*, vol. 1, *Domestic Enterprises*, London: Routledge. Academic but invaluable companion to Child and Yuan (1996).

Brown, R. Ampalavanar (1996) *Chinese Business Enterprise: Critical Perspectives on Business and Management*, London: Routledge, 4 vols. Academic and historical, but worth browsing through if you see it in a library; look for the chapters on relationships and on branding.

Bucknall, Kevin (2002) *Chinese Business Etiquette and Culture*, Raleigh, NC: Boson Books. Does not add significantly to earlier works on the subject, but very readable and approachable.

Burstein, Daniel, and Arne de Keijzer (1998) *Big Dragon*, New York: Touchstone. Brave and surprisingly optimistic look at China's future, which sees the Asia Crisis as a passing event.

Chai, Joseph C.H. (1997) *China: Transition to a Market Economy*, Oxford: Clarendon. Good update, though some of the material on trade regulations has been overtaken by events.

Chen, Albert H.Y. (2004) *An Introduction to the Legal System of the People Republic of China*, 3rd edn, Hong Kong, Singapore, Malaysia: LexisNexis. Best general introduction to PRC law.

Chen Huan-Chang (1911) *The Economic Principles of Confucius and His School*, New York: Columbia University Press.

Chen Min (1995) *Asian Management Systems*, London: Routledge. Academic but well-written comparison of four business systems: Chinese family, Chinese state-owned enterprise, Korean and Japanese.

Chi Fulin (2000) *Reform Determines Future of China*, Beijing: Foreign Languages Press. Exposition by a respected Chinese state economist; cut through the obfuscation, and there are some useful clues about where China's economic policy may be going.

Child, J. (1994) *Management in China during the Age of Reform*, Cambridge: Cambridge University Press. One of the classics on the subject, a very detailed and well-written study; essential for managers as well as academics.

Child, J. and Yuan Lu (1996) *Management Issues in China*, vol. 2, *International Enterprise*, London: Routledge. Very useful collection of academic but relevant articles.

China Economic Review (2008) *China Business Guide 2008*, Hong Kong: China Economic Review. Gazetteer and reference guide which first-time travellers in particular will find extremely useful.

—— (2008) *China by Numbers 2008*, Hong Kong: China Economic Review. Useful summary of statistics, though these should be handled with care.

Chong, Alan (1995) *The Art of Management: Sixteen Strategies of Zhuge Liang*, Singapore: Asiapac. Application to management of the sayings and deeds of the Three Kingdoms hero, Zhuge Liang. One of Asiapac's bizarre comic-book guides to management; fun.

Chu Chin-ning (1991) *The Asian Mind Game*, New York: Rawson Associates. Whilst some aspects show their age, this is a splendid idiosyncratic tour of three separate areas: Chinese strategic thinking (Sun Tzu, 36 Strategies etc.), a tirade against Japan, and easy-to-read synopsis of Chinese philosophy and customs, plus some sensitive insights on Korea. Written for American executives. Overall, an excellent read.

Clifford Chance (1994) *Establishing a Representative Office in China*, London. A how-to-do-it guide by one of the largest legal firms in China.

Cradock, Sir Percy (1994) *Experiences of China*, London: John Murray. Memoirs of a former ambassador, special adviser on Hong Kong and 'China hand'; an excellent 'whiff of gunsmoke'.

Croll, Elisabeth (2006) *China's New Consumers: Social Development and Domestic Demand*, London: Routledge. Academic in tone but full of useful information.

Crow, Carl (1937) *400 Million Customers*, New York: Halcyon. CC set up first as an agency in China in 1916. Less has changed than you might think.

Cua, A.S. (1998) 'Confucian philosophy, Chinese', in E. Craig (ed.) *Routledge Encyclopedia of Philosophy*, vol. 2, London: Routledge, pp. 536–49.

de Keijzer, A.J. (1992) *China: Business Strategies for the 90's*, Berkeley, CA: Pacific View Press. Good easy-to-read introduction. Despite its age, still one of the best books for managers on this subject.

Deacon, R. (1974) *A History of the Chinese Secret Service*, London: Frederick Muller. Interesting insights on organisation and the reverse Opium War (Vietnam).

DeKrey, Steven J. and David M. Messick (eds) (2007) *Leadership Experiences in Asia: Insight and Inspiration from 20 Innovators*, Singapore: John Wiley. Despite the title, this is a series of articles by several observers rather than innovators, but contains some useful insights on organisation, leadership, ethics and managing people.

Deng Xiaoping (1987) *Fundamental Issues in Present-Day China*, Beijing: Foreign Languages Press. Not an easy read, but useful for the reader who wants to know more about why Deng inaugurated China's third great revolution of the century.

Economist Intelligence Unit (1994a) *Investing, Licensing and Trading Conditions Abroad for China*, London: EIU. Showing its age now, but still more detailed than most contemporary publications.

—— (1994b) *China Market Atlas*, London: Economist Intelligence Unit. Badly needs updating, but again, no comparable publication has yet emerged.

—— (1995) *Moving China Ventures out of the Red into the Black*, London: Economist Intelligence Unit/Andersen Consulting. Good study, again getting on in years, but has some useful advice for companies.

Euromonitor (1995) *China: A Directory and Sourcebook 1994*, London: Euromonitor. This could be regarded as essential for any company doing, or aiming to do, business in China. Sections 1 and 2 cover economic and consumer market surveys, 3 provides guidance on doing business in China, including law, formation, investment and addresses, 4 provides sources of marketing information, 5 has profiles of over 400 state and local enterprises, and 6 is a statistical factfile. Needs updating, but still very valuable.

Fang, Tony (1998) *Chinese Business Negotiating Style*, Thousand Oaks, CA: Sage. Good summary of the subject; recommended.

Financial Times (1999) 'Financial Times survey: the Philippines', 28 September. Special insert with up-to-date information on the Philippines economy.

Fleming, Peter (1959) *The Siege at Peking*, London: Rupert Hart-Davis.

Gao Shangquan and Chi Fulin (1995) *Theory and Reality of Transition to a Market Economy*, Beijing: Foreign Languages Press. Heroic attempt at making economic policy sound interesting. Available from Friendship Stores, should you wish to make the attempt.

Hall, David and Roger Ames (1987) *Thinking through Confucius*, Albany, NY: State University of New York Press. Sometimes technical but mostly highly readable account of Confucianism by two of the world's foremost Confucian scholars.

—— (1997) *Thinking from the Han: Self, Truth and Transcendence in Chinese and Western Cultures*, Albany, NY: State University of New York Press. Sequel to the above; intense but very important comparison of East–West systems of thought. Some philosophical background required.

—— (1998) 'Li', in E. Craig (ed.) *Routledge Encyclopedia of Philosophy*, London: Routledge, pp. 594–5. Encyclopedia article summing up a key concept in Chinese philosophy; referred to frequently in our text.

Hansen, Chad (1996) 'Chinese philosophy and human rights: an application of comparative ethics', in G.S. Becker (ed.) *Ethics in Business and Society*, Berlin: Springer, pp. 99–127. Academic but useful comparison of approaches to ethics and human rights.

Hexter, Jimmy (2007) *Operations China: From Strategy to Execution*, Boston, MA: Harvard Business School Press. Aimed mainly at large corporations, but thoughtful and has background information that may be of value to others.

Hofstede, Geert (1991) *Cultures and Organizations: Software of the Mind*, Beverly Hills, CA: Sage. An updated version of Hofstede's classic (if flawed) research on organisation behaviour.

Hsieh Tsun-yan (1996) "Prospering through relationships in Asia", *The McKinsey Quarterly* 4: 4–13. Another look at the importance of *guanxi* in commerce.

Huang Quanyu, Joseph Leonard and Chen Tong (1997) *Business Decision Making in China*, London: Haworth Press. Strongly recommended as one of the few English-language works on the subject.

Huang, Ray (1990) *A Macro History of China*, Armonk, NY: M.E. Sharpe. Excellent overview but not a quick read. Particularly good at drawing inferences (some debatable) from period to period and looking at underlying causes.

Hucker, C.O. (1978) *China to 1850. A Short History*, Stanford, CA: Stanford University Press. Probably the best short history; recommended for background reading. Unfortunately uses Wade–Giles romanisation which gives it an archaic look. Less academic than Huang but perhaps the best history of its type.

Hughes, Richard (1972) *Foreign Devil*, London: Century. Highly recommended. Despite its date, many of Hughes's reflections remain as valuable as ever. The perfect airport read for the Far East-bound traveller.

Huo Da (1992) *The Jade King*, Beijing: Panda. Novel about the Chinese Muslim community in Beijing; a unique glimpse into an all but forgotten Chinese community.

I Ching (1992), trans. Thomas Cleary, Boston and London: Shambhala. Pocket version of a Chinese classic; initially impenetrable, but worth dipping into.

International Journal of Advertising (1997), special issue on advertising and branding in China, 16(4). Recommended for a number of articles, especially

the distinction between 'name' and 'real' agencies (Swanson) and brand
naming (Huang and Chan).

Jiang Wei (1994) *Chinese Business Strategies*, Singapore: Asiapac. A surprisingly
useful introduction to Chinese approaches to business strategy, with examples
from the literary classics and real case studies; we say 'surprisingly' because
this is in fact a 'graphic novel' ('comic book' to older readers). This is one of
a series of similar works from Asiapac.

Jianguang Wang (ed.) (1995) *Westerners through Chinese Eyes*, Beijing: Foreign
Languages Press. Interesting, though some of the stories are best taken with
a pinch of salt.

Jones, Stephanie (1997) *Managing in China: An Executive Survival Guide*,
Singapore: BH Asia. The best informal guide currently on the subject.

Khu, Josephine M.T. (2001) *Cultural Curiosity: Thirteen Stories about the Search for
Chinese Roots*, Berkeley, CA: University of California Press. Interesting and at
times moving accounts of overseas Chinese returning to the mainland, and
their impressions and what they found there.

Laozi (1990) *Tao Teh Ching*, Boston and London: Shambhala. Good pocket
translation of the work now usually known as the *Daodejing*; very valuable
for understanding Chinese thought, today as in classical times.

Latourette, Kenneth Scott (1934) *The Chinese: Their History and Culture*, London:
Macmillan. Good cultural history, complements Hucker, above.

Lemoine, P. (1994) 'Mediation prospers in China', *Dispute Resolution Journal*
49(2). Useful description of the mediation process, common for settling
disputes in China.

Li Cheng (1994) 'University networks and the rise of Qinghua graduates in
China's leadership', *The Australian Journal of Chinese Affairs* 30 (April): 1–30.
Interesting look at one form of relationship-building in China.

Liu Shengjun (2006) 'Pepsi's "painful marriage" in Sichuan', *Asian Case Research
Journal* 10(2): 281–302.

Luo Yadong and Min Chen (1997) 'Does *guanxi* influence firm performance?',
Asia Pacific Journal of Management 14: 1–16. Assessment of how *guanxi* matters
to businesses.

McKinsey Quarterly (2006) *Serving the New Chinese Consumer*, special edition of
McKinsey Quarterly. Contains a number of useful articles on emerging trends
in Chinese consumer markets; well worth a look.

Mann, J. (1989) *Beijing Jeep*, New York: Simon & Schuster. Excellent story from
the boardroom, though remember to update the story; Beijing Jeep is now a
considerable success.

Mao Zedong (1954) *Strategic Problems of China's Revolutionary War* (speech
delivered 1938), Peking: Foreign Languages Press.

Meridian Resources (1998) *Managing in China: Recruiting and Retaining
Employees*, Washington, DC: Meridian. One of a useful series of small
pamphlets, with a good bibliography.

Moise, Edwin E. (1994) *Modern China: A History*, London: Longman. The
most recent and in some ways the best, for our purposes, of the
three histories. Unfortunately it does not do justice to earlier history, a
basic understanding of which is necessary; see Hucker or Huang, above,
for this.

Mok, Vincent, Dai Xiudian and Godfrey Yeung (2002) 'An internalization approach to joint ventures: Coca-Cola in China', *Asia Pacific Business Review* 9(1): 39–58. A good case study showing how attitudes to joint ventures have changed over time but how they remain a useful tool.

Moser, Michael J. (ed.) (2007) *Managing Business Disputes in Today's China: Dueling with Dragons*, The Netherlands: Kluwer Law International. Practical and useful guidance on resolution of Chinese–foreign business disputes under Chinese law.

Naughton, Barry (2007) *The Chinese Economy: Transitions and Growth*, Cambridge, MA: MIT Press. Interesting and updated introduction to the Chinese economy since 1949.

Negotiating: Opening Moves; *Negotiating: The Middle Game*; and *Negotiating: Closing the Deal?*, Videos 3–5 in the Working with China Series, Intercultural Training Resources, Inc., n.d.

Ng Sek Hong and Malcolm Warner (1997) *China's Trade Unions and Management*, London: Macmillan. Up-to-date study by two leading China business scholars; focuses in particular on the role of unions in state enterprise.

Palmer, Michael and Chao Xi (2007) 'Collective and representative actions in China', national report to the University of Oxford Centre for Social-Legal Studies and Stanford Law School joint project on the globalisation of Class Actions. Useful information about civil litigation and court systems in China.

Plafker, Ted (2007) *Doing Business in China*, London: Business Plus. Useful work by a leading financial journalist.

Porter, R. and M. Robinson (1994) *The China Business Guide*, Keele: Ryburn Publishing/Keele University Press. Keele's China Business Centre and CBTG's joint production for teaching use.

Purves, W. (1991) *Barefoot in the Boardroom*, Sydney: Allen & Unwin. This is a light but real, tell-it-as-it-is guidebook. Hardly academic but a clear Western view of life by a JV general manager.

Pye, Lucian W. (1992) *Chinese Negotiating Style: Commercial Approaches and Cultural Principles*, Westport, CT, and London: Quorum Books. Overview of negotiating attitudes and problems from a US point of view.

Rae, Ian and Morgen Witzel (2008) *The Overseas Chinese of Southeast Asia: History, Business, Culture*, Basingstoke: Palgrave Macmillan. General survey of Southeast Asian cultures and countries, with several chapters on business culture and practices.

Rice, D. (1992) *The Dragon's Brood: Conversations with Young Chinese*, London: HarperCollins. Interesting insights, not strictly relevant to business but good for attitudes.

Robison, Richard and David S.G. Goodman (eds) (1995) *The New Rich in Asia*, London: Routledge. Pre-1997/8 crash of course, a useful multicultural study of the new elites in what used to be called 'tiger economies'.

Roll, Martin (2006) *Asian Brand Strategy: How Asia Builds Strong Brands*, Basingstoke: Palgrave Macmillan. Looks at the branding strategies and techniques used by Asian firms, making the point that many Asian companies and managers are still weak in this respect.

Saich, Tony (2004) *Governance and Politics of China*, Basingstoke: Palgrave Macmillan, 2nd edn. Interesting insights on the political system in China.

Schlevogt, Kai-Alexander (2002) *The Art of Chinese Management: Theory, Evidence and Applications*, Oxford: Oxford University Press. Interesting if at times very technical analysis of how Chinese companies manage, with implications for Western management.

Schneiter, Fred (1992) *Getting Along with the Chinese for Fun and Profit*, Hong Kong: Asia 2000. Humorous, affectionate if not terribly rigorous look at East–West personal relations. Light reading.

Schroeder, Greg (2007) 'The career paths of Chinese graduates', Graduate Management Admissions Council Research Report.

Seagrave, Sterling (1996) *The Soong Dynasty*, London: Corgi. Recent Chinese history as family quarrel; terrific read with some insights.

Seligman, S.D. (1990) *Dealing with the Chinese: A Practical Guide to Business Etiquette*, London: W.H. Allen. Informal, easy to read for incoming businessperson.

Shabad, T. (1972) *China's Changing Map*, London: Methuen. Geography of China; out of date in terms of demography, but useful physical overview.

Shaw, S. and J. Meier (1993) 'Second generation MNCs in China', *The McKinsey Quarterly* 4. Useful look at the development of foreign ventures in China in the 1990s.

Shenkar, Oled (1990) 'International "JV" problems in China: risks and remedies', *Long Range Planning*. Although old, the JV management problems this article describes continue to occur in China today.

Shih, C.Y. (1990) *The Spirit of Chinese Foreign Policy: A Psycho-Cultural View*, Basingstoke: Macmillan. Very academic, but has some valuable pieces on the Chinese decision-making processes.

Spence, Jonathan (1997) *God's Chinese Son: The Taiping Heavenly Kingdom of Hong Xiuquan*, London: Flamingo. Account of the Taiping Rebellion, which began the downfall of the empire and the sequence of events that led to today; some interesting observations on the impact of foreign cultures on China.

Starr, John Bryan (1997) *Understanding China*, New York: Hill Wang. Fairly up-to-date text by an American sinologist; hypercritical and very pessimistic about China's future, but does have some useful chapters.

Stewart, S. (1990) 'Where the power lies: a look at China's bureaucracy', *Advances in Chinese Industrial Studies*, vol. 1, New York: JAI Press. Dated but still valuable.

Stewart, S. and Ip Kam Tim (1994) 'Professional business services in the People's Republic of China', University of Hong Kong, unpublished monograph, November. Very useful, though difficult to find.

Strange, Roger (1998) *Management in China: The Experience of Foreign Businesses*, London: Frank Cass. Academic but useful, with some case studies.

Su Chenting, Ronald K. Mitchell and M. Joseph Sirgy (2007) 'Enabling *guanxi* management in China: a hierarchical stakeholder model of effective *guanxi*', *Journal of Business Ethics* 71: 301–19. Theoretical examination of *guanxi* and the nature of relationships.

Sun Li and Yu Xiaohui (1992) *Metropolis*, Beijing: Panda Press. Novel about a north Chinese city in the throes of economic and social reform; no direct business relevance, but an extraordinarily fine account of life in modern China; hard to find.

Tang, Jie and Anthony Ward (2002) *The Changing Face of Chinese Management*, London: Routledge. One of the best recent books on management in China, with a strong focus on social/cultural influences and organisation.

Tao, Julia (1996) 'The moral foundation of welfare in Chinese society: between virtues and rights', in G.S. Becker (ed.) *Ethics in Business and Society*, Berlin: Springer, pp. 9–24. Very good account of the subject.

Tsang, Eric W.K. (1998) 'Can *guanxi* be a source of sustained competitive advantage for doing business in China?', *Academy of Management Executive* 12(2): 64–73. Another useful look at the importance of *guanxi* in commerce.

Tseng, C., P. Kwan and F. Cheung (1995) 'Distribution in China: a guide through the maze', *Long Range Planning* 28(1): 81–91. Academic but important, in a field where not enough has been written.

—— (1996) 'Business strategies, East Asian', *International Encyclopedia of Business and Management*, London: ITBP. Good generic work, with plenty of relevance to China.

Tucker, Spencer C. (1999) *Vietnam*, London: UCL Press. Long-overdue updating of Vietnam's situation; should be required reading for anyone interested in the country.

van Gulik, Robert (1989) *The Chinese Lake Murders*, 4th edn, London: Sphere.

Wang, Guiguo (2003) *Wang's Business Law of China*, Hong Kong: LexisNexis. Sketchy and hard to find but important for lawyers.

Wang, Wei (2006) *The China Executive: Marrying Western and Chinese Strengths to Generate Profitability from Your Investment in China*, Peterborough: 2W Publishing. Focuses heavily on the need to build relationships with business partners, customers and employees.

Wank, David L. (1996) 'The institutional process of market clientelism: *guanxi* and private business in a South China city', *The China Quarterly* 137: 820–37. Worth looking for; good example of how a *guanxi* system works.

Warner, Malcolm (1992) *How Chinese Managers Learn*, London: Macmillan. A bit dated but useful for approaches and attitudes to formal and informal management education programmes in China. Warner and John Child, mentioned above, are probably the two best British-based writers on China.

White, Theodore H. (1978) *In Search of History*, New York: Warner Books. Account by veteran journalist of his years in China with Mao, Zhou Enlai *et al.*

Wilson, Dick (1995) *The Big Tiger*, London: Little, Brown. One of the better, and certainly bigger, Western journalist surveys of modern China. Not popular with Chinese readers as he plays to the Western liberal gallery.

Witzel, M. (1998) '*Guanxi* East and West', in Yuanhui Lin and Oliver Lau (eds), *Proceedings of the 1998 Annual Conference of the Academy of International Business Southeast Asia Region*, Nanning: Guangxi People's Publishing House. Conference paper summarising current writings on *guanxi*.

—— (1999) '*Guanxi* East and West', *Financial Times Mastering Management Review*, January. More accessible version of 1998, above.

—— (1999) 'China: the world's oldest brand', *Financial Times Mastering Management Review*, September. Account of British–Chinese trade in the eighteenth century, when 'China' had many of the connotations of quality that the Chinese now associate with the West.

Wu Janglian (2005) *Understanding and Interpreting Chinese Economic Reform*, New York: Thomson Texere. An insider's view of China's post-Mao economic reform.

Wu Jie (1996) *On Deng Xiaoping Thought*, Beijing: Foreign Languages Press. Good distillation of Deng's economic and social ideas, preferable by far to seeking to tackle the voluminous originals.

Xi, Chao (2005) 'Transforming Chinese enterprises: ideology, efficiency and instrumentalism in the process of reform', in J. Gillespie and P. Nicholson (eds), *Asian Socialism and Legal Change: The Dynamics of Vietnamese Renewal and Chinese Reform*, Canberra: ANU Press & Asia Pacific Press, pp. 91–114. An analysis of law and policy of China's state-owned enterprise reforms.

—— (2006) 'In search of an effective monitoring board model: board reforms and the political economy of corporate law in China', *Connecticut Journal of International Law* 22: 1–46. Academic study of corporate board reform and law-making in China.

—— (2006) 'Institutional shareholder activism in China: law and practice', *International Company and Commercial Law Review* 17(9): 251–62; 17(10): 287–94. Describes institutional investors' involvement in the governance of portfolio companies in China.

Xu Bai Yi (1990) *Marketing to China: One Billion New Customers*, Chicago: NTC Business Books. Perhaps it toes the Party line but a comprehensive guide to the four Ps in China. Rather out of date now, but not much has come along to supersede it.

Yan, R. (1994) 'To reach China's consumers, adapt to Guo Qing', *Harvard Business Review*, September–October. Controversial in places, but worth a read.

Yang Zhongfang (1988) *The Psychology of Advertising*, Yunnan People's Publisher. In Chinese.

Yang, Mayfair Mei-hui (1994) *Gifts, Favors and Banquets*, Ithaca, NY: Cornell University Press. Do not be put off by the title; this is the best work we have seen on the subject of *guanxi*-building.

Yau, Oliver H.M. (1994) *Consumer Behaviour in China*, New York and London: Routledge. Reports on a research study into the effects of Chinese cultural, experiential and environmental matters on consumer satisfaction. Technical.

Yeung, Henry Wai-Chung (2002) *Entrepreneurship and the Internationalisation of Asian Firms*, Cheltenham: Edward Elgar. Very academic, but worth looking at for insights.

Yeung, I.Y.M. and R.L. Tung (1996) 'Achieving business success in Confucian societies: the importance of *guanxi* (connections)', *Organizational Dynamics* 25(2): 54–65. Another useful, if academic, look at the role of *guanxi*.

Zhang Yi and Zhang Zhigang (2006) '*Guanxi* and organizational dynamics in China', *Journal of Business Ethics* 67: 375–92. A more recent academic look at *guanxi*, which offers some helpful explanations of the concept.

Index

BUSINESS ESSENTIALS
from Routledge

Doing Business in India

Pawan S. Budhwar, Aston Business School, UK
Arup Warmar, Loyola University, Chicago, USA

This brand new and indispensable textbook covers a wide range of issues and topics for students and researchers in the fields of International Management, International HRM, Cross-Cultural Management, Business Communication and Asian Business.

Written by academic experts, the book presents key information on topics including:

- geography
- politics
- legal system
- historical background
- economy and economic factors
- national infrastructure
- regulatory environment (convertibility of local currency, sectors open to foreign investors, extent of foreign ownership allowed)
- how to negotiate in India
- privatisation
- hot sectors for investors
- incentives for foreign investors
- competitive environment
- advertising and marketing
- promotion
- distribution
- conducting / implementing business (i.e. strategies for investing in India, mode of entry)
- possible business structures
- culture, business customs, practices and etiquette
- greetings, gestures, conversation and related issues.

Hb: 978-0-415-77754-4: **£85.00**
Pb: 978-0-415-77755-1: **£22.99**

Visit **www.routledge.com/asianstudies**
to order copies or for further information.

Routledge
Taylor & Francis Group